The Language of Sexuality

THE LANGUAGE
OF SEXUALITY

by
Alan Richter

McFarland & Company, Inc., Publishers
Jefferson, North Carolina, and London

Library of Congress Cataloguing-in-Publication Data

Richter, Alan, 1951–
   The language of sexuality.

   Bibliography: p. 147.
   Includes index.
   1. Sex — Terminology. I. Title.
HQ23.R53   1987   306.7'014   87-42520

ISBN 0-89950-245-8 (acid-free natural paper)

Printed in the United States of America.

McFarland   Box 611   Jefferson NC 28640

PREFACE

My interest in writing a book on sexual language arose out of my work a few years ago as an editor on an English dictionary. Initially I was amazed at the mass of ordinary innocent-looking English words that also happened to have sexual meanings or connotations. Why, I asked myself, should this be the case? Why should sexuality give rise to an unrivalled variety of terms in English? Furthermore, I was curious to find out what logic, if any, existed within this linguistic multitude. Were there definite classes or types of words that could be identified? What were they?

At first I conceived of this book as a dictionary but soon realized that since dictionaries should be comprehensive and authoritative, in this field that could mean a lifetime's work. I also felt, anyway, that the dictionary format alone was not conducive to discourse. The extensive glossary at the end of this book, however, offers substantial lexicographical content by way of compromise.

I plan to discuss the ideas about the language of sexuality in Chapter 1 and then illustrate them with the relevant terminology in the later chapters.

My acknowledgments and gratitude are due to all the authors listed in the Bibliography (page 147).

CONTENTS

Preface   v

1. The Language of Sexuality   1
2. The Language of Sexual Intercourse   23
3. The Language of the Female Sex Organs   39
4. The Language of the Male Sex Organs   53
5. The Language of Other Aspects of Sexuality   66
   - ACTIONS   66
     - Caressing (Foreplay)   66
     - Masturbation   67
   - ORAL SEX   69
     - Anal Sex   71
     - The Anus and the Buttocks   73
     - Miscellaneous   74
     - Orgasm   75
   - PEOPLE   75
     - Prostitute   77
     - Homosexual   79
     - Bisexual   82
     - The Brothel   82
   - STATES   83
     - Menstruation   83
     - Pregnancy   85
     - Lust   85
     - Erection   87
   - AIDS AND OBJECTS   88

Glossary   91

Bibliography   147

Index   149

1. THE LANGUAGE OF SEXUALITY

Any serious analysis of the language of sexuality must first separately illuminate the roles of both sexuality and language in human social life. Let us begin with sexuality: What is it? Most people would have no doubts as to what constitutes the sexual, though they may have difficulty defining it or circumscribing it. The Freudian revolution of this century alone has vastly expanded our frame of reference for sexuality. Clearly, sexuality is not only about bodily organs and reproductive functions. The etymology of the term *sex* itself gives little help — it is from the Latin *secare* meaning to cut or divide, which suggests a biological derivation. But even a Freudian recognition of the extension of sexuality into the domain of childhood and infancy, and into the heart of such phenomena as dreams, jokes, etc., does not really capture the centrality of sexuality in human experience and in our human world.

To bring out this centrality one has to try to imagine a world *without* sexuality. This requires a well-developed imagination that can somehow "imagine away" what is so basic and assumed in our world. If, after this, nothing sensible or nothing human is left over, we could justly assume that sexuality is central to our experience and our world. This "imagining away" is nothing other than a philosophical or phenomenological armchair experiment.

Perhaps it is best to attempt this strange philosophical experiment first on some comparatively fundamental concept. We can begin to see the essential nature of space and time, for example, if we try to "imagine them away" or imagine a world in which both these concepts do not have any application. Such a world is barely imaginable to us and if such a world could exist it would not be accessible to human experience. This is a conclusion that the philosopher Kant arrived at when considering the grounds of human experience.

1

Now try "imagining away" sexuality—imagine a world in which sexuality does not exist at all, not in one particular form, but in *no* form at all. This entails imagining a world in which there are no sexes, no sexual activity, no sexual desire, no sexual perceptions or sexual thought. Though it may seem logically possible for *a* world still to exist without sexuality, even perhaps for creatures to exist in such a world, it clearly would be alien to our human world in any of its variations. That we can still imagine a world at all perhaps makes sexuality less fundamental than, say, time, but we need to compare sexuality to other specifically human or animal qualities or faculties to show its *human* centrality. Take the sense of smell, for example; if we lost our sense of smell we could still easily imagine surviving as human beings. Some readjustments would be necessary, certain experiences would no longer be possible, and the perfume industry would collapse. But smell does not appear to be *necessary* to our definition of ourselves as human beings. Sexuality, on the other hand, appears to be indispensable in defining ourselves as human beings; it appears to be a necessary aspect of human experience, much like space and time. If you take sexuality away you threaten to take humanity away with it.

This phenomenological argument, if it holds, holds irrespective of the variety of forms of human sexuality. The centrality of sexuality in human experience does not alone, however, explain the variety of sexual terminology. But before attempting to explain this phenomenon we need to look at the notion of language. Language, in a very oversimplified sense, is a system or means of expression and communication. And like sexuality, language is a central aspect of human life. Though it takes on different forms and is open to great changes over time, language is nonetheless also *necessary* to human life. Try imagining it away! Life forms without expression or communication would not be human, let alone animal.

One of the main features that distinguishes language from animal communication is that it is not confined to the instinctive level. With the aid of grammar, common to all human languages, we can create new sentences and new meanings. We can describe objects, situations, actions that we have never seen before. Through self-reflection, we can describe ourselves and how or why we have described things. The development of vocabulary actually opens up new dimensions for our experience by extending our thought and by enabling its expression. The crucial point is that language does not simply reflect some objective reality; rather, we actively construct our reality with the use of language. All this means that the world is not simply given to us, we interpret it, we name it. Furthermore, we select what we are to perceive, interpret and name. Different peoples with very different languages, it has been claimed, consequently see the world differently. In this respect the world of human experience portrayed in this book can only safely apply to English speakers, though in different places and at different times.

The relationship between language and reality is not a one-way affair. Instead there is a true interdependence between them; language not only reflects the world but also determines how we see the world. Within limits we choose our language (or how to express ourselves verbally), just as we choose our sexuality (or how to express it). This is nothing other than our existential freedom and to that extent we can talk about constructing reality (or realities). But we are also limited in our range of choice by our inherited genetic makeup, our environment, and by the history and culture that we happen to be born into. So our reality which presupposes language, history and culture must have underlying perceptions, attitudes, and theories. One of the most important underlying notions in language, which has a direct connection with sexuality, is the notion of *gender*.

Gender exists in all languages since all languages reflect the sex difference in nature; the relationship between sex and gender, however, varies greatly. In the earliest recorded or written languages, Sumerian, Akkadian, Hebrew, etc., the sexual difference is reflected in inflected forms (especially by affixes) and it is the female gender which receives the inflection — implying a norm of masculinity. In many modern languages, for example French and German, and in some earlier languages such as Latin and Hebrew, we find that language as a whole is pervaded with gender, that is, grammatical gender. Nouns, whether animate or inanimate, are either masculine, feminine or neuter, and other parts of speech correspond to the stated gender of the nouns. The existence of grammatical gender must reflect the way speakers saw or conceived of the world at some earlier period in time. Grammatical gender adds force to the argument that sexuality is so central to human experience. That stones, trees and stars should be imbued with gender is perhaps parallel to the child's early conception of the world in which everything is *animate* until the distinction animate/inanimate develops.

This book, however, is concerned with the English language, and English, unlike French or Latin, has *natural gender*, or so the linguists and grammarians tell us. Natural gender means that sex and gender correspond and that inanimate objects have no gender or are neutral. In general that is the case with English, though it is not entirely natural. Certain anomalies exist which bring out the historical and cultural underpinnings of the language and illuminate the earlier point that through language we construct rather than simply reflect reality. That the word *man* is an ambiguous term is at the heart of the matter, for *man* can refer to the species of human beings or to the male subset of this species. In the former sense it "embraces" woman and according to the rules of grammar it must be coupled with a *he*. We need to look behind language here to grasp the ideology underlying it.

Marx said that the ideas of the ruling class are the ruling ideas. The same can be said of language: the language of the ruling class is the ruling language, for language is a vehicle for ideas. Spender in *Man Made Language* has traced the history of natural gender in English. According to her the linguistic notion that "man embraces woman" was relatively unknown to English speakers before Thomas Wilson in 1553 suggested that it was natural to place male before female, no doubt reflecting the status quo of male dominance, whether natural or otherwise. In Old English *man* had the generic sense of human being while the male was referred to as *wer* (related to Latin *vir*) or *weap(n)man*; more on these terms later. The suggestion "man embraces woman" was incorporated by John Kirkby into his *88 Grammatical Rules* of 1746 in which rule 21 stated that the male gender was more "comprehensive" than the female one. And finally in Britain in 1850 this view was fully legitimized by none other than an act of Parliament which stated that *he* also stood for *she*.

Not surprisingly all the grammarians that Spender refers to were males, as were the honorable members of the British Parliament in 1850, and what was natural for all of them may not have been so for women. All this goes to show the societal and political underpinnings of language, and the fact that language does not reflect a pure reality but helps to construct a reality, based on theories, attitudes, and values whether consciously held or not.

The question of natural gender in English raises the issue of sexism. Interestingly the term *sexism* itself is a very new term in English. The earliest quotations for it in dictionaries are in the 1960s. And the term *sexual politics* was coined as late as 1970 by Kate Millett. Barnhart's *Dictionary of New English* which captures new words and new meanings in English since the 1960s lists *sexism, sexist, sexploitation* and *sexual revolution*. Barnhart's second dictionary, which begins in the 1970s, lists *sex clinic, sex object, sex shop* and *sex therapy*.

Sexism is a neutral term, for it can be applied equally to females as to males. But the recorded history of sexuality, which includes the period of spoken English, is one of male superiority and so a more useful and accurate term would be one that refers to male sexism. Feminists have recently put forward many words for this phenomenon and the term that I will use for this book is *androcentrism*, used by Morgan in *The Descent of Woman* (1972). *Androcentrism* shares an ideological transparency with *sexism* and makes room for the term *gynocentrism* should we need to make use of it. The other suggested terms seem to be too ideologically cluttered, namely *phallocentrism* and *patriarchy*, though there will be occasions for their use. We shall be seeing that the language of sexuality is overwhelmingly androcentric, though not always clearly phallocentric or patriarchal.

A further way in which "man embraces woman" shows its linguistic self is in grammatical constructions where *a person* or *one* is the subject. For example, in the sentence "a person (one) should always obey his language master" the term *his* is required by the rules of grammar as the neutral possessive adjective or determiner. According to Miller and Swift *they* and *their* have been used for over 400 years by eminent writers as a singular pronoun and adjective despite all the attempts by grammarians to keep it down. Dictionaries that actually bother to list *they* and *their* in this sense still mark them as nonstandard.

In the example I gave above I intentionally used the word *master*; the way this word contrasts with its opposite, *mistress*, brings out another general feature of androcentrism in English, for there is a radical polarization between many male and female terms. Think simply of the connotations of *mistress*. Other examples are the *bachelor/spinster* pair and the *boy/girl* pair. Although these pairs form gender opposites their connotations stretch them unequally apart; the terms *girlie, call girl*, etc. have few equivalent counterparts with *boy* (though boy has, for instance, derogatory racist connotations). The etymology of the word *girl* itself is interesting: its obsolete meaning is youth and it appears that *gōr* was Low German for boy and *-l* is the female suffix.

Polarization is most acute in swear terms; we find nothing to match *motherfucker* or *son of a bitch*, where much of the insult is (probably unconsciously) transferred onto the mother of the person concerned. This polarization in meaning is a clear reflection of an androcentric and patriarchal view of the world and must point to the male's control of the construction of new meanings in language, which ultimately reflects male power going back at least throughout the history of what we know as the English language. Recently Daly in *Gyn/Ecology* has attempted to balance the negative connotations with positive ones for such downtrodden terms as *spinster*.

As a final example of androcentrism in English let us look at one of the primary functions of language, viz, naming. Firstly, many names have sexual connotations which usually refer to sexual organs, for example **Peter**, **Dick**, **Mary Jane**, etc. This could be seen as reducing a person to a sex object but could also more pleasantly be seen as a simple acknowledgment of the primacy of sexuality. This phenomenon, however, is shared between the sexes. But we do find a disparity with conventional names in English. Female names often consist of male names with suffixes added, for example: *Georgina, Paulette*, etc., which give a sense of derivation much like Eve being derived from Adam's rib. The suffixes also are often no more than diminutives, thus reflecting social hierarchy. Furthermore, to maintain this hierarchy, many names that were applied to both males and females at an earlier time have more recently dropped out of use for males but not vice versa; a few examples are *Beverley* and *Shirley*. And finally, titles reflect an androcentric view of the world — *Mr.* as opposed to *Miss/Mrs.* requires no comment.

Although androcentrism may have characterized most of the history of sexuality since recorded times, it nevertheless has not made for a homogeneity of sexuality through history. That is, even within the confines of an overriding androcentrism, mankind has been capable of almost anything in sexual matters. Clearly, 1980s Western sexual attitudes and behavior is merely one variation on an infinitely improvisable theme. And like all other viewpoints in history it is in a state of continual change.

A brief glance at classical Greece for example will show different sexual viewpoints. Sexuality and eroticism had an accepted central place in Greek life and many forms of it were regarded as healthy; homosexuality and pederasty were acceptable and fashionable, masturbation was regarded as normal rather than sinful, and prostitution seems to have been a well-recognized occupation. Greek society, then, seems to have been free of many of the taboos more recent societies have fallen prey to.

Openness to varied sexual experience has much to do with the overriding religious ethos of a society. Sexuality takes on very different forms under Taoism, Hinduism, Christianity, etc. For an account of the different paths that sexuality followed under different religions through history see Tannahill's *Sex in History*. Perhaps in the 1980s in the West, since religion has lost much of its constrictive and repressive grip, sexuality and its expression is going through further liberalizing changes. In addition to an historical examination of societies one could just as easily examine present-day primitive societies, for the wealth of anthropological data available simply adds to the argument for the existence of extreme variations on the theme of sexuality.

I have argued that the history and anthropology of sexuality should be reflected, at least partly, in the languages of the societies under inspection. Different societies naturally evolve their own terms and metaphors for sexuality; ancient China, for example, spoke of the *Jade Chamber*, the *Jade Stalk*, *Golden Lotus*, and so on. However, since I am dealing with the language of sexuality in English, it is the language and terminology principally in the last five hundred years (for that is how far back modern English goes) that really matters here. But obviously English did not spring out of nowhere. In highly oversimplified terms we know that modern English is a rich blend of three language currents: the primary Old English (sometimes called Anglo-Saxon), the very strong Norman (French) influence, and the subsequent learned adoptions of elements of Greek and Latin vocabulary, which coincided with the development of modern English.

Of particular importance is the duality of Old English and Norman (including Latin and Greek), which has led in modern English to the existence of two terms for many things: for example, **copulate/ fuck**, *expire/die*, *defecate/shit*, *deity/god*, and so on. What is interesting is the relationship between these two streams or classes of words. Usually the Old English, or Anglo-Saxon, form is simple and informal. "Anglo-Saxon" today has an informal meaning itself, referring to commonness or plainness, and in the sexual context this means nothing other than vulgar (the etymology of *vulgar* leads back to *vulgaris*, Latin, meaning "of the common people or the multitude"). The best known "vulgar" terms are the so-called four letter words and as an illustration of the historical vicissitudes of an Anglo-Saxon sexual term let us look at the case of the best-known four letter word in English, perhaps even the best-known four letter word in the world today, thanks to the growing universality of English, namely, **fuck**.

Fuck first appeared in English in print in the 16th century when it was used as a vulgar term for copulation. However, vulgarity in the 16th century was widespread, acceptable and, true to its etymology, commonplace. Perhaps because the written word had not gained much power by then, spoken language, though vulgar, could not be suppressed or made the subject of a taboo quite so easily as the written word. However, the Puritanism of the 17th century was so powerful that by the 18th century **fuck** had virtually disappeared from print.

According to Montague (in *The Anatomy of Swearing*), the first dictionary to contain the word was John Florio's Italian-English dictionary *A Worlde of Wordes* in 1598. The first English dictionary to have the word was Skinner's *Etymologicon Lingua Anglicanae* in 1671. Bailey's *Universal Etymological Dictionary* of 1721 gives the word as does Grose's *Classical Dictionary of the Vulgar Tongue* in 1785, though Grose used asterisks for the middle two letters! And by the time the 1811 edition came out the term was dropped. Samuel Johnson in his famous *Dictionary of the English Language* in 1755 decided to omit the word, and excused himself by saying that the taboo would gradually fade away by itself as "civilization advanced"! The grand *Oxford English Dictionary*, which was begun in 1884 and continued until 1928, avoided the word, as did the 1933 supplement; only the new supplement of 1972 included it.

In 1936 Eric Partridge challenged post–Victorian prudery and included the word in his *Dictionary of Slang and Unconventional English*, to anticipated protests, and even he had to use one asterisk (for the vowel this time — a slight improvement on Grose's dictionary 150 years earlier). The first English dictionary this century to print the word unashamedly — without the veil of asterisks — was the *Penguin Dictionary* of 1965. This led to the banning of the *Penguin Dictionary* in certain countries. The first American dictionary to print the word was the *American Heritage Dictionary*, which took the plunge in 1969 and was itself banned in various states of America.

Many dictionaries have now followed suit and included **fuck**, though it is interesting to see the variations in the way the word is labelled. The *Oxford* dictionaries give the label "vulgar or taboo word" while the *Chambers 20th Century Dictionary* says "long taboo . . . still vulgar" and the *Collins Dictionary of the English Language* uses the label "taboo." **Fuck** only appears in the Addenda to *Webster's Third New International Dictionary* (1976) and is labelled with "usually considered obscene." The word now appears in print more frequently, and bolsters the argument for changing its label to slang or even informal. The recent edition of *The Random House College Dictionary* labels it "slang (usually vulgar)."

We appear to be moving away from the written word back to the spoken word, thanks to the technology of television, computers and videos. Respectability may now be tested out not only in print but also, more realistically, on television. It is worth recalling that the term **fuck** and its variants are more often than not bleeped off television and radio — the auditory equivalent of the asterisk.

Fuck is one of a group of well-known four letter words, all Anglo-Saxon, or Old English, in origin, that are uncomplicated, easy to pronounce, and monosyllabic — so, not surprisingly, **monosyllable** itself became a euphemism for the monosyllable **cunt**. But besides the commonly-known four letter words, other older sexual terms are also Anglo-Saxon in derivation — for example, the now obsolete **swive**, which in Old English means to revolve as well as to **fuck**. A present-day English equivalent to **swive** would be the word **grind**, having the same sexual connotation.

The two streams, Norman (including Latin and Greek) and Anglo-Saxon, that flowed together to make up the core of modern English also helped to make English a particularly rich language. But more importantly, these two streams also reflect the divisions in class that have existed throughout the history of English society. One would not argue that the two different streams or sources of modern English have two separate classes of speakers, but, rather, that the upper or educated class in general has since the Norman invasion been associated with the use of French (and frequently, therefore, Latinate) words in English, while the peasants and working classes have been associated with the Anglo-Saxon vocabulary. In the yard it is a *pig*; served up on the master's table, it is *pork*.

The two-stream theory is only a part of the story of the variety of sexual discourse, as is the over-simplified view of different classes in society. For a fuller account of this variety we need to move from the sociopolitical field to the field of knowledge and science. According to Foucault in *The History of Sexuality*, volume 1, it is the *proliferation* of discourses on sexuality arising after the Middle Ages that conveys the secret strength of sexuality. Foucault claims that the unitary sexual discourse of the Middle Ages was theological in character — the language of the flesh, penance, etc. Consider the popular phrase **living in sin**. Terms for the genitals show a similar story: **pudenda** is from the Latin *pudere*, meaning to be ashamed.

This singlemindedness was shattered only in later centuries by the development of new discourses (and perhaps by the concomitant weakening of the church). Sexuality became the legitimate subject of learned investigation in fields such as biology, demography, medicine, psychology and psychiatry. Sexuality became scientifically studied and talked about; a concomitant supposition was that its truths could thus be known. An important distinction exists between the *scientia sexualis* of the West and the *ars erotica* not only of the East (China, Japan and India) but also of ancient Rome, the Arabic world, etc. The West does not lack an *ars erotica*; we can see interesting cultural and artistic metaphors in the English language for sexuality. The blossoming and rapid expansion of the *scientia sexualis* in the West in the last few centuries, however, is unique to mankind.

Science is really a process of self-discovery, so that we learn as much about ourselves as about the world. Self-discovery with regard to sexuality is relatively recent. Freud must be regarded as the central figure in the process of the *scientia sexualis*, though some acknowledgment should be made to the sexologists who preceded him, such as Krafft-Ebing and Ellis. Freud, the psychoanalysts and the sexologists certainly developed the scientific discourse of sexuality in psychology and psychiatry, and helped to establish such terms as *sadism, masochism, libido, erotogenic zones, autoeroticism* and *narcissism*.

Scientific language, however, is only a small part of the language of sexuality, though its influence on ordinary terminology may be greater than is usually acknowledged. The mass of terms in the area of sexuality can be divided roughly into levels of acceptability and spheres of usage. Though the borders are far from clear at times, we can distinguish official or technical (often scientific) discourse from colloquial discourse, which itself subdivides into the informal, euphemistic, slang and taboo. To give examples of these levels, to **copulate** and **coit** would be technical or scientific terms, to **have sex** would be an informal expression, to **sleep with** and to **play the national indoor game** would be euphemistic expressions, the second perhaps in addition "jocular"; to **lay** and to **screw** would be slang terms, and perhaps to **fuck** could still qualify as a taboo term.

Terminology from each of these levels or strata should provide insights into the multifaceted nature of sexuality. I have already mentioned the formal/technical/scientific discourses that blossomed in the past few centuries elucidating a *scientia sexualis*. For examples of scientific sexual discourse, which shall not be discussed at much length in this work, medical textbooks are the best source. Informal, euphemistic, slang and taboo discourses have been around for centuries, though they have had their ups and downs. For example, euphemistic expression had its heyday in Victorian society when sexuality in general was regarded, in parts of society at least, as a taboo. Euphemism is an attempt, usually motivated by kindness, to deal with taboos. But however delicate the euphemism is, it must bear some resemblance to what it points at, and so inevitably becomes associated with it, and eventually a new euphemism is needed to circumvent the taboo. Euphemisms are first created by altering or replacing a taboo word (by abbreviating it or abstracting from it). The more oblique or indirect the replacement is, the better. The number of euphemisms for a term are generally proportionate to the strength of the taboo.

Slang as a linguistic phenomenon has blossomed only relatively recently, but is now profuse. It must be pointed out that the slang in this book is almost exclusively *recorded* slang, that is, words and phrases that have entered into print. There is much slang about today that has not yet achieved this status, for a variety of reasons; it will not be recorded in this book, but it is nonetheless genuine. Defining slang is somewhat of a problem. The dictionaries variously give the following definitions of slang, or of the usage label used to flag words regarded as slang: terms having extreme informality, limited currency, considered not to form part of Standard English, of restricted usage, racy, inappropriate for writing and formal speech, and so on.

Flexner, in his preface to Wentworth and Flexner's *Dictionary of American Slang*, maintains that a large slang vocabulary results from three major factors: an acceptance or openness to new concepts, the existence of many diverse subgroups in society, and the intermingling of these subgroups. He points out that primitive societies have very little slang or no slang at all because their lives are structured by ritual, few new concepts come into existence, and, as important, there are no significant subgroups. Slang therefore really owes much of its existence and recent proliferation to, on the one hand, the ever greater influence of science on society, which has given rise to new and varied ways of seeing the world, and, on the other hand, to the modern technological and mobile society that has been shaped by the applications of science, making subgroupings so much more common. The fact that Western society has been composed of mainly male subgroups until recently — at work and play — helps to explain the predominantly androcentric element in sexual slang. Recent psychological studies still tend to show that females use a higher percentage of technical and euphemistic terms for sex than males.

Partridge in *Slang Today and Yesterday* gives a varied list of reasons why slang is employed: high spirits, wit (he says "sex is responsible for much that is amusing in slang"), to be different, to be picturesque, to be startling, to escape clichés, to lend concreteness to abstraction, to soften stings, to ease social intercourse, to induce friendliness, to show belonging, to be secretive, and so on. These features all point to the creativity of slang; Partridge quotes Carl Sandburg, who expresses it succinctly: "Slang is a language which takes off its coat, spits on its hands — and goes to work."

The difficulty with studying slang is that it is essentially a spoken language; because it is not a written language it can go beyond the rules of written English. This often makes etymologies difficult if not impossible to trace. Another lexicographic challenge is the predominance in certain sexual areas of literary and euphemistic terms over true slang terms simply because the former categories belong to written, recorded language more than to spoken language. One of the features of slang that has given it reason to be employed in spoken language was the desire to be secretive, to be understood only within a certain group, something that no doubt was of much use in sexual matters. This characteristic was developed to a fine art perhaps most famously in Cockney rhyming slang (where, for example, *plates of meat* are *feet; trouble and strife* is *wife,* and so on).

In England, and especially in London, rhyming slang was used and enjoyed by people from all classes of society, indicating its colloquial acceptance into the English language. A phrase such as "to get down to brass tacks" (*brass tacks* being the rhyming slang for *facts*) is now considered to be standard idiomatic English. Further success of rhyming slang is evident in the extent to which it traveled to America and Australia. Rhyming slang embraces the ordinary matters of life, and often in a humorous way; there are many interesting rhyming slang terms with sexual references covered in later chapters.

The humor of so much rhyming slang especially in sexual matters helps to turn touchy subjects into talkable ones, and the wit of rhyming slang helps to lighten and enliven its subject matter. To give an example, calling someone a **berk** (or **burk**) seems quite a harmless way of referring to someone you regard as rather silly or stupid. **Berk**, however, is none other than rhyming slang for **cunt**, for it is a contraction of *Berkeley Hunt* or *Berkshire Hunt*. Calling someone a **cunt** would be a much more offensive form of address.

Though slang can and has been applied to all sorts of situations in life, certain topics in the hands of slang seem to take on a special character. Wentworth and Flexner claim that the concept having the most slang synonyms (in American English, that is) is drunkenness. I think the following chapters, however, will give the edge to synonyms for sex, though in all fairness sexual terms are heterogeneous, while terms for drunkenness are homogeneous. Before explaining this difference let me first point out the similarities between drink and sex. Both involve actions, objects and experiences which are what the terms describe; drinking, the action, may parallel having sex, and drink itself, the object, may perhaps parallel the sex organs with regard to slang terminology. Sex, however, involves relationships between people and also has considerably more functions than drink and in this sense is heterogeneous.

Morris in *The Human Zoo* lists ten functions of sex; they are: procreative, pair-formation, pair-maintenance, physiological, exploratory, self-rewarding, occupational, tranquilizing, commercial and status-seeking. Drinking could only apply to about half of these functions. Nonetheless there is something to be learned from a comparison between slang terms for drunkenness and slang terms for sexuality. Synonyms for being drunk often describe or point to the feeling of being high, happy, unselfconscious, oblivious to the suffering of the world, and so on. And in this sense the experience of sexuality and sexual satisfaction is rather similar — sexual arousal and orgasm also make us high, happy, unselfconscious and oblivious to the suffering of the world.

Sex involves relationships while drink does not. Sometimes sex is tied to love, and related emotions, but curiously we do not find a very large slang lexicon for love, perhaps because it is too amorphous a concept or too complex. Anyway its physical side is covered by sex, as are its extremes, for example, infatuation, which is expressed in such terms as *being hooked on, head over heels about, crazy about*, etc.

Another lesson to be learned from the comparison between slang terms for sex and drink is related to the causes or origins of these terms. Wentworth and Flexner point out that most of the terms for *drunk* originated and became popularly used during Prohibition. This effectively means that *repression* was the chief impetus to the development of new terms. Repression is obviously of great importance in the history of sexuality, especially with regard to language. Even in the research for this book were the shackles of repression evident. In the library in the British Museum some works about sex and so-called "dirty books" have been singled out and stored separately; many are kept in what is called the Private Case. The history of the Private Case is documented in Fryer's *Private Case—Public Scandal*.

A taboo, which is a public or common prohibition based on repression, with societal backing, touches on vitally important areas of life, and is evident in a variety of different forms. For example, Young divides his book *Eros Denied* into such sections as excluded words, excluded images, excluded actions and excluded people: four different kinds of taboo. The existence of so many different discourses for sexuality originating in the past few centuries may indicate the existence of a taboo as surely as an absence of terms. Even Foucault admits that talking about sex acts as a block against repression; that is, the creation of new discourses is a way round the taboo of sexuality. Foucault puts it this way: "What is peculiar to modern societies, in fact, is not that they consigned sex to a shadow existence, but that they dedicated themselves to speaking of it *ad infinitum*, while exploiting it as *the* secret" (page 35).

Freud's writings on the subject hint at the idea that civilization could only really take off with the help of repression and taboo. If sexuality were allowed absolutely free expression, society (even animal societies) would break down. Only with the emergence of the reality principle, as opposed to the pleasure principle, can society ever develop, and the reality principle is, partly, a recognition of prohibitive rules governing behavior. Civilization is clearly one way of coming to terms with the reality principle and harnessing it at the expense of the pleasure principle. This is the essence of sublimation, which, like repression, is one of Freud's classic ego defense mechanisms.

Repression and sublimation are perhaps too abstract to have much bearing on the actual words that make up the corpus of sexual language, though they certainly determine denial and avoidance of sexual terms in speech, writing and thought. The strongest evidence for the workings of repression (and perhaps also sublimation) in our language can be found in certain words that definitely have no sexual denotations or connotations (that is, they have no standard, slang or euphemistic meanings), and yet can be shown, usually through etymological quarrying, to have repressed sexual content.

Thass-Thienemann in *The Subconscious Language* claims that language (all languages, not only English) is shaped by repression as a result of the anxiety experienced through unconscious sexual fantasies and that the sedimentation of language, which etymologists trace, reflects the common sexual fantasies of people. Thus the original meanings of certain words have been repressed because of their anxiety-provoking sexual content. The word *existence*, for example, etymologically reflects the notion of "standing out" and thus may be considered as pointing to the penis. Adjectives like *outstanding* and *swell* are further examples of possible phallic metaphorical origins.

The aim of the present work is to show how much of our ordinary language or terminology serves to provide metaphors for describing or understanding sexual activities, attitudes, organs, and so on. But what is fascinating is that we can also see quite the reverse. Thass-Thienemann tries to show that at least some of our ordinary language or terminology is in fact metaphorical and based on sexual description. Sexuality, itself a basic human experience, is also basic to understanding other phenomena through metaphors based on sexuality. Thass-Thienemann shows us that our understanding of creation is often in sexual or generative terms (this is reflected in myths from many different societies); *material* (the products of creation), for example, etymologically reflects *mater*, or mother.

A most interesting argument given in Thass-Thienemann's book is in connection with irregular verbs — verbs (in English) that have irregular forms in past and past participle forms, such as *know, can, may*. According to Thass-Thienemann the original forms are not simply missing, or did not simply fade away, but, rather, were blocked or repressed, for these terms all originally evoked sexual fantasies. We are familiar with the sexual connotation of **know** from the Biblical meaning of **knowledge**, while *can* and *may* both etymologically reflect potency or sexual power. This demonstrates the implication of sexuality not only in the content of language but also in its very form or structure, that is, its grammar.

One other Freudian ego defense mechanism that may well have a bearing on the language of sexuality is the phenomenon of reaction-formation. Reaction-formation is the doing or saying of the opposite of what is really felt or intended. In *The Antithetical Meaning of Primal Words*, Freud explains that dreams can sometimes mean the opposite of what is manifested, and he ties in this notion with philological research he had recently become aware of: he refers to Abel, whose researches in ancient Egyptian led to the strange discovery that certain words had two meanings, one being the very opposite of the other. This situation is found also in modern languages and examples can be given though they may seem to lack pertinence. In English, for example, to *clip* can mean to fasten or hold things together, or quite the opposite, to cut something apart. In slang usage also we find for example that *bad*, in black American slang, can mean good.

The possible relevance of all this to the language of sexuality is that sexual terms which have taken on derogatory or offensive connotations may well be reflecting some sort of unconscious reaction-formation or antithetical meaning — why else, then, should words like **cunt**, **prick**, etc., be used in such emotionally negative ways. It is worth reflecting on Freud's last words in *The Antithetical Meaning*: "we psychiatrists cannot escape the suspicion that we should be better at understanding and translating the language of dreams if we knew more about the development of language" — an open invitation to the sort of work done by Thass-Thienemann.

We need to look beyond the psychology of ego defense mechanisms, however, to understand the full scope of sexual repression. This involves taking up a sociological and anthropological viewpoint on the notion of taboo. The notion of taboo should be of some use in elucidating some of the more common themes that keep cropping up in the terminology of sexuality. One of the most general features of taboo is the existence of a boundary across which certain actions are not sanctioned by social custom. The incest taboo, for example, does not permit sexual relationships between children and their parents or between siblings. In some sense sexuality in general can be, however, and has been, regarded as a taboo subject. Why should this be the case? What sort of boundaries does sexuality itself straddle?

The most basic boundary encountered by sexuality is the body itself. Sexuality normally involves two people (hence sexual relationships); even masturbation in some sense presupposes another, though a fantasized or projected other. The issue here is individuality and isolation; engaging in sexual activity, in a sense, obliterates the notion of one person. In sex one enters a partnership and in so doing one overcomes one's physical isolation and to some extent even one's own individuality. Bataille, in *Eroticism*, says that human sexuality must be understood in terms of substituting a feeling of profound continuity for the individual's normal isolated discontinuity or experience of separateness. For this reason he finds a very close relationship between sexuality and death. Sex cheats death for it temporarily allows this feeling of continuity and the overcoming of individual isolation, which death brings absolutely. (The language of orgasm in Chapter 5 will show this connection.) On the physical level, sex leads to reproduction, which is another way of overcoming death. Sex, through reproduction, and death, together, are the two essential tools of evolution. On the physical plane sexual intercourse involves a mingling of bodies and bodily juices through the opening of orifices and the exuding of fluids. This crossing of the borders of oneself and joining or mingling with another is precisely what constitutes the danger of sexuality, where desire triumphs over taboo; desire has to be regulated, controlled, even legislated. Since the sex organs are the chief instruments in the action of mingling bodies, or the crossing of body boundaries, they become imbued with special status and taboo. This is one reason, among many, for the vast terminological potpourri for these organs. Ample evidence for this will be provided in chapters 3 and 4.

Since sex is a bodily affair in general, we must go beyond the central focus of the sex organs and acknowledge that the whole body or its entire boundary—the skin and hair—is one continuous erogenous zone. Different parts of it have been emphasized by different societies and at different periods in history. The foot has in certain societies had special erotic status; the foot-binding practices of the Chinese serves as a good example. This phenomenon could be interpreted in Freudian ego defense terms as a type of displacement. The foot displaces the sex organs in response to repression in connection with the sex organs, but the result of the displacement needs explanation; what is it about the foot that makes it a suitable genital substitute? In *The Sex Life of the Foot and Shoe*, Rossi provides many good reasons, stressing such matters as the phallicism of the toes and the sensitive curve in the arch of the foot. Rossi concludes that "'Foot' and 'shoe' are new four-letter entries eligible to be included in the dictionary of erotica and the language of sex."

The juxtaposition of the foot and shoe illustrates another important distinction that should be made in order to understand sexuality and the language of sexuality, namely the distinction of nature from culture. Distinctions, pairs, or binary systems such as nature/culture recur throughout an analysis of the language of sexuality. This very analytic structure could probably be traced back to the male/female distinction we are all familiar with. That is, sexuality itself provides the most basic example of a binary system and can even help in our attempts to understand other binary systems. But returning to feet and shoes, the feet, like the genitals, are part of the body and our bodies tie us to nature.

Sexuality has been extremely adept at straddling both areas, nature and culture. The sexuality of shoes is but one example; we need only think of pointed toes, high heels, and decorations on shoes such as fur, to be aware of erotic overtones. There are some sexual terms borrowed from the world of clothes but clothing is really another language all to itself. We say a great deal sexually simply by the way we dress; words are unnecessary or secondary here. Partially sharing the culture of clothing are such phenomena as cosmetics that alter or enhance the body's appearance.

Other cultural activities that virtually explain themselves as sexual, in some sense, are dancing and sports, both of which are bodily activities and usually involve two or more people. We shall see, in fact, in later chapters, that sports and dance give rise to many sexual terms, or rather, that the metaphors for sex are often taken from the two areas. In the case of sports the very structures of many games, predominantly androcentric in character, seem to parallel the aims of intercourse. We should remember that sports were primarily if not exclusively a male activity.

One major sporting image is of propelling a ball into a goal, net or pocket, or over a post, boundary or net, or through some opening. There appears to be a two-way borrowing — in the later chapters we shall see how sporting terms have been imbued with sexual meanings but we should also be aware that some sporting terms have been acquired from sexual meanings, for one small example, the *kiss* in snooker.

The advent of culture has brought mankind to a restructuring of nature and the body. Society can be seen as responsible for such familiar distinctions, or binary systems, as clean/dirty and sacred/profane. These distinctions presuppose the existence of culture since nature on its own is neither clean nor dirty, sacred nor profane. What this means is that society or culture has imposed rules on the natural expression of sex (and other activities) so that certain forms of sex are allowed, while others are not and are regarded as taboo; some forms of sex are regarded as clean while others are regarded as dirty, and some forms of sex are regarded as sacred while others are profane.

Douglas, the anthropologist, has defined dirt as "matter out of place," as dictated by society. Semen, blood and sweat, if regarded as out of place, will be seen as dirty. Douglas' definition certainly illuminates the taboo of menstruation. The paradigm of dirt is probably encapsulated in excrement, and Freud has pointed out the relationship of excretion to sexual development through the notion of anal eroticism. Using Douglas' notion, it should follow that dirty words, or dirty language, is simply language deemed to be "out of place"; one purpose of this book is to come clean on this point.

The cultural imposition of the sacred/profane distinction in sexuality has a long history. Foucault has already pointed out that in Europe until the 18th century sexual practices were governed by canonical law. Sexuality has a long history of religious control, and religious overtones to sexuality go way back to temple prostitution. The fact that the notion of sin is so strongly associated with sexuality, and that regard for the body is the source of this sin, indicates the power of the church in determining the rules that govern sexual matters. All this may explain why there are a number of religious terms that have entered the language of sexuality.

Perhaps we can find out more about the way we think of sexuality by comparing it with other basic human activities. Without necessarily invoking Sigmund Freud, we can discuss eating and excreting. Both of these functions are, like sex, natural and bodily, and furthermore, both have been the targets of enculturation as has been sexuality. With eating I naturally include drinking, though drink in the alcoholic sense is not implied; some societies have no alcohol so this need cannot be regarded as basic or essential even if some of its florid terminology may suggest otherwise. Orality and anality are, or can be, both regarded to some extent as erotic, though for our purposes we shall look at the strict functions of eating and excreting, conscious nonetheless of the sexual overtones. Not surprisingly our language exhibits terms for eating and excreting with fair variety, paralleling the terminology for sexual activity though not with the same magnitude. What is interesting, however, is the annexing especially of food and eating terms to sexual terminology. There must be strong parallels between eating and sex if one can take language from another; the mixing of metaphors must imply a strong common viewpoint. Let us therefore look at these activities, including excretion, to see what they might share with one another.

Firstly, we could note that society separates sexuality and excretion from eating; that is, there is a taboo against open, public sex and excretion but no such taboo about eating openly and in public. It seems unlikely that we would find a society where eating is private. It is not too difficult, however, to imagine societies where excretion is an open public affair. One may even find that open, public sex is the norm in certain places. In our society we should note that **privates** or **private parts** refer to the sex organs and organs of excretion.

Buñuel, in his cinematic masterpiece *The Phantom of Liberty*, exploits this private/public distinction by showing a group of people sitting around a table on lavatory seats — an image of public excretion — then one person discreetly excuses himself, leaves the room and goes to what we, the audience, expect from appearances to be a lavatory. However, this small room turns out to be a private larder crammed with food. Having locked the door the man then tucks into the food. After this private meal he returns to the communal lavatory. Woody Allen tells a story about Sweden, a country he imagines to have become so free in sexual matters that it has created a taboo about eating — eating can only be done privately and alone. Allen tells of a man being approached to buy pictures of a grilled cheese sandwich, and of someone checking into an hotel at night with a mixed green salad.

In Western society sex and excretion share a further property, namely that participants undress (at least partially) and expose the body, though usually to different degrees in sex and excretion; eating is, however, exempt from all this. This highlights further related functions of clothing, beyond sexual appeal, namely, to cover or hide the body or special parts of it. We can therefore analyze our chosen activities in terms of naked/clothed and or visible/invisible dimensions. One can argue that the body, having organs situated where they are, makes undressing inevitable. But this masks the function of clothes; in some societies the face and the mouth are covered. We could imagine societies where the face only is covered while the genital region is left unclothed, thus undressing would occur for eating but not for sexual intercourse or excretion.

So far it seems that where sex and excretion are similar, while eating is the odd one out, we can blame the positioning of organs on the body. However, we can find an issue where sex and eating are similar, while excretion is the odd one out, and this is with regard to heterogeneity/homogeneity. Sexual appetite and the appetite for food vary considerably, whereas excretion seems to be boringly homogeneous. This appears to be the case since food and sex are basic drives or needs. That is, with food and sex there is the aim of obtaining something that is necessary for survival, future survival and good health, whereas with excretion, though it is necessary, there is simply an elimination of bodily wastes. It therefore cannot be regarded as a basic drive.

It is precisely this notion of sex as a basic drive, comparable to eating, that explains why so much of the terminology of sexuality employs food and eating metaphors. Since eating is regarded as more basic, for immediate survival, than having sex, it is not surprising that we understand sexuality metaphorically in terms of eating but not vice versa. Orality is (according to psychoanalytical thought) the first stage in sexual development so its primacy with regard to metaphorical language should be obvious. Note also that many other phenomena besides sex can be understood by using the metaphor of food and eating — for example, concerning abstract notions, we talk of *raw* facts, ideas that are *fermenting, half-baked* theories, and so on.

Having initially tried to explain the taboo of sexuality in general in terms of crossing boundaries I should point out that one particular, specific sexual taboo has been with us a long, long time, namely incest. If language is anything to go by, this apparently universal taboo reflects an androcentric world view. It is the taboo of incest which gives the term *motherfucker* such power and force. Androcentrism is also evident in an Elizabethan phrase for one type of incest, namely, **returning naked to the womb**. But returning to *motherfucker*, there is an interesting distinction between *a* motherfucker and *the* motherfucker, the former is offensive while the latter is a slang term (mainly American) for the boss or top dog — perhaps unconsciously recognizing Oedipus who had intercourse with his mother but also killed his father who was the king. *Bastard* is another word somewhat similar to *motherfucker* in terms of abuse, but *bastard* seems now to reflect a less powerful and declining taboo, namely that of illegitimate birth.

Other states or activities related to sex, besides sexual intercourse, also qualify as taboos. These states include puberty, menstruation and pregnancy. Puberty is the halfway mark between childhood and adulthood, and the dangers of this transition period may well explain the elaborate rituals so many societies indulge in to mark the tribal initiation into adulthood and the responsibility (especially parental responsibility) that full sexuality brings with it.

The onset of menstruation is, of course, linked to puberty, and it too is regarded by many societies as a dangerous phenomenon and as a taboo. Though in strict biological terms menstruation does indicate a boundary (between periods of ovulation), its "dangers," or the taboos surrounding it, are probably much better understood in terms of matter, namely blood, "out of place." Blood, even to primitive man, must have been held in high regard, for it symbolizes life, and it must have eventually become apparent that menstruation had some connection with childbirth; why else did only postpubertal females menstruate?

Tannahill in *Sex in History* refers to the bloodiness of many puberty rites and mentions certain tribes of Australia and New Guinea where the penises of pubescent boys are cut along the undersides, with the ensuing blood referred to as "men's menstruation." This action, it has been argued, results from a realization that blood somehow enables childbearing, and therefore to produce blood may somehow magically endow men also with the power of childbearing. Finally, pregnancy can be seen as a state of danger for it too straddles a border, between adulthood and parenthood. These dangerous, or taboo, states are well reflected in our language; we find a variety of slang, informal and euphemistic terms for these states, especially menstruation and pregnancy, thus reflecting their special status in society.

2. THE LANGUAGE OF SEXUAL INTERCOURSE

The introduction spoke of a specturm in language from technical and scientific terms through informal expression and euphemism to slang and taboo; to **coit, copulate, have sex, sleep with, lay** and **fuck** were the category examples provided. The historial vicissitudes of the word **fuck** were also briefly discussed. Since this word has survived in English for centuries despite repression and appears to be the most successful of nontechnical or slang terms for **sexual intercourse**, itself the most common formal term, we should look more closely at this word **fuck**.

Perhaps part of the success of **fuck** is related to its phonological properties. Without going into technical details we should simply recognize that it is made up of two consonant sounds which can be described as "hard," and one vowel sound which can also be described in this way. It is worth comparing **fuck** phonologically with **cunt** and the mostly British *bloody*; both also have "hard" consonant sounds, and they both share the same vowel sound with **fuck**. Perhaps this combination of sounds goes some way in explaining the force or strength of these terms. But part of the success of **fuck** also certainly lies with its grammatical and semantic flexibility; it serves not only as a verb and a noun, but also allows for such constructions as *fucker, fucking* (noun and adjective), phrasal verbs such as *fuck around, fuck off, fuck up*, adjectives such as *fucked-up, fucked-out* and the Freudian dreamword, *motherfucker*.

Before discussing some of these interesting variations we should first look into the etymology of the term. Unfortunately not much has been provided etymologically for **fuck**. The *Oxford Etymological Dictionary* chooses to ignore it. The *Oxford English Dictionary* (new supple-

23

ment) relates **fuck** to the Middle English *fuken* and tentatively relates it to the German *ficken*, meaning to strike, though nothing earlier or more definite is given. The term has also been tentatively related to the Latin *futuo* meaning to copulate. The *Merriam-Webster's Ninth Collegiate Dictionary* and the *New Collins Dictionary* relate the word to the Dutch term *fokken*, which the former translates as to breed, while the latter translates as to strike.

If **fuck** is in fact derived from words meaning to strike then it raises interesting questions about sexuality. We may note here that to *fuck up* means to mess up while to *fuck* someone *up* can mean to confuse someone or to beat someone up violently. We should also remember that the child often conceptualizes the sexual act (the primal scene) as an aggressive act, which is why fright or fear often results in the child when this scene is witnessed. Furthermore, sadism and masochism have often been postulated as inherent attributes of all sexual activity. It is not so surprising, therefore, that in addition to **fuck** (which shows aggression etymologically) there are many other verbs in English which denote not only sexual intercourse from an androcentric point of view but also aggression; examples of these terms are to **bang**, **poke**, **thump**, and so on.

It should be obvious that these words are androcentric and phallocentric in character, that is, they describe the sex act from the male's point of view, and more precisely from the penis's point of view. **Fuck**, however, in its primary sexual sense, is intersexual and does not pay too much regard to the active/passive distinction. To indicate sexual intercourse one can say "she fucked him" without any contradiction or linguistic unease, and even without necessarily implying activity/passivity; "she poked him," though, sounds quite ridiculous. **Fuck** is also used in homosexual slang to denote anal intercourse which I shall discuss from the terminological viewpoint in Chapter 5.

One major nonsexual sense of **fuck** is cheating or being done over, especially in the phrases to *fuck someone over*, to *be fucked* or *get fucked*. This connection, between sexuality and cheating, bears some relationship to violence or aggression, for cheating is often done in a violent or aggressive manner. However, the connection can only really make sense in historical perspective. In societies where sexuality is, or was, so controlled (by the church usually) and governed by rigid rules, most or much of sexual activity must be or have been regarded as illicit, particularly masturbation, fornication, adultery and homosexuality. In this way sex becomes associated with cheating or tricking one's society,

religion, and so on. Also where a double standard applies to men as
against women, certain forms of sex can be regarded as cheating the
women. It would be interesting to see if, in societies that do not have
powerful restrictions and taboos about sex, we would find sexual terms
that also have a cheating sense.

That cheating in the sexual sphere is, or has been, so important
in our culture is evident simply from the number of words we find for
the cuckold. *The Slang of Venery* lists over fifty synonyms for a cuckold.
Perhaps the most commonplace term for sex that clearly exhibits this
other, cheating, sense is the word **screw**. Like **fuck**, **screw** is gram-
matically versatile; it is both a verb and a noun and it allows for phrasal
verb constructions. As a verb **screw** can mean both to have sexual intercourse and to cheat. And as a noun, in addition to its sexual senses
of an act or instance of sexual intercourse, and of a person who **screws**
(e.g., a good **screw**, a good **fuck**), it has a slang meaning (in Britain)
of a prison guard, with overtones of crime — all in addition to its standard meaning of a fastening device with a thread. Etymologically
screw is rather obscure from our point of view; it is derived from Latin
meaning a sow, from the suggestion that the sow's tail is spiral-shaped,
like a screw or, more exactly, like the thread of a screw. The spiral motion in working a screw obviously has some bearing on the sexual
sense, for it roughly resembles the motion in the sexual act. On the
subject of hardware, there is the word to **nail** which is modern slang
for having sex, though this term carries much more aggressive and androcentric overtones.

Sticking to the theme of cheating, however, one should also mention to **rip off** (or "**rip off a piece**") and to **trick**, both modern slang
terms for sexual intercourse derived from the language of prostitution,
an institution which openly exhibits the connection between sex and
cheating in a number of senses, perhaps the central ones being the
client who cheats on his wife or lover, and the prostitute who cheats
or, rather, tricks her client or tricks with her emotions. A **trick** is also
a noun referring to a prostitute's client. **Rip off** also has strong aggressive overtones. Other terms which can refer to both sexual intercourse and cheating are: to **diddle**, **ferret**, **job** and **jump**, all now obsolete in the sexual sense though still alive in the sense of cheating or
robbing. **Treason** is another old euphemism for sexual intercourse.

Interestingly the phrasal verb to *screw up* and the adjective *screwed-
up* parallel to *fuck up* and *fucked-up*. To *screw up* or *fuck up* something
means to mess it up, which implies failure, while *screwed-up*, like

fucked-up, suggests confusion and neurosis. Perhaps the very sex act itself, which can result in tiredness and exhaustion, in some way explains the sense of failure and confusion that these phrasal verbs suggest. Curiously an old, now obsolete, sense of the word *tire* is to fail. It is noteworthy that to **shag** is an old, but still currently used, British slang term for sexual intercourse and also means to tire out or exhaust. This word must be related to the words *shag*, meaning matted hair or wool, and *shaggy*, which points to the fact that hair is a strong sexual signifier.

I began this chapter with **fuck** as it appears to dominate sexual slang today, as it did in the past. However, the themes of aggression and cheating are perhaps not primary or even major themes in sexual terminology, though they are important especially in understanding sexism in language. As was stressed in the first chapter, since sexuality is a central aspect of human experience, consequently we ought to find evidence for this in sexual terminology. There is considerable metaphysical terminology for sexuality that can be called up as evidence. Most of the basic or central verbs in the English language can take on sexual connotations, though they are euphemistic or informal rather than slang uses. Metaphysics, in an oversimplified way, is concerned with such general notions as *being, having, doing* and *knowing*. All of these verbs have application in the sexual sense, with the possible exception of *being*, perhaps, since *being* is holistic rather than a particular state, action or activity (though there are some sexual "be" expressions, mainly euphemistic or formal, such as to **be intimate with**, to **be coupled with**, or to **be there**). The language of love however is full of *being* phrases and so could be seen to make up for sexuality—think simply of "love is being...."

To provide examples for the above claims about metaphysics and sex, we have: **having it**, **having it off** and, the classic euphemism, **having sex**. Allied to *having* is *getting* and *taking*, which provide **getting some**, **getting there**, **taking someone** (usually androcentric) and **possessing someone** (again androcentric, and a combination of *having* and *taking*). Then there is **doing it** (see *Maledicta* IV, 2, where well over a hundred examples, from "admirals do it fleetingly" to "writers do it literally" are given), and finally **knowing a woman**, which is Biblical and formal. Knowledge, which is at the heart of metaphysics, thus also has a sexual sense—**carnal knowledge**—and so brings philosophy and sexuality closer together. Note also that to **conceive** can be understood either sexually or epistemologically. Another basic English verb is to *make*; not only is this verb a synonym for intercourse (as in **make it** and **make out**), it also finds sexual expression in **making love**, which is perhaps the most common euphemism nowadays, **making babies**, **making the scene**, etc.

These last phrases with the word *make* place an emphasis on the more successful and positive side of sexuality. Other terms also connect sex with success — perhaps the best known is to **score**, which implies that having sex is in fact winning it; **score**, incidentally, also has the slang meaning of obtaining narcotics or drugs, something illicit and dangerous. Another term for doing successfully and for having sexual intercourse is to **quiff**, though now both senses are obsolete. Curiously, **quiff**, the noun, also has meant a lock or curl of hair on the forehead, a meaning it could well have obtained via the sexual symbolism of hair. Dictionaries simply state for **quiff**, "etymology unknown."

Hole in one is another quaint metaphor for sexual intercourse which carries with it sporting (golf) overtones of great success. **Hole in one** and **score** as well as **win** and **prize**, which is Elizabethan, naturally bring to mind sport, so not surprisingly we find such colloquialisms for sexual intercourse as **the first game ever played** and **the national indoor game**. **Sport** itself has an old sense of amorous sport or sexual intercourse. More specific sporting terms give rise to such terms as **couch rugby**, **tick-tack**, which is another term for sexual intercourse as well as meaning, in standard English, a board game predating backgammon, and **tilting**, from the art or sport of jousting.

Given that sex is so basic to our lives it is no surprise that the words *game, play* and *work* all take on sexual connotations; in fact our lives can be seen to consist of working, playing and sleeping, all of which have sexual overtones. We have already mentioned phrases for sexual intercourse with the word *game* in them. The word *play* is also found in additional phrases such as to **play hanky panky**, **play at in and out** and to **play at in and in** (both used since the 17th century), and the word *work* appears with sexual meaning in such phrases as to **work up** (androcentric and phallocentric) and the euphemism **night work**. Sleep gives rise to **sleep with**, perhaps the best-known euphemism. **Grafting** is an Elizabethen term for sex and now has a slang meaning of to work. It should be noted that some of the terms in other phrases also embody other sexual meanings; for example, to **play with oneself** is to masturbate and to **be on the game** is to be engaged in prostitution. The terminology of these other sexual themes will be discussed in Chapter 5.

Much of sexual terminology is obviously less metaphysical or occupational than the foregoing examples, and more straightforward or up front. In fact much of sexual slang, unimaginatively and often crudely, simply describes the positions of sexual intercourse; thus most of the slang terms are merely verbs or verbal constructions. Those verbs which are straightforwardly positional such as to **hump, lay, mount** and **ride** are all, like **fuck**, intersexual, though only **lay** really allows for the active/passive distinction — **getting laid** is applied equally to males and females. Other terms that actually specify or describe the position of the act are to **lie with** and the now obsolete to **horizontalize** or **horizontal refreshment**. Other quaint horizontal turns of phrase are: to **see stars lying on one's back**, or to **study astronomy**. **Riding Saint George** or **riding the dragon upon Saint George** describes sexual intercourse with the woman on top, as does a **reverse western**; while to **dog** refers to entry from the rear on all fours. Sexual intercourse in the standing position gives rise to **doing a perpendicular** which is also called an **up-right** or a **knee-trembler**. The various positions for intercourse, heterosexual and homosexual, give rise to a language all of its own with oriental as well as occidental (often technical or medical) terms. These terms are sometimes shorthand for detailed descriptions, but I shall omit them here and simply refer the reader to sex manuals and to medical books on sexuality. There are, however, some colorful androcentric phrases for types of sexual intercourse — examples of unsuccessful sexual intercourse, that is, without ejaculation, are: a **flash in the pan**, a **dry hump** and a **dry bob**; **shooting in the bush** and **shooting over the stubble** refer to a self-explanatory outcome, given that **bush** and **stubble** are terms for the female public hair, while **double fire** and **double payment** refer to two ejaculations in the course of sexual intercourse.

Keeping to the theme of positions, though, we may note that prepositions feature quite strongly in the language of sexual intercourse. We have already mentioned to **play at in and out**, to **play at in and in**, to **work up** and to **rip off**. Some other expressions that use prepositions are: **in Cupid Alley, in Cock Alley, in love lane**, to **do over**, which also means to cheat or trick, and to **do/have a hoist in**, now obsolete. There are also androcentric puns on the preposition *under* as in the terms to **undergo, understand** and **undertake**.

Many verbal expressions for sexual intercourse do not describe positions but instead describe actions or activities, in however vague or general a way. These terms are predominantly euphemistic and informal. Examples of these terms are to **bounce, grind, roll, tumble** and so on, all intersexual. From the androcentric pont of view there is: to **dock, plug, shove, split** and **stuff**, among many. An interesting old term for sexual intercourse is to **pump**, interesting because as a noun it can refer to both the male and the female genitals — probably because pumps consist of both levers and containers. From terms for the female genitals we find such verbs as: to **hole, nock** and to **stretch leather** (obsolete). And from the gynocentric viewpoint we find: to **bear, give oneself, let in, cure the horn**, etc.

Certain descriptions of sexual intercourse go beyond describing actions and describe instead the ensuing result; examples are: to **couple with**, which goes way back to the 15th century; **congress** and **union** which are both very formal; the now obsolete to **fit ends**, or to **fit end to end**, as well as to **make ends meet** which also has an idiomatic meaning of earning a living. To **accommodate** is perhaps from the female's point of view, but **lovers' knot** is intersexual as is **addition** and **multiplication**, perhaps in view of the results. The coupling of male and female in sexual intercourse is even reflected in the language of certain nonsexual activities such as in the terminology of hardware in which male and female parts refer to instruments or devices that project into something or that receive a projected part. Sex thus serves as the metaphor for identifying certain cultural or technological artifacts.

Though sexual intercourse can be conceptualized as a violent attack (the **fuck** group of words), the metaphor of conquest can be employed without necessarily having sadistic or violent overtones. This theme, which is almost always androcentric, gives rise to such euphemisms for sexual intercourse as: to **occupy, charge, invade**, etc., likening the female to a fortress (*fortress* even sounds like a female version of a fort because of the suffix -*ess*). Related to conquest is the word **venery** which has two meanings — the sport or practice of hunting and the pursuit of sex. Incidentally, *The Slang of Venery*, the privately published sexual slang dictionary in the Private Case in the British Museum library, was first classified under hunting. Hunting and conquest obviously lead on to the theme of deflowering, for the conquest is often of a virgin. The terminology for this is a mixture of aggressive terms and charming idioms which are self-explanatory: to **punch, puncture, crack a teacup, crack a judy**, and the Shakespearean to **pick the lock**, which brings to mind the chastity belt.

The introduction discussed the nature/culture distinction that runs through the language of sexuality. The first aspect, on the nature side of this polarity, is the theme of animality. Sexuality shows up our connection and continuity with the natural world, which includes the animal world; it points to our innate animality or beastliness. Emphasis is usually placed on the relative "lowliness" of the animal world, thus sexuality is shown *not* as a distinguishing feature of humanity, whereas in fact human sexuality *is* quite unique — very different from animal sexuality and considerably more complex.

The verb to **ride** in the sexual sense goes way back to Middle English, and this is an obvious metaphor for the sexual act. To **mount** is another term with a long history. Not surprisingly, then, to **horse** was once a term for sexual intercourse, from the 17th to the 20th century, though now it is obsolete. Both to **bull** and to **ferret** were also terms for sexual intercourse, and both of these terms can also mean to cheat. The deer and the cat also come in for some of the action since both to **tom** and to **rut** have been used as euphemisms for human copulation. Grose defines [to make a] **dog's rig** as "to copulate till you are tired and then turn tail to it" and **rabbit** exemplifies the rabbit's well-known propensity for frequent copulation, inferred from frequent reproduction. **Goose** is an interesting term for sexual intercourse because of its derivation: it is rhyming slang from **goose and duck** meaning **fuck**.

The primacy of **fuck** as a term for sexual intercourse is evidence in rhyming slang. But why, we must ask, was **goose and duck** selected as the rhyme for **fuck**? There must be a myriad other options that could have been chosen. To **goose** is also American slang for prodding someone in the anus, though this meaning appeared later than rhyming slang; Partridge also provides senses of *to goose* which mean to condemn by hissing, to spoil or ruin, or to make a fool of — and these slang senses appear to predate the sexual sense of *goose*. In addition to **goose and duck** as rhyming slang for **fuck** there also is **Russian duck** (the English frequently look elsewhere to coin sexual euphemisms, hence also **French letter**, etc. — see Chapter 5) and **lame duck** which hints of post-coition. Another rhyming slang term is **cattle truck**.

Reviewing all the animals that get mentioned or are implied in sexual terminology we find: horse, bull, ferret, dog, rabbit, goose, duck, cattle, cat and deer, as well as sow or pig (via the etymology of **screw**), almost all of which are familiar creatures today and, centuries ago, even more familiar to people, even in urban areas. These animals conjure up images of farming and **husbandry**, which itself is an old term for sexual intercourse, as are **tillage**, to **plough** and to **ear** (to plough for corn), all now obsolete. Lastly, on this theme, there is the euphemistic expression to **do the beast with two backs**.

The theme of animality, under the cloak of nature, leads on to the theme of the body. Terms for sexual intercourse that use terms for the body are mostly all euphemistic for they do not refer to the genitals but rather to other parts of the body (which Freud, for instance, called displacement) or to the body as a whole (the Freudian "abstraction"). One exception is to **hole**, derived from the noun meaning the female genitals. Starting with terms for the body as a whole, we have to **flesh** or to **flesh it**, used since the 16th century but now obsolete. Turning to more specific parts of the body, since the genitals are in the middle region of the body where the buttocks are as well, we find many terms for sexual intercourse that reflect this anatomical region. We have to **rump** and **rump work**, to **do a wet bottom** and **buttock ball**, to **tail** and to **shoot in the tail**, which also has overtones of animality.

Next in spatial closeness to the genitals are the legs, which lead up to and join at the genitals. Perhaps because of this, and also perhaps because they are capable of such flexible movement, they serve as an appropriate euphemism for genital activity; further explanation may be needed for why leg terms predominate rather than, say, belly terms. The association by some of sex with lowliness or baseness could account for this phenomenon. Examples of leg terms, now mostly obsolete, are: to **throw a leg over**, to **play at lift leg**, **leg business** and the arithmetic **four-legged frolic**. One Elizabethan expression, employing the leg euphemism with aggression, is to **stab in the thigh**. Allied expressions for deflowering and losing one's virginity are: to **break her leg above the knee** and to **be wounded in the thigh**, respectively. Finally going to the extremes of the anatomy, and of euphemism, we find to **foot** used by Shakespeare, though this is an educated pun on the French *foutre* meaning to **fuck**.

Moving upwards from the genitals we find a few euphemisms such as to **wriggle navels** and to **join giblets**. And before reaching the face as a source of metaphor, **titty** must get a mention as gay slang for heterosexual intercourse. To **ear** has already been mentioned, in connection with ploughing, as a term for sexual intercourse. **Lip work** is another obsolete term which trades on the pun between the lips of the mouth and those of the female genitals. Other idiomatic euphemism also go to both bodily extremes: **making faces** and **making feet for children's stockings/shoes**.

If **ball** was left out of this section you may think a relevant term had been overlooked. This modern term for sexual intercourse may not, however, be derived from the familiar round objects, testicles, but perhaps rather from the grand dance. *Having a ball* has become an ambiguous phrase, as is *the secret policeman's ball* — is it a dance or a raffle? But at least we see some joy of sex shining through in this modern slang term to **ball**, though **ball** is only a plural away from negative connotations; *balls* and *balls-up* both derive their negative sense from the sexual meaning. We shall return to the theme of dance later, but while on the subject of *having a ball* we should note that some very early terms for sexual intercourse reflect joy; to **joy** and to **enjoy** go back to the 16th century, as does **gaying it**, though this would probably be differently understood nowadays. Other terms of this nature for sexual intercourse are: to **have a bit of fun** and **delight**, and, leading in true reaction-formation style from pleasure to pain, we find: **tender agony**, **sweet agony** and **sweet death**. The introduction discussed the connection and relationship between sex and death, which makes **buried alive** and **last act** or **last liberties** logical euphemisms for sexual intercourse.

Another important theme that surfaces in sexual terminology is food. The introductory chapter dealt with the close relationship between eating and sex. It was Freud's view that the oral stage is the first of the stages of psychosexual development. So sexuality is already present in earliest childhood and the mouth may very well serve as the first erogenous zone. We find terms for sexual intercourse in food terms and in eating terms. Beginning with food, the first grouping of terms can be seen to equate sexual activity to the primary nature of food; that is, something necessary for survival. **Ground rations**, a 20th century slang term, perhaps most obviously stresses survival. **Meat** is generic for the body, in the same way that **flesh** is, and both are obviously also regarded as food, often of a necessary kind. Related terms for sexual intercourse are: **a bit of meat**, **mutton**, and to **put four corners on the spit**. It should be noted that **meat**, like **pump**, is one of those rare all-purpose sexual words, for in addition to sexual intercourse it can refer to both the male and the female genitals. From meat to fish: **a bit of fish** is an obsolete term for sexual intercourse derived from **fish**, meaning the female genitals. **Sard** is a term going back to the 10th century, now obsolete, which has a fishy etymology — *sarda* is Latin for fish (reflected in the English term *sardine*).

Vegetables are also held in high regard as essential food, and they too give rise to sexual connotation. To **get**, **give** or **have one's greens** were terms used in the 19th century; more specifically we have to **be among the cabbages** and a **bit of cauliflower**, both androcentric terms. Necessity is also seen in grains, perhaps explaining the phrases to **get one's oats** and to **sow one's wild oats** which reflects the follies of male youth — sowing wild oats instead of good grain. Finally, from among substances regarded as essential, there is to **salt**, now obsolete. Salt is an essential mineral and the etymology of *salary* brings this out — it means "salt money." However, Partridge suggests that the sexual intercourse sense of the term is derived from a slang meaning of the noun *salt*, meaning a sailor, especially an experienced one. A further thought is that salt is used as a flavoring in food, and in this spicy sense could provide some rationale for the sexual connotation of the word, as is also reflected in the word **relish**, meaning sexual intercourse.

From food as a main course, or as a necessity, we move on to food as desserts: **pudding** is an obsolete term for sexual intercourse, though it can also refer to the penis, while **crumpet** refers to women in general as sex objects. The sweetness (and sting?) of sex is evident in to **hive it** and **honeyfuck**, now both obsolete, though the term *honeymoon* and endearments such as *honey* and *sugar* retain the sweetness today. Other desserts or similar foods are **a hot roll with cream** and **a bit of jam**, the latter phrase being applicable in other ways besides food, since *jam* can also mean a very close or tight fit as well as a jazz performance. There are two apposite American slang terms exclusively androcentric in character, namely to **have one's banana peeled** and to **have one's nuts cracked**. **Taking a slice** and **a bit on a fork** further unite sexuality with food, though the latter phrase can also refer, androcentrically, to the female genitals. Since sexual intercourse from the female's point of view involves taking in the penis, and eating involves taking food into the mouth, we find such exemplary gynocentric phrases as to **feed one's pussy**, and the pejorative to **feed one's monkey**, to **get the sugar stick**, to **take in beef** and to **take in cream**. The connection between sex and feasting is reflected in the now obsolete **beanfeast**, while the close relationship between sex and the act of eating is reflected in Shakespeare's euphemism to **taste** as well as in the more modern terms to **nibble** and to **have a nibble**. Sexual intercourse is referred to in terms for food, eating, meals, feasts and utensils, thus exploiting the whole gamut of orality in sexual terminology.

Food and eating, like sexuality, straddle the border of nature and culture. Having already looked at nature, through the themes of animality and body, we should now turn to the cultural metaphors that abound for sexuality. The ambiguities inherent in the word **ball** involve dance and music, both of which serve as metaphors in the vocabulary of sexuality since they all share a pulse, a rhythm and excitement. Dance terms referring to sexual intercourse, now obsolete, are to **dance the sheets**, to **dance the goat's jig**, to **dance the matrimonial polka**, and so on, and the ontological and cosmological to **dance the beginning of the world**. Dance phrases show references to such diverse themes as the body, animality and bedding. To **jig** is of course an old term for sexual intercourse, a jig being a fast kind of dance, while to **shake** is an old euphemism; *the shake* is also a popular recent dance. The names of other modern dances also have sexual ovetones, such as *the twist* (euphemism for a **screw**?), *the hustle* akin to **hustle** meaning to copulate, and *beguine*, a South American dance, derived from French *beguin*, meaning flirtation.

Music, of course, is a natural partner to dance, and we find many interesting musical terms that also have sexual references. One word deserving a paragraph to itself is **jazz**. The *Oxford English Dictionary* originally did not list the word at all, though the new supplement rectifies this omission by listing six uses for the noun — the first being the music and the fourth being sexual intercourse — and three for the verb, the last being sexual. The OED supplement does not provide an etymology for the word but states that the connection with *jasm*, meaning energy, has not been demonstrated. The *Oxford Dictionary of English Etymology* suggests that *Jas* is a pet form of the name Charles, the name of some early Negro musician. *Merriam-Webster's Third New International Dictionary*, *Merriam-Webster's Collegiate* and *Random House* do not provide an etymology, nor does the *Chambers 20th Century Dictionary* nor the *New Collins Dictionary of the English Language*. Some dictionaries simply decare that **jazz** is a "Negro word." The notion that jazz music has its very name entwined in a reference to sexual intercourse may well provide insight into the nature, the vitality, and the rhythm of the music. It may also provide new shades of meaning to some song titles like *Jazz Me Blues*, etc. Historically jazz evolved in New Orleans, especially in its places of entertainment — like brothels — making further sense of the name that the music received. Linguistically and in other ways jazz reflects one of the closest relationships between art and sexuality.

The roots of jazz clearly are in Africa, and curiously we find that the names of certain types of African music show definite connection with sexuality. **Kwela** is a type of black South African beat or jazz music, but the word is derived from the Nguni (Zulu, Xhosa and Swazi languages) *khwela*, a verb meaning to climb on or mount which can also be taken in the sexual sense. And **patha-patha** which is a type of sensuous African dance music (popularized by Miriam Makeba in the 1960s) is derived from the Nguni *patha* meaning to touch; *touch-touch* has obvious overtones of sexual intercourse. Funk, which is a type of modern jazzy music with a heavy beat, deserves a mention here simply because of its phonetic resemblance to **fuck**; this resemblance is exploited in musical names and titles

Other terms which have both sexual and musical meanings are the now obsolete **strum** and **thrum** (an early 17th century term), both of which imply sexual fingering. Then there is to **fiddle** which has at least three distinct meanings, the obsolete one of having sex, the central one of playing the fiddle, and finally the sense of cheating. The word is derived from the Latin *vitulari*, meaning to celebrate, which could account for the first two meanings; but the third sense, that of cheating, has somehow entered the language with a more tenuous link to the word's etymology. **Playing the trombone** and **tromboning** are other androcentric examples of having sexual intercourse. Finally Grose provides us with the now obsolete **blanket hornpipe** which he defines as "the amorous congress," combining the realm of the bed with that of music — a hornpipe is an obsolete reed instrument.

The mention of bed leads to the next general theme in the language of sexual intercourse, namely that of place. Since sexual intercourse must take place somewhere, many of the words that describe these places have acquired, by simple association, sexual meanings. To **go to bed with** must be among the most common euphemisms for sexual intercourse (ranking with to **sleep with**). This variety of euphemism goes back at least to Elizabethan times when **bed sports**, **chamber work** and **chamber combat** were employed. **National indoor game** is self-explanatory in this category, but to **fornicate** and **fornication** need explanation. Both words are derived from the Latin *fornix*, the original meaning of which was an arch, vault or vaulted room. In Latin, the word also took on the meaning of brothel. Interestingly, the word is also etymologically related to the Latin *furnus* meaning a furnace; this conjures up the notion of heat, which figuratively can mean passion or ardor, which is but a step away from sexual desire.

Another modern euphemism for sexual intercourse is **nooky**. This could be derived from *nook* meaning a corner, angle or narrow recess—that is, a place where sex can be practiced in private, or it could be a variation on **nick**, a term for the female genitals. Partridge, however, suggests that **nooky** may be derived from **nug** which is an obsolete word for sexual intercourse. **Nug** is definitely related to nudge, meaning "to gently push with the elbow." *Monty Python*, the recent television comedy series, gained some currency for the charming euphemism **nudge, nudge (wink, wink)**.

Related to the notion of place, through the focus in the room on the bed, are the objects associated with it, such as sheets, blankets, etc. We have already discussed **dance the sheets** and **blanket hornpipe**, both now obsolete, as is to **polish one's arse on the top sheet**. Linen naturally brings to mind clothing and sewing, which have both contributed some terminology. The clothing terms are all androcentric: to **do a bit of skirt**, the Cockney terms to **have a bit of skirt** and to **have a bit of fluff**, to **get into her pants**, and the older to **go underpetti-coating**. The sewing metaphors are also androcentric and have an aggressiveness about them since the needle has a sharp point—to **stitch**, to **sew up** and **ladies tailoring** indicate this. Only to **thread the needle** gets away from that sharpness since it focuses on the eye of the needle; presumably the penis is equated with the thread so only accuracy and shape are emphasized.

Having discussed space, which is implied in the notion of place, let us turn to time and causality, which both generate sexual terminology. Time is reflected rather simply in terms that refer to the evening or bedtime, such as **night work**, and the older **night physic**. Love in the afternoon is expressed (with linguistic inexactitude) by the term **matinee** (from the Latin for *morning*), while to **wind up the clock** is an educated 18th century euphemism that Partridge suggests may derive from a passage in *Tristram Shandy*. Curiously one winds up a clock to keep everyday life going or when "time stops"—something sometimes felt to occur during sexual intercourse—one also winds up the clock to keep it going—something experienced or rather desired during intercourse. Finally, there is the screw-like action of actually winding a clock.

Causality is reflected in terms or phrases that exhibit knowledge of the result (sometimes) of sexual intercourse, namely procreation. Some straightforward terms are: to **make babies**, the less happy to **make piggies**, and such phrases as: to **make faces**, to **make feet for children's stockings** or to **make feet for children's shoes**. Not just Cockneys euphemistically refer to sexual intercourse simply as **it**, elsewhere in Britain we find **that there** as a euphemism. Yiddish provides to **yentz** derived from the German *jenes* meaning that or that thing. **Yentz** also means to swindle or "screw" someone and so adds to the long ambivalent list of terms including **screw**, **diddle**, etc. There is also an Australian slang term for sexual intercourse, namely **root**, as a noun and a verb. **Root** seems to reflect primacy or essence as well as origin or derivation, though the term is most likely to come via another older slang meaning for the noun, namely the penis.

The realm of mystery also supplies some sexual terminology; we find that **alchemy** and to **do miracles** goes back to Elizabethan times. **Mysteries of love** may remind us of the dual nature of sexuality, ranging from the **art of pleasure** to **sexual science**, and on the scientific side we find the euphemism to **exchange DNA**. Many qualities emphasized in sex provide terms or phrases for sexual intercourse, usually euphemistic. First there is heat or warmth, which provides to **smoke**, to **get one's ashes hauled** and to **light the lamp**. Firmness and softness are both captured in the intersexual idioms **a bit of hard for a bit of soft** and **a bit of snug for a bit of stiff** and wetness enters with to **give juice for jelly**. There is also to **lubricate**, to **take the starch out of** and to **bury the hatchet where it won't rust**. The death metaphor is dug with to **bury the bone**.

Much of the terminology for sexual intercourse that we have discussed is euphemistic and the history of the word **fuck** goes some way in showing this. Since **fuck** is perhaps the central English slang term for sexual intercourse, and has suffered the vicissitudes of repression, we find such replacements for it as **firk** (which could be derived from **fuck** and **dirk**, the penis as a sword), **frig**, though this has now come to mean to masturbate, the Elizabethan **fucus** which is juxtaposed with **fuck** in many English dictionaries, **futter**, and **foutering**. These terms all clearly point a finger towards **fuck** whereas rhyming slang terms, by sometimes dropping the second, rhyming, part may succeed as euphemisms. Not so, however, for some of these terms, which retain their second or last term. I have already mentioned the rhymes with *duck* and *truck*; others are **Friar Tuck** and **Colonel Puck**.

Since having sex can be very healthy for one it is not surprising that **medicine** has been used euphemistically, and from this we get to **relieve** as opposed to **do an inside worry**. Many terms for petting are also used euphemistically for sexual intercourse, for example, to **fondle**, to **huddle** and to **cuddle** — all showing the close communication involved in sexual intercourse. Communication itself serves as a theme:

we find such Elizabethan terms as to **talk**, to **converse**, **parley** and **discourse**, which brings us to the sounds of sex.

Finally, sexual intercourse can be reduced to **bangs** and **whimpers**. Sound-related modern terms are **grumble and grunt**, **groan and grunt** and **gasp and grunt**, though the rhyming term here is **cunt**. **Twang** is another auditory term (now obsolete) for copulation, with musical overtones; compare it to **strum** and **thrum**. And finally there is **making whoopee** — derived from the exclamation *whoopee*, which is usually said out of joy or excitement.

3. THE LANGUAGE OF THE FEMALE SEX ORGANS

There happen to be more terms for the female genitals than for the male — possibly but not necessarily a result of androcentrism. But no term can be discussed before one of the most well-known of all terms, that chiefly used for the female genitals, **cunt**.

Though the *Oxford Dictionary of English Etymology* does not list the word, the new supplement to the OED cites its use from as early as 1230. Chaucer used the word in the 14th century, and it has been considered vulgar only since about the 16th century — so vulgar that Grose's *Dictionary of the Vulgar Tongue* places two asterisks between the C and the T and defines the entry as "a nasty name for a nasty thing." The *Oxford English Dictionary* relates the word via Middle English *cunte* to Old Norse *kunta* and to similar Middle Low German and Middle Dutch terms. Partridge seems to think that **cunt** is unlikely to be related etymologically to the Latin *cunnus* meaning a wedge, but that *cu*, or *cwu*, in Old English appears to mean quintessential femininity; in Old English *cwithe* means a womb. Partridge even suggests that this perhaps explains why the cow is a sacred animal in India!

Merriam-Webster's Third New Interational Dictionary relates **cunt** to the Middle High German *kotze* meaning a prostitute, and suggests a relationship to the Old English *cot* meaning a den or cottage. Interestingly, **den** is an obsolete literary term for the vagina, while **cottage** now has the slang meaning in some English-speaking countries of a public lavatory where male homosexuals loiter (it is also called a **tearoom** or **teahouse**). The term **vagina** is derived from the Latin meaning a **sheath**, which perhaps sounds androcentric, even aggressive, especially as it may conjure up images of swords. However, the term is widely used in anatomy for other bodily parts. For a

39

a genuine weapons metaphor we find the word **quiver** for the female genitals — which in standard English means a case for arrows.

Related to **cunt** is the term **quim**; Partridge suggests that it is derived from the Celtic **cwm** meaning a valley or cleft. **Quim** has been a vulgarity since the 17th century. The *Oxford English Dictionary* relates the word etymologically to *queme* which, as an adjective, means pleasing, fitting or suitable. Already, then, we have seen through etymology that terms for the female genitals point to such themes as containers and to contours or **shape**, which is itself a euphemism. Perhaps this distinction between container and shape lies in, or is explained by, a deeper distinction, namely between the **vagina** and the **vulva**, or the internal and the external parts of the female genitals, between the visible and the hidden. In a paper entitled "The Vulva: A Psycholinguistic Problem" (*Maledicta* IV, 2), Mildred Ash shows that there is an astonishing absence of the word **vulva** from our vocabulary. **Penis** is always matched with **vagina** and the word **vagina** is usually used also to refer to the **vulva**. Psychoanalysis may try to explain this phenomenon in terms of the **vulva** causing anxiety (in both sexes) for it reminds one of the lack of a **penis**. However, although this strange linguistic practice may exist in the medical or technical sphere, we find that the informal, euphemistic and slang terms for the female genitals clearly exhibit reference to both the **vagina** and the **vulva** — that is, to containers, and to slits, etc.

Let us begin with the container words. Not surprisingly these divide into natural and cultural groups, though the vast majority are cultural items. Beginning with the nature items: **nature** itself has been used as a euphemism for the female genitals. Other natural terms (conjuring up the ancient element of water) are **peculiar river**, **pond**, **shell**, **bog** and **quagmire**. Involving the element of earth are **den** and **pit**, as well as variations on **pit**, namely **bottomless pit** and **pit of darkness**.

Of terms reflecting culture we find such domestic examples, now mostly obsolete, as **oven**, **kettle** and **pot** as in **melting pot**, which all also involve heat or warmth and conjure up the element of fire. Other domestic containers are **pitcher** and **box**, which also has the slang meaning of a coffin. Other domestic container terms relate to clothing or clothes-making, such as **pocket** and **case**, especially in **needle case** and **jewel case**, though these are linguistically androcentric. On a larger, nondomestic scale we have such manmade conversions of nature as **mine of pleasure** and **quarry**, and, also perhaps manmade, we have **vacuum**. **Lock**, **padlock** and **keyhole** all have androcentric overtones of chastity and fidelity in women. And religion contributes with **pulpit** and **shrine of love**, while Shakespeare provides us with **treasury**. The full gamut of connotation or emotional response to the female genitals is present in **bog** to **treasury**.

Closely related to container words are passage words; the vagina is as much a passage, a birth canal, as a container. However, we find fewer terms in this category, perhaps because androcentrically the passage is not as significant sexually as the container. Some of the more pejorative terms are to be found in this category; we find: **ditch**, **dike** (though this has now acquired another sexual meaning, namely, a lesbian), **drain**, **furrow**, **gutter**, **waste pipe**, and so on. The term **twat**, a vulgarism used since the 17th century, and its etymologically related **twatchel** or **twachel**, all mean a passage, though a different etymology has been proposed relating **twat** to *two*, that is, the two major labia (see *Maledicta* IV, 2). Other passage terms are more recent and really take their sense from traffic or transport systems with overtones of prostitution; we find: **main avenue**, **turnpike** and **Venus's highway**.

Moving from container/internal/vagina terms to shape/external/vulva terms we find again a division into natural and cultural terms, though this distinction is not always clear. Is **cleft**, **crack**, **cut**, **gap**, **gash**, **hole** or **slit** natural or cultural? It should be pointed out that these general terms also generate further terms for the female genitals. Taking **hole** as general, we also find: **black hole**, **fuck hole**, **manhole**, **poke hole**, **queen of holes** and the Elizabethan pun **whole**.

Some terms are, however, clearly cultural, such as **noose** which implies that men or penises will be trapped. **Wheel** is another cultural term that goes as far back as the 16th century, while more recently we find **hoop**. Ambiguities persist between nature and culture with the following words: **ring**, **crease**, **circle** and **corner**, while terms that are also related to the appearance of the body are found in **grin**, **wound** and **wrinkle**, though it should be noted that the appearance is of other parts of the body, especially the face, and have been typically euphemistically transferred. There are a number of terms that seem to be on the border between the themes of container and shape, namely, **cranny**, **crevice** and **nooky**, though this last term is used more often to refer to sexual intercourse. **Notch**, **nock** and **nick** sound related to **nooky** though **nick** has other connotations, namely of stealing and of the devil.

In *Literary Women*, Moers refers to the themes that women

commonly use to describe their sex organs. Most prominent, she thinks, is the theme of birds, though other prominent themes are flowers and landscape, in spite of the opinion of some males that landscape, or more generally, external reality, is a male prerogative. These themes are all derived from nature. The origins of animal life can be found in plant life, and so plants can really be credited with the invention of sex. Even in human sexuality, plants play a significant role; many perfumes or scents are extracted from plants and many sexual messages are conveyed by flowers. Even the euphemistic phrase **birds and bees**, which refers to the sexual facts of life, hints at the plant world that birds and bees pollinate.

Flower itself is a common euphemism for the female genitals. More specifically, but now quite obsolete, we find **flower of chivalry**. And examples of flowers with sexual meanings are: **daisy** and **rose**. Etymologically **daisy** is derived from the Old English *day's eye* and we shall soon see the sexual significance of the eye. Both **daisy** and **rose** must have acquired sexual meaning by virtue of their appearance. In the past, medicinal theory made use of the doctrine of signatures, which states that similarities between plants and human body parts signify certain powers for those plants; this theory provided some logic to what are regarded as aphrodisiacs. The etymology of **flower** itself, through the idea of flowing, is related to a woman's monthly flow. Also to **deflower**, meaning to break the hymen through intercourse, makes clear sense, given the sexual meaning of flower. Flowers and plants lead on quite naturally to the theme of landscape, and in particular to **garden**, perhaps sexualized via grass, which conjures up the pubic hair—also a strong signifier of the female genitals. And on the garden theme we also find **patch**, **green grove**, **pleasure garden**, **garden gate**, **garden of Eden** and, related to this, **promised land**. **Nursery** notes the generative powers while the **lowlands**, **midlands**, **mount pleasant** and **Shooter's hill** add further spatial dimensions to the landscape theme. Other geographical names, though with obvious sexual innuendo, are: **Holloway**, **Cape Horn** and **Cape of Good Hope**.

Moving from the natural landscape to the human, or cultural, one we find many terms for buildings having sexual connotations. The container idea is found in housing terms such as **thatched house, the thatched house under the hill** (a book title in the 18th century) and **house under the hill**. **Eve's custom house** is a euphemism which invites the response "where Adam made his first entry." **Lodge** is an Elizabethan euphemism, while **hotel, Cupid's hotel, Cupid's Arms** and **Cock Inn** are all more recent euphemisms. **The world's smallest hotel** refers to the androcentric riddle whose explanation is: "because you've got to leave your bags [that is, testicles] outside."

Moving on to shapes or parts of buildings we find such terms as **blind entrance, forecastle, front door, front window**, etc. A typical distinction is here present between vulva and vagina terms; **front door** for example is contrasted with **front attic, front room** or **parlour room**.

Though birds and flying may feature in female literary descriptions or metaphors, we find only such terms as **cuckoo's nest, rooster**, and such pejorative terms as **fly-trap** and **fly-cage**. The animal that seems to have become most prominently associated with the female genitals in the language of sexual terminology is the cat. **Cat** itself has been so used, as has **chat** from the French, **malkin** which is an old Scottish term for a cat but can also mean a hare, and **kitty**. But the most well-known of cat terms is **puss** and **pussy**, which date from the 17th century. **Puss** also has slang meanings for the face, the mouth and (in homosexual slang) the anus. How this feline word acquired its sexual meaning must have something to do with the fur of a cat, both visually and through tactile sensation.

Focusing on the pubic hair goes some way in explaining the choice of animal terms for the female genitals. Besides the cat the furry rabbit features strongly. Though **cunny** may well sound like a diminutive of **cunt** or a variation on the Latin *cunnus*, it actually is an obsolete form of *cony*, a rabbit. **Bunny** is another term for the female genitals (the advent of the Playboy bunny may echo this, though the nickname "Bunny" is usually thought of as innocently affectionate). **Scut**, in fact, means a rabbit's tail, in addition to its genital reference. One other furry animal that has only recently entered the realm of sexual slang is **beaver**, which also has slang meanings of a beard and of a bearded man. The phrase **wide open beaver** has come to signify explicit pictures of the female genitals in pornographic magazines.

Other animals that find their way into sexual slang are **fish** (and many different kinds of fish shall be dealt with under the theme of food), **rooster** and **coyote**, which show variation from the domesticated to the wild, and **monkey**, which is possibly derived from something like *monkey business* or *to monkey around*. Animality in general is expressed in the early 18th century phrase **mark of the beast**, emphasizing the lowliness of the sex organs; this characteristic, though, is not greatly emphasized in the terminology for the female genitals, which we have seen emphasizes other characteristics such as furriness. **Leather** and **leather lane** both refer as much to animality as to the body, for leather has another slang meaning of skin.

The body, then, is the next theme to explore. Since the female genitals consist of an aperture, we find such terms as **hole** and **orifice**, but these shapes are not peculiar to the genitals; the mouth and anus are also body orifices and so not surprisingly we find terms for the female genitals borrowed from these other two orifices. The proximity of the anus gives rise to such terms, often ambiguous, as **tail**, **piece of ass**, **toby**, now obsolete, and **fanny**, which retains different meanings on different sides of the Atlantic—in Britain it refers to the female genitals while in North America it refers to the buttocks. The genital sense is probably derived from the famous novel *Memoirs of Fanny Hill*, by John Cleland (1749). **Gut entrance** and **front gut**, both now obsolete, also obliquely refer to that other orifice since *gut* is a term with a very general reference; ambiguity disappears with **'twixt wind and water**.

The other primary bodily orifice is the mouth and this gives rise to such terms as: **nether mouth**, **mouth thankless**, **gully** and **gully hole**, based on the slang meaning of *gully* for the throat. Other related mouth terms are **mute**, **grin** and **yawn**. The lips, which are ambiguous anyway, explain **hotlips**, while the tongue and cunnilingus are implied in **Lapland**. **Lapland** also gives rise to another meaning, namely, the **lap**, which itself is euphemistic for the female genitals.

Curiously, the nose makes an appearance in the now obsolete **gigg**, which Grose defines as "a nose . . . and woman's privities" (*gig* now has a musical meaning). The **eye** also comes into use in sexual terminology, as with the phrases **long eye** and **blind eye**. These euphemisms go back to Shakespeare's day. Partridge explains the genital usage as follows: "**eye** because of the shape, the garniture of hair, and the tendency of both organs to become suffused with moisture" (*Shakespeare's Bawdy*, p. 102). Related to **eye** is another Shakespearean phrase: **naked seeing self**, where *self* puns on *I/eye*. The variation **blind eye** as well as **blind entrance** parallels other terms such as **mute**, euphemistically pointing to functions for the genitals other than that of seeing or speaking.

The heart gives rise to **pulse** and possibly **pump**. Finally, on the theme of the body, **tit** must be mentioned for although today (and going back at least to the 17th century) **tit** is a slang or informal term for the female breast, it did have a slang meaning now obsolete, of the female genitals, though this is probably derived from abbreviations of **tit-bit** or **titmouse**. In retrospect, it certainly seems that many terms for the female genitals are simply derived from, or related to, other bodily orifices.

As with terms for sexual intercourse, we find necessity — such as eating — reflected in many of the terms for the genitals. Both **meat** and **fish** are such terms, as is **bread**, though given its other slang meaning — of money — this is probably prostitute's slang. Related to meat we find **bacon**, **hotbeef** and **mutton**, while fish is made more specific with **ling**, **trout** and many shellfish such as **cockles** (though this really refers to the labia and so is always in the plural). The word **lobster** is interesting, making sense through the *-ster* suffix, which originally denoted female agency (as in *spinster*), added appropriately to **lob** which is slang for penis (it should be noted that *-ster* nowadays often has a deprecatory sense, as in *trickster, gangster*, etc.). Other shellfish are: **oyster**, **periwinkle**, from *peri* meaning round and **winkle** meaning penis, and **whelk**.

Next on the menu are vegetables, which provide us with **cauliflower**, probably through its connection with **flower**, **mushroom**, and **cabbage**, with its variants **cabbage patch** and **cabbage garden**. Desserts are fruitful too and provide **fig**, **papaya** and **plum** which is Shakespearean and possibly explained from its shape — some even have grooves down one side. **Cherry** specifically refers to the hymen or virginity, as does the term **pitcher**, as in to **crack a pitcher**; the breaking of glass is even found in Orthodox Jewish marriage rituals, performed symbolically by the bridegroom. Another dessert is **cake**, while *cakehole* is slang for the mouth; related to this are **cookie** and **knish** (Yiddish for a dumpling).

Related to food are terms for food containers that also double as terms for the female genitals. Examples are: **honeypot**, **jam pot**, **milk jug** or **milk pan**, **salt cellar** and **sugar basin**. Of these contents **honey** and **milk** refer to semen, thus rendering the container words androcentric: **jam** is simply equivalent to **jam pot**, and like so many nouns for the female genitals it has a verb form meaning sexual intercourse; **salt**, the verb, also means to copulate.

On a larger scale we have **coffeehouse** and **coffeeshop**, both qualifying as container terms. And referring to the pubes, we find **hair pie** and more recently **hairburger** and **furburger**. These last two terms, which use hair as the genital signifier, emphasize the relationship between sexual intercourse and eating, and hint at cunnilingus. **Delicate**

glutton, **dumb glutton**, **suck and swallow** and **bite** view the vagina as voracious; psychologists even encounter *vagina dentata*, or a vagina with teeth, in sexual fantasies. Related to eating is **fork**: to **have a bit on a fork**, meaning sexual intercourse, is the usual expression, but the fork here is that of the legs rather than the eating utensil. **Supper** is another term that makes a meal of the genitals and also carries with it a reference to time, the evening. Related to food, but perhaps pointing more towards the generative powers of the female genitals, we find **pipkin** and **seedplot**. Finally, **yum-yum** explains itself.

Already we have seen that a number of terms for the female genitals are androcentric, such as **manhole**; other examples are: **man trap**, **masterpiece**, **male catcher**, **cream catcher**, **magnet**, which attracts opposite poles, and the probably patriarchal **private property**. **Punse** from Yiddish may derive from the German *punzen* meaning to **punch**, which itself is slang, meaning to deflower — another androcentric conception. Other terms simply form opposites to the male genitals, for example: **needle-case** to **needle**, and **ladder** or **Jacob's ladder** to **Jacob**. From the woman's point of view, even though these terms may be male-created, we find terms related to money, no doubt reflecting the potential earning power of prostitution; examples are: **money** itself, **chink** (which is also a slang term for money, especially in coin form, as well as for prison), **coin-slot**, and the container words **purse**, **wallet** and **shake bag**, while **commodity**, **merchandise** and **ware** reflect a wider economic viewpoint. **Breadwinner** sounds like prostitute's slang while **spender**, unless referring simply to the urinary function, might consider the female orgasm. **Poontang** is black American slang and possibly a variation of the French *putain*, prostitute.

The next cultural theme is that closest to the body, namely clothes. **Gusset**, a piece of material used to strengthen a garment, is one term now obsolete, **muslin**, the fine cotton material, is another, while **placket**, which is a hole or slit in a petticoat or dress, doubles appropriately for the female genitals. **Venus's glove** is self-explanatory though with overtones of manual sexual activity, while **hat** is charmingly and jokingly defined by Grose as: "A woman's privities: because frequently felt."

Sports and pastimes provide rich terms too: **Bull's eye**, **target** and **sport of Cupid's archery** make a neat trio without any need for an explanation. **Wicket** may at first recall cricket, or croquet, but is more likely to be related to the sense of a window, casement or gate. **Saddle** clearly ties in with the riding metaphor, while boating gives rise to **boat**, probably inspired by the shape, though again it is a container word. Many sports are performed in a **gymnasium**; related as container words to this are **workshop** and **premises**.

Music contributes the following terms: **lute**, possibly from its body's shape, and **fiddle**, which is paired with **fiddle stick**, while to **fiddle** and to **strum** both mean to copulate. Dance provides the terms **cooch** — derived from a pseudo-oriental female dance which involves sinuous twisting of the torso, also known as *hootchy kootchy* — and **nautch**, which in standard English means a traditional Indian dance performed by women or girls.

In the first chapter we saw that naming was one of the primary functions of language. It is perhaps the earliest manifestation in the development of language in children. Giving a name to the genitals may simply be an attempt to personify them but can also impute to them a life of their own, especially if their owner wishes to avoid responsibility for their actions. The names chosen for the female genitals are, not surprisingly, common female names: **Mary Jane**, or **Lady Jane**, **Fanny**, and so on. *Jane* is a feminine form of *John* and is also used to signify women generally — "me Tarzan, you Jane." Placing *Miss* before a name yields **Miss Brown** and the punning **Miss Laycock**, while **Mother of all Saints** reflects motherhood. **Bookbinder's wife** also makes a reference to motherhood, since both punningly manufacture in sheets. **Itching Jenny** probably makes reference to the female ass or donkey — and **scratch** seems to be the solution; incidentally, **scratch** also has the (American) slang meanings of money and the devil. Then there are the classically oriented names such as: **Venus's mark**, **Cupid's Arms**, **Cupid's Hotel**, and so on. Finally, androcentric naming is found in **tickle Thomas**.

Names also appear, but with a different purpose, in **Joe Hunt** and **Charlie Hunt** or **Charley Hunt**, sometimes shortened to **Charlie/Charley**, **Berkeley Hunt** or **Berkshire Hunt**, usually shortened to **Berkeley** and to the well-disguised **berk** — all exhibiting rhyming slang on **cunt**, and in so doing enphasizing **cunt**'s centrality in the slang terminology of the female genitals. These terms, though, are used not anatomically but rather to describe someone as a fool. Another rhyming slang term is **growl**, from **growl and grunt**, though for some curiously auditory reason **groan and grunt**, **grumble and grunt** and **grasp and grunt** are all taken to mean sexual intercourse even though their rhyming partner is **cunt**. **Sharp and blunt** is another variation on the rhyme perhaps especially antithetical in its meaning so as to increase the disguise. Back slang provides **tenuc** as well as **naf** or **naff**, which is **fan**, abbreviation of **fanny**, backwards.

Cunt is, and has been, such a powerful taboo word that even words approximating it in pronunciation have acquired its meaning; **constable** (pronounced with the same sound as in **cunt**) and **cunning** were both Elizabethan euphemisms, and puns, for the female genitals. Then, taking the disguise even further we find **thingstable** in which the troublesome first syllable has been replaced by **thing** (itself an old euphemism, though much more commonly used for the male genitals than for the female). Variants on the feminine **thing** are **real thing**, **another thing**, **old thing** and **nothing** (and **O**), which is the antithesis of **thing** meaning penis, a linguistic move Freud would have been proud of. The female *zero* (**O**) together with the "phallic" symbol for *one* (1) could, at a stretch, be seen as the basis for the binary system at the heart of the computer era.

Euphemism continues with **article**, **etcetera**, **tivy** or **tivvy**, presumably derived from *activity*, and, emphasizing the female's control in sex, we find **controlling part** and **regulator**. Then emphasizing, more specifically, nimbleness or speed, we find **agility** and the ever-popular **snatch**. **Snatch** also means seizure and has slang meanings of kidnaping and robbery, activities more usually portrayed androcentrically; sexual terminology thus shows many points of view, including the male being seen as the victim.

Other euphemisms which express delight in that part of the female anatomy are **best**, **center of bliss**, **funny bit**, **the naughty**, **novelty**, **pretty**, and **quaint** (which is really a version of **cunt**). On a religious plane we find the following euphemisms, mostly now obsolete: **heaven and hell**, an antithetical pair if ever there was one, **Lord knows what**, **saint's delight** and **vice**, which though having religious overtones is probably simply derived from the instrument with two jaws. **Undertaker** unites sexuality and death by simply punning on the missionary or matrimonial position of the woman who takes the man from under. Finally there is **oracle**, which brings the oral and the genital together. One variation on **oracle** is the oxymoron **dumb oracle**. **Mot** and **motte** could both be derived from the French word meaning a word, perhaps in reference to the **monosyllable**. Grose relates **mot** to **mort**, meaning a wench or prostitute. **Oracle** also has a variation in **hairy oracle**, which introduces the last theme: tactile characteristics.

We have already seen that the animals featured in this chapter do so usually because of their soft fur. **Hairy wheel, downy bit, fleece, muff** and so on all extend this theme. The general terminology of pubic hair or **pubes**, derived from the Latin *puber* meaning adult, is included here because most of the terms for pubes are applied to the female.

Many of the terms are simply extensions of genital terms; for example we find: **cunt curtain, twat rug**, and **quim bush**. Since the pubes consist of hair we find also many terms for hair such as **fur**, and the literal **furbelow, silent beard, stubble**, and **fuzz**, not to mention **toupee** and **wig**. There is even a term for a pubic wig, namely **merkin**, for which most dictionaries simply give "etymology unknown," though Bailey's *Universal Etymological Dictionary* states that it is from the French *mère*, meaning mother, with the suffix *-kin*, a diminutive — that is, a small mother. **Merkin** also means an artificial vagina.

The vegetable kingdom provides us with **bush** and **bushy, furze, hedge, forest, moss**, and many others, and Shakespeare contributes **brakes**, meaning thickets, and **ling**, which, in addition to its genital reference through its fish meaning, can refer to the pubes via its Scottish meaning of heather. **Strawberry patch** is used specifically for reddish pubes, as does **red ace**; the **ace of spades** refers to black pubes as well as to the genitals itself, while **figleaf** has an artistic heritage.

The animal world contributes **feather** or **feathers, fleece, kitten's ear**, perhaps because it is roughly triangular and hints at **puss** or **pussy**, and **scut**, which doubles also for the genitals itself. One term combining the vegetable with the animal kingdoms is **gorilla salad**. Finally, turning to cultural artifacts, we find **rug, shaving brush, plush, mat** and **Mata Hari** which bears a resemblance to *mat of hair*; Mata Hari was both a dancer and a spy and dancing and cheating are both significant themes in sexual terminology.

The above list of terms provides us with a wide variation in the tactile quality of pubic hair, though the characteristics of shape and even color also feature. It is the theme of shape that characterizes the next few terms: **curls, curlies** and **short and curlies**. Only these terms for pubes are intersexual. The last example extends in the phrase "to have someone by the short and curlies" (more usually in the United States "short hairs"), which is an intersexual version of "having someone by the balls."

On the subject of the female genitals, it is a curious, perhaps telling, fact that so few terms are available for the **clitoris**. *The Slang of Venery*, a privately published manuscript of 1916, provides about 1,000 terms for the **vagina/vulva** but only nine for the **clitoris**. Perhaps this, more than anything else, shows the androcentric nature of sexual slang. Furthermore most of these terms are fairly recent; **clitoris** itself was coined in the 17th century. We do not find terms for the clitoris in Shakespeare or in the work of other Elizabethans. The clitoris, often shortened to **clit**, has been much misunderstood in the past and even its etymology is puzzling. Most dictionaries insist that it is derived from the Greek *kleitoris* which is related to *kleiein* meaning to close — perhaps to be understood in terms of the fact that unlike the male phallus the clitoris has no urethral opening. The name *Clytemnestra* of Greek mythology may have some connection, since Clytemnestra was portrayed as a strong, manlike woman, while the clitoris is seen as the female phallus. The Latin term, according to Rodgers in *Gaytalk*, is *naviculans, navicula* meaning a little boat, which explains such expressions as **little boy in the boat** or **man in the boat**, no doubt conceived of in view of the position and shape of the clitoris in relation to the vulva. But note that it is not little girl or woman but little boy or man, emphasizing the homology with the male phallus; relative position also explains such phrases as **peeping sentinel** and **little ploughman**, using a land metaphor in contrast to a boat at sea. Other terms for the clitoris are the classical **penis muliebris** and the camp **jointess** (feminine of **joint**), **sensitive spot**, **fleshy excrescence**, **bud**, which makes reference to the plant world, and **button**, which implies touching with the fingers. Finally there is **little shame tongue** (a translation from the German).

Two other areas of the body still need to be discussed. One area is the bottom or buttocks, but I shall postpone this discussion until the final chapter, since the buttocks are intersexual and serve as a source of pleasure and of arousal to both males and females, heterosexuals and homosexuals. The other area, the **breasts**, however, should be discussed in this chapter, since they serve as a powerful signifier for the female, even more potently than pubic hair since they are more noticeable and prominent; even with clothing, they leave an impression, outline or shape that unmistakably distinguishes women from men.

Besides **bosom** and **bust**, which are common euphemisms for the breasts but which also have wider references, perhaps the most common term, regarded as slang, is **tits**. **Tits** was used from the 17th century onwards and is no doubt derived from animal **teats**, used as early as the 10th century. **Titties** is the diminutive form, while **titty** can also be used to refer to sexual intercourse (gay slang). Another common slang term is **boobs**, which in the singular means a blunder or embarrassing mistake. This is seemingly androcentric, but could be matched by other terms for mistakes such as *cock-up*. **Boobs** is probably related to **bubs** and **bubbies** which all show some etymological resemblance to *baby*, because the breasts serve to feed babies. *Bub*, incidentally, is also a slang term for drink. **Poonts** should be mentioned here as it could be derived from **poontang**, or, like **boobs**, could be derived from *poon*, an Australian slang term for a stupid fool. The function of the breasts gives rise to a number of terms, such as **fountain**, the Elizabethan **milky way**, **milk shop**, **milk-shakes**, **dairy arrangements**, **udders** and so on.

The shape of the breasts gives rise to many, sometimes obvious but often obscure, terms such as, from the theme of food, **apples**, **coconuts**, the punning **chestnuts**, and **melons**, and from other diverse sources, **knockers**, **cliff**, **pantry shelves**, **bulbs**, **globes**, **hemispheres**, Shakespeare's **world**, the musical **kettledrums**, **jugs**, and many others. **Blubber**, **dugs**, and **heavers** all contribute to **meat market** which is pejoratively androcentric.

Position or place gives rise to the following bodily terms: **fore buttocks**, **upper works** and **top ballocks**, while **neck** has been used as an Elizabethan euphemism. All these terms illustrate displacement. Since the breasts consist of mammary glands we find such terms as **mammets**, **mollies** and the nostalgic, punning **memories**. The differing fruits used to describe the breasts show variation in sizes; other variations are captured in **pointers**, **droopers**, **piggies**, and so on. The effects that the breasts have on others is perhaps suggested in **charms**, and possibly also in **bazooms** (a corruption of bosoms). The military fireworks suggested by this *bazooka*-like word continue with **barbettes**, derived from an 18th century term for a mound within a fortification from which cannons could be fired, and **turrets**. **Charleys** or **charlies** may be connected to **charms** — perhaps those charms displayed by the mistresses of Charles II, though Partridge thinks it derives from the Romany *chara*, meaning to touch or fondle.

Finally, rhyming slang gives rise to a number of terms for the breasts. Perhaps the best known British term is **bristols** derived from **Bristol City** which rhymes with **titty**. That **bristols** perhaps conjures up bristles, which is quite antithetical to breasts, shows how successful the disguise of Cockney can be. Other rhymes on **titty** or **titties** are mostly now obsolete: **thousand pities**, the British **Manchester City**, the American **Jersey City**, the Australian **Lewis & Witties** (a store), **cat and kitties** (extending the feline imagery in female sexual terminology), **towns and cities** and the **tale of two cities**, often swapped around to the "sale of two titties." Rhymes on **breast** itself are, appropriately, the buxom **Mae West** (which became the American name for an inflatable life jacket) and **east and west**, while rhymes on **tits** are **threepenny bits**, **brace and bits** and the Australian **tracy bits** or **tray bits**. Finally, **jubes** could be rhyming slang for **boobs**, but as likely it could be derived from *jujube*, a lozenge that one sucks.

This leads on to the terminology of **teats** or **nipples**, often shortened to **nips**. As with breasts, men too have nipples but usually the terms are applied to females. Function gives rise to **dinners** and **dugs**, a term that was standard English in the 16th century, and was possibly derived from an old Germanic term meaning to suckle (**dugs** also of course refer to the breasts as a whole). Shape is evoked in **buttons**, **knobs**, **rose buds**, and **strawberries**, which covers artifacts, flowers and food. Other terms, which are also used of homosexual males, are **ninnies**, **nums**, **piggies** (also used of breasts and toes) and **puppies**, which is close to **paps**, an old term for nipples, probably of Latin origin.

4. THE LANGUAGE OF THE MALE SEX ORGANS

The words **cock**, **dick** and **prick** are today probably the most common slang or colloquial terms for the **penis**. Although **prick** is not literally a four-letter word it may be regarded as such for practical purposes. These three terms embody three different themes, each of which is of central importance in the terminology of the male genitals. **Prick** is a rather tame example of the theme of aggression, **cock** is a classic example of the theme of animality, even though etymologically it may not quite bear this out, and **dick** is a typical proper name, among other things, that is used for the penis.

The discussion of the language of sexual intercourse in Chapter 2 took notice of the prevalence of aggression, violence and conquest, especially in the context of androcentric terminology. The means of aggression are now identified in the terminology for the penis. **Prick**, and its variant **prickle**, have been used since the 16th century and were regarded as standard English until the 18th century. **Prick** and the verb *to prick*, meaning to pierce, are related in meaning to **sting**, which also refers to the penis.

Things which pierce or are pointed can be both natural objects and cultural artifacts. Among the natural objects we find **thorn, coral branch, stem** and **horn** from the vegetable and animal kingdoms. Cultural items, however, provide the vast majority of terms with aggresive overtones. The most blatant of these terms is **weapon** which shows a curious similarity to the Old English term for man, namely *waep(n)man*; if these two terms are in fact related it would show that man in general can be, or has been, characterized or identified by his **weapon**, or penis.

From the generic term, **weapon**, we find such examples as: **sword**, which goes back to Shakespeare's time, and other terms for

53

sword, namely, **dirk, bilbo** and **bayonet**, which originally meant a short dagger, a meaning now obsolete. Other related terms exemplifying weaponry are **lance** and **pike**. These terms refer to warfare in the 16th century or earlier. Weapons which predated these are **arrow** and **dart** (and **dart of love**) — illustrations of Cupid often show him shooting an arrow. Later discoveries in the science of warfare provide us with **pistol** and **gun**. Policing provides us with **copper stick**, a 19th century term referring to a policeman's truncheon. Other weapons are **club**, **poker** and **rammer**, though these terms are as much instruments as weapons.

Two terms perhaps related to the theme of aggression but derived from verbs are **wang**, or **whang**, and **wop**, both meaning to beat or strike, **wop** being derived from *whop*. **Shoot**, of course, should also be mentioned, though it refers to the action of ejaculating, and may well have etymological primacy over the weaponry sense.

Although many dictionaries suggest that **cock**, meaning penis, is derived from the watercock, spout or tap sense, this meaning itself is related to and derived from the male of the domestic fowl which we find in English from as early as the 13th century. A more recent meaning of **cock** is of a mechanism for discharging a firearm, though this meaning must be derived from the tap sense which was already in use in the 15th century. Partridge provides a quotation from the early 17th century to show the sexual meaning of **cock**, though it could well have been used even earlier in this sense. **Cock** also, used informally, has a generic sense of man or fellow, while a verbal sense exists, meaning to stick out or stand out — a clear reference to the erection of the penis. Pejorative senses exist in the phrase a *cock-up* (similar to a *fuck-up*), meaning a mess or disaster. Partridge even provides a further slang sense of **cock** in ancient oaths to mean God, clearly a masculine God.

It should be stressed that the cock is a domestic animal; as with terms for the female genitals, terms for the male genitals are usually taken from domestic animals, or at least from creatures that are, or were, encountered fairly regularly in everyday life. Th cock is actually a bird, showing that birds are not solely the metaphorical property of the female genitals; other birds also feature in the language of the male genitals. One is **cuckoo** — probably to match the female's **cuckoo's nest**, though it could be a variation (through imitative sound) of **cock**, and shows a close resemblance to *cuckold*, in which the penis is the means by which to cuckold a husband. **Cuckoo** also has a slang sense of mad or crazy, a state sometimes identified with sexual arousal.

Canary is another bird, but only makes sense against the background of its other slang senses, namely, a knave, a jailbird (perhaps from yellow prison clothes) or most likely, a modified codpiece; **codpiece** itself is a euphemism for the penis. **Pecker** could perhaps be assimilated to the bird category if the sexual sense is in fact derived from the woodpecker. To peck at something is to try to make a hole in it. Another relevant slang sense of **pecker** is appetite; *to peck* means to eat. **Goose's neck** also fits in the bird category and its usage is probably explained by its shape; it also coheres with rhyming slang usage of **goose (and duck)** meaning **fuck**.

Another animal that denotes the penis is **donkey**, usually meaning a large penis, though it may be derived from **dong**, and similar terms such as **dingle-dangle**, **flap-doodle**, and so on, which refer to the way a limp penis hangs. **Nag** and **pony** are other equine animals with sexual meanings. **Live rabbit** is matched by the female **cunny** and **bunny** which perhaps explains why to **rabbit** means to copulate. **Goat**, like **rabbit**, is also a sexual term probably because of the connotations of sexual prowess. **Snake**, **worm** and **lizard** are self-explanatory, and thus feature in Freudian symbolism; **schlong**, from Yiddish, also means snake. **Lizard** is etymologically derived from the Latin *lacertus* meaning **muscle**, which is itself a euphemism for the penis, while the English *muscle* itself is derived from the Latin *musculus* which is a diminutive of *mus* or mouse, and **mouse** is another animal euphemism for the penis. **Mickey Mouse** is a variation of this, adding familiarity through the name, while **mole**, the burrowing animal, can also mean a penis.

Parts of animals' bodies are also employed in the language of the male genitals. **Horn** is probably the best known, obviously derived from the projecting growth on certain animals' heads. **Horny** is a related term meaning sexually aroused. **Horn** usually refers to an erect penis; obsolete variations are **old horny** and **old Hornington**. The horn also refers to cuckoldry since imaginary horns were meant to appear on the forehead of a cuckold, and we find such Shakespearean terms as *horned* and *horn-mad* meaning cuckolded. **Pizzle** is yet another term that in standard use only refers to the penis of a bull. It is derived from Germanic terms meaning sinew. Finally there is **tail**, which was used in the sexual sense as early as the 14th century and only became slang or vulgar from about the 18th century onwards; **tail** also refers to the female genitals, as well as to the buttocks, and the verb to **tail** means to copulate.

Tail, then, is one of those multi-purpose sexual terms like **meat** and **pump**; it has also been used most prolifically as a prefix in the terminology of sexual slang. Though now many of these terms are obsolete, we find: **tail-pike**, **tail-pin**, **tail-pipe**, for the penis, **tail-gap**, **tail-gate**, **tail hole**, for the vagina or vulva, **tail-feathers** for the pubic hair (female), **tail-juice** for semen or urine, and **tail-wagging**, **tail-work**, **tail-tickling**, for sexual intercourse. The word **penis** itself comes from the Latin *penis* meaning a tail. The significance of **tail** in sexual terminology probably indicates the emphasis that society must have placed in past centuries on the lowliness or beastliness of sexual activity, especially from certain religious or theological points of view; the devil, we must remember, was usually portrayed with a long tail. **Schwantz** is from Yiddish and German, also meaning tail.

The theme of animality leads on to the theme of the body. The human body provides the opportunity for much displacement with regard to terms for the penis, as we have already seen for the female genitals. As with the terminology for sexual intercourse, the leg serves as a useful euphemism and so we find such phrases as: **best leg of three**, **first leg of three**, and **middle leg**. The arm provides **short arm** and the torso provides the formal and Shakespearean **loins**, and the less literary **gutstick**.

The face also features in **eye-opener**, though to be understood either by its effects rather than by any physical resemblance, or in relation to **eye** meaning the female genitals, and **nose** which is already presaged by **horn**, trading on a similarity of shape. The nose's other similarities to the genitals have been indicated by Freud's friend Fliess, who showed organic parallels in mucous membrane and cartilage placement. The tongue also comes in for a mention via the word **lingam** which is Sanskrit for penis (**yoni** being Sanskrit for vulva or womb). **Lingam** is etymologically related to the Latin *lingua* meaning language or tongue. This possible relationship between tongue (especially in its linguistic sense) and penis is of great interest to psychoanalysts. According to Lacan, and others, the phallus is the first symbol that a child acquires and thus the penis is the first signifier — at the origin of language itself. This androcentric view, however, is not supported by the terminology of sexuality, for we find both **mot** (French, meaning word) and **velvet** (also slang for the tongue) used for the female genitals.

Other bodily terms that are used for the penis are **bone**, especially used of erections, **marrow bone**, suggesting semen, **muscle** and

gristle, which is cartilage. **Joint** probably finds justification in that the penis is joined to the body (**joint** also has a slang meaning of place or building, as in the phrase "casing the joint," however, this seems quite unconnected for logically it would have a female reference). Finally, **organ** must be one of the more common euphemisms for the penis, and one that is frequently used in jokes because of its various references; technically the penis is an organ, in its standard English sense. Etymologically **organ** is related to the words *work* and *orgasm*, events not unrelated to the penis.

The theme of food provides us with a full shopping bag. **Meat** must be mentioned again here, though it refers also the female genitals and to sexual intercourse. The different varieties and creations of meat provide us with **banger** (a kind of sausage, with overtones of **banging**), **baloney** (or **balogna**), **salami**, **hotdog** and **wiener** (another kind of sausage). All these terms trade on the similarity in shape to a penis, and there are some hot and spicy overtones.

The vegetable world provides us with **Irish root** and **root** (to **root** is Australian slang for having sexual intercourse) and **stalk**, and **carrot**, **cucumber**, **pickle** and **rhubarb**, all of which are approximately penis-shaped. **Radish** is another vegetable; it resembles the glans of the penis. Desserts provide **banana**, from its shape, and perhaps explains why **monkey** is a term for the female genitals. **Pudding** is more likely derived from the sausage-shaped puddings, though **pud** may not be the shortening of **pudding** but rather of **pudendum**, the Latin term for the male genitals. Other desserts are **roly-poly**, which is a jam roll pudding (bringing with it all the connotations of **jam**), **lollipop** and **sugar stick** which must conjure up fellatio more vividly than most of the food terms.

Other food terms, though perhaps more marginal, are **cream-stick**, **gravy-maker** and **milkman**, all derived from the seminal fluid that the penis ejaculates. Cutlery also makes an appearance in **fork**, hence the female version a **bit on a fork**, and **blade**, which has aggressive overtones. Finally appetite and tastiness, again emphasizing fellatio, are exhibited in **yum-yum**, which is also used for the female genitals.

Cultural items abound in the terminology for penis; in particular, we find instruments, especially hand-held instruments, with masturbatory overtones. From the rudimentary objects like **bat**, **club**, **hand-staff**, **pipe**, **blank**, **pole**, and so on, we can move on to tools proper: **tool**, itself, is one of the more popular euphemisms for the penis, and another general term is **gadget**, derived from French meaning a tool. More specifically we find: **screwdriver**, which obviously refers to **screwing**, **piston**, **hammer**, **pile-driver**, which hammers repeatedly, **key**, which evokes its female partner **keyhole**, the multipurpose **pump**, and the generic **machine**.

Related terms are **dipstick** and **joystick**, pointing to action and result respectively. **Pointer**, which knows where it's heading, is yet another term for the penis. Other specific instruments and objects are **pin**, **needle**, **bodkin**, which is a large needle and an archaic term for a dagger, **lipstick**, perhaps for the way it emerges from its holder, and **candle**, which appropriately melts away when lit. **Schmuck** and **putz** are both Yiddish words for the penis, meaning in standard German a decoration, finery or an ornament. The terms have the same pejorative usage as **prick** has, namely to describe a stupid, silly person.

The flaccid and erect state of the penis are captured by separate groups of words. Most terms for the penis refer to the erect state, however there are some for the flaccid, hanging or limp penis. Examples are **tassel**, **pendulum**, **dingle-dangle**, **lob**, archaic for drooping, and **doodle**, perhaps derived from *cock-a-doodle-doo* or from its meaning of idle activity. Other interesting cultural artifacts are **pencil**, which may be derived from the diminutive of the Latin *penis* meaning a tail, and **pen**, which is derived from the Latin *penna* meaning a feather (originally pens were quills).

Codpiece is the only term from clothing and though used to refer to the penis its etymology points to the testicles or scrotum. In fact in the 14th century **cods** or **codpieces** meant testicles; it is derived from the Old English term *cod* or *codd* meaning a bag or husk. **Wand** is primarily a gay slang term for the penis, with obvious angelic or magical overtones. Finally **yard** can be assimilated to the theme of cultural items, especially hand-held implements, for its original meaning was a rod or staff. **Yard** was perhaps one of the most generally used of all the literary terms for the penis in the 17th and 18th century, but became obsolete by 1850.

The theme of music provides a number of fairly predictable terms. **Fiddle-stick** and **fiddle-bow** both pair up with **fiddle**, meaning the female genitals. Shape gives rise to **flute** and its variation **silent flute**, emphasizing another nonauditory function, **drumstick** and **trombone**, which already has **bone** connotations, but is also played by sliding in and out. There is also **bugle**, a kind of **horn**, and finally there is **organ** with its musical reference.

Many terms for the penis are couched in female terms, in relation to female parts or in hopeful relation to female expectations. Of the former variety we find **hair-splitter**, **hair-divider** and **beard-splitter**, all using the pubic hair to symbolize the female genitals. **Rump-splitter**, **tickle-tail** and **tickle-toby**, and **plug-tail** seem to keep options open, while **whore-pipe** and **trapstick** are self-explanatory. **Tit-bit**, though used for the female genitals, is also used occasionally for the penis, being literally the bit for the **tit** in its female genital sense. **Ladies' delight**, **ladies' lollipop** and **ladies' treasure** elucidate the theme of hopeful expectations, as does **eye-opener**, which has already been mentioned.

Of the three most common terms for penis, **dick** still has to be discussed. **Dick** is mostly thought to be the proper name, especially the nickname for Richard. However, it may be derived from a contraction of *derrick*, either the proper name or the lifting crane or the framework in oil fields — each with sexual overtones, though the sexual use of **dick** in the 19th century predates some of these senses. Furthermore, **dick** may be short for **dickery-dock**, which is rhyming slang for **cock**.

Another common name with sexual reference is **Jack**, which like **dick** can refer to any man or fellow, though it also means a lifting device, which seems appropriate. Furthermore jack could be derived from the Latin *jacere* meaning to throw, which is at the root of *ejaculate*. **Jack-in-a-box** or **jack-in-the-box** emphasizes the erectile ability of the penis as well as playing on **box**, which can mean the female genitals. **Jack Robinson** adds a further variation emphasizing speed or short-lived duration.

Jock is the Scottish variation of **Jack**, nickname for John, meaning any fellow, and it too is slang for the penis, and may explain the derivation of the word *jockstrap*, which is a support for the genitals, worn especially by athletes. **John Thomas** is another name for the penis, emphasizing commonness, as is **Peter**, which is etymologically significant, being from Greek meaning rock, that is, something hard. Dictionaries are at a loss for the derivation of the recent phrasal verb *to peter out*; perhaps this is derived from the sexual sense of **peter**, especially emphasizing the limits of male virility. **Peter** may have been adopted in its sexual sense from its closeness to *pee*; **peepee** is a common, children's term for the penis.

Likewise, **Willy**, another name for the penis, may have its childhood equivalent **weewee**. *Wee*, of course, also means small but as a verb is perhaps derived from *water*. Since the penis is also a urinary organ we find such terms as **water-engine** and **waterworks**, which are intersexual terms for the genitals. **Willy** has positive connotations from the phrase *willy-nilly*; affirmation or agreement is also found in **Roger** (*R* for received, appropriately), another name, which has Germanic origins (related to the term *spear*). To **roger** is of course a slang term meaning to have intercourse with a woman. **Johnson** may simply be the son of John, a common name, but could perhaps point to **Doctor Johnson**, of dictionary fame, which was a 19th century euphemism for the penis; Partridge suggests that perhaps this name came to be used because "there was no one that Dr. Johnson was not prepared to stand up to."

We now turn to names from biblical sources. The first name in this category is **Old Adam**, from which all sex (or sin) began. Next is **Abraham**, which was a 19th century slang term for the penis, perhaps appropriate in that the name is derived from Hebrew meaning "father of a multitude," related to one of the biblical injunctions to man, namely, to be fruitful and multiply. **Abraham's bosom** was used for the female genitals. Similar pairing is found in **Jacob**, with its female partner **Jacob's ladder**. **Jezebel**, also 19th century usage, is an unusual name for the penis since it refers to a female character in the bible. Partridge offers an explanation from the book of Kings: "and he said throw her down. So they threw her down."

Nebuchadnezzar, who was king of Babylon, features as a result of the phrase to **take Nebuchadnezzar out to grass**, meaning to have sexual intercourse, said of males. *Grass* can refer to the female pubic hair; grass is also green, and **Nebuchadnezzar** likes **greens**, that is, sexual intercourse. (*Grass* and *green* also explain a nonsexual slang meaning of **Nebuchadnezzar**, namely, a vegetarian.) **Nimrod** is another biblical figure — already with **rod** in the name — who was a mighty **hunter**. Finally, on a classical bent, there is **Polyphemus**, a cultured reference to the penis as "one-eyed." **Cyclops** is another euphemism, now obsolete.

Names also feature in rhyming slang for the penis. We find the following: **Hampton Wick**, **Pat and Mick**, **stormy Dick** and **uncle Dick**, all displaying rhymes on **prick** which must be regarded as a, if not the, central slang term for the penis. In *Slang and Its Analogues*, Farmer and Henley provide synonyms for the penis under **prick**, though, amazingly, they collect terms for the female genitals under the euphemistic **monosyllable**, and terms for sexual intercourse under **greens**. **Uncle Dick** exhibits one other feature besides rhyme, namely, family relationship. **Uncle**, itself, is also used for penis, as are **big brother** and **little brother**, presumably depending on when used.

Finally, there is a motley collection of euphemisms for the penis. In general there appear to be many more euphemisms for the female genitals than for the male genitals, perhaps because so many of the terms are male created and used androcentrically, perhaps reflecting straightforwardness with regard to the penis, while reflecting mystery, respect, disgust or fear with regard to the vagina/vulva. The most obvious euphemisms for the penis are those that reflect the generative powers of the genitals. Examples of this are: **life preserver, baby maker**, and **tree of life**. Tree gives a visual image of uprightness; **tree of love** is another variation. The tree also provides us with **stump** or **carnal stump** or the even more euphemistic **carnal part**.

We have already seen how the notion of shape explains an overwhelming number of terms for the penis. More specific shapes, especially that of the glans, perhaps explain the euphemisms **bishop** and **bald-headed hermit**. **Bishop** requires explanation; its sexual sense could be in reference to a bishop's mitre or derivatively to the bishop piece in chess. The religious overtone adds to the strength of the euphemism. More straightforward terms for the glans, based on physical resemblance, or position, are **acorn, bulb, crown, German helmet** and **head**, making references to the vegetable kingdom, the body and to cultural artifacts; **glans** is even derived from the Latin *glans* meaning an acorn.

The foreskin or prepuce of the penis also deserves a mention; slang terms for it include **blinds, curtains**, and **onion skin**. These terms, curiously, refer to cultural artifacts except for **onion skin**, which simply refers back to **onion** meaning glans. To **draw the blinds**, means to pull back the foreskin. An **unsliced bologna** (*bologna* being a kind of sausage; also **baloney**) is an uncircumcised penis, as is a **goy toy** from the Hebrew *goy* meaning a gentile, while **nipped in the bud** refers to infant circumcision.

Moving from clipping to color: **rubigo** is an old Scottish colloquialism for the penis dating from the 16th century. Partridge suggests that it could be from Latin *ruber* meaning red, though the *rub* in **rubigo** might lead to a more functional explanation. From **meat** as the term for penis, we also find such usage as: **dark meat** and **jungle meat** for a black man's penis, and **white meat** and **light meat** for a white man's penis. **Black jack** and **black snake** are variations on **dark meat**. Behavior perhaps gives rise to the odd euphemism **tantrum**, which in standard usage means a fit of temper; perhaps the exertions of the penis in intercourse or orgasm go some way in explaining the sexual sense of this word. **Impudence** is yet another behavioral term suggesting mischievousness; a relevant meaning of **impudence** is immodesty. And then there is **devil** which gets put into **hell**, though it visits **heaven** also, both terms referring to the female genitals.

Of the most general euphemisms for the penis, masculinity is the emphasis in **manhood**. Even more abstract than masculinity is existence itself; **thing** must be the least descriptive euphemism for the penis. **Thing** is derived from the Old High German *ding* which shows a marked similarity to such recent euphemisms for the penis as **dingle-dangle**, **dong**, and so on. **Thing** also pairs with terms for the female genitals such as **nothing** or **another thing**, though **thing** can also refer to the female genitals itself.

It is yet another term for the penis, though more commonly used for the female genitals. Related general terms, which are also used of both sexes, are **concern** and **affair**. Number provides us with **unit**, something regarded as an entity or singular whole; time gives us **night stick**, night being the period when the penis is usually sexually active, and **lullaby**, since sex is often followed by sleep. Finally, relationship provides one of the most common euphemisms, namely, **member**, which gives rise to the idea of joining; **member for Cockshire** plays on the (British) parliamentary meaning of the word.

The word **testicle** comes from the Latin *testiculus*, the diminutive of *testis* meaning a witness. An old custom of testifying to the truth involved placing the hand on one's testicles. The most common term nowadays for testicles is **balls**, which appears to be a contraction of **ballocks** which itself means testicles, the *-ock* suffix simply indicates a diminutive, as in *hill/hillock*. **Bollocks** is a variation of **ballocks**, though this has come to be used mainly as an interjection meaning nonsense, and is equivalent to the interjection *balls! Balls-up*, meaning a shambles, is yet another variation using sexual terms, in line with *fuck-up* and *cock-up*. Shakespeare gives us **bawl**, a pun on ball, perhaps based on the idea that males bawl when hit or kicked in the balls?

Balls, and all its variants, obviously exploits the quality of the shape of the testicles. Many other terms used similarity of shape to gain this sexual meaning. From the natural world we find **stones**, one of the oldest terms for the testicles, recorded in the 12th century, **pebbles**, now obsolete, and **rocks**, a more recent term. The vegetable kingdom provides many terms all based on shape. The nut is perhaps the central figure, perhaps bearing some relationship to the other slang reference of *nuts* meaning crazy, especially in the phrase *nuts about* meaning crazy about. We find **nuts**, **chestnuts**, **coconuts** and **nutmegs**. Note that **chestnuts** and **coconuts** as well as **orbs** and **apples** all apply not only to the testicles but also to the female breasts; both are pairs of organs, both, very roughly, have a rounded shape, and both secrete milky substances. **Charleys** is another such dual purpose term. **Love apples**, which is an archaic word for tomatoes, however, applies only to testicles, as do **damsons**, **gooseberries** and **eggs**.

Cultural items also offer similarities in shape; we find **marbles**, which relates back via the substance marble (Greek *marbaros*) meaning **stone** or **rock**, **goolies**, which are a type of marbles, and **seals**, because according to Partridge "they seal a sexual bargain." **Ornaments** and **magazines**, derived from a cartridge of a firearm, add to the cultural diversity. The way the testicles hang from the body also gives rise to a number of terms such as **danglers**, **tallywags** and **whirlygigs**, and even gives rise to musical considerations with **ding-dongs** and **gongs**. **Thingumbobs** may also fit into this dangling theme since bobs can mean hanging objects. Because of its general unspecified meaning, **thingumbobs** makes for typical euphemism. Even weight finds a mention in **pounders**, which is a 17th century term.

The value of the testicles, in providing semen to fertilize the ovum, is captured in such phrases as **family jewels**, **crown jewels**, **diamonds** (which, in the mines in southern Africa are called **stones**), and **meggs** which may be derived from a slang sense for coins. **Meggs**, however, could simply be a contraction of **nutmegs**. **Knackers** seems to stand all alone. A knacker is a dealer in, and slaughterer of, old horses. *Knackered* means worn out and tired, and can describe how the male feels after sexual intercourse, so perhaps could explain how **knackers** came to mean testicles. One other possible etymological explanation is via the word *knack* which means a trick or the nifty ability to do something; the testicles enable the "trick" of fertilization to occur.

Finally, there are the rhyming slang terms for the testicles. Perhaps the best known of these is **cobblers** from **cobbler's awls**. Interestingly an awl is a tool for piercing holes — a subtle reference to the testicles' partner? Like **balls** and **bollocks**, **cobblers** is used especially as an interjection to mean nonsense. **Orchestra stalls** is another rhyming slang term and may sound related to the term **orchids**. **Orchids** bear a physical resemblance to testicles. In fact the derivation of **orchid** points to the Greek *orchis* which means a testicle, and brings to mind the doctrine of signatures in the plant world. Another rhyming slang term is **Beecham's Pills**, presumed to be a rhyme on "testi-kills" (testicles); this is usually shortened to **pills** and is used in much the same way as **cobblers** is used. **Pills** are also usually round and spherical. **Tommy Rollicks** and **Johnny Rollicks** are names which both rhyme on **bollocks**, as do **flowers and frolics**, as well as **fun and frolics** — a phrase that perfectly matches the verb to **ball**.

Culls is an obsolete term for the testicles. It is an abbreviation from **cullions**, used by Chaucer, and is derived from *couillons*, French, meaning testicles, which itself comes from the Latin *coules* meaning a bag. This leads to terms for the scrotum. **Scrotum** is derived from the Latin *scrotum*, which is related to the Latin *scrautum*, which like the Latin *vagina* means a sheath. **Bag** is the general colloquial term for the scrotum and its more specific variant is **jelly bag**. **Cod** is derived from the Old English *cod* or *codd* meaning a bag or a husk or a pod, and, in the plural, **cods** refers to the testicles; the 20th century term *codswallop*, meaning nonsense, is probably derived from the term **cods** and is akin to **balls** or **cobblers**. Other terms for the scrotum simply paraphrase **bag**, for example, **basket** and **baggage**.

Terms for the penis, scrotum and testicles all together are **bag**, and the more specific **bag of tricks**, **kit**, **gear**, which was standard English from the 16th to the 19th century, and **Adam's arsenal**, which has aggressive overtones. Other terms make some play out of the arithmetic, such as: **the rule of three**, an 18th century phrase which also suggests a rule or ruler, that is, an erect penis, as well as male dominance. **Meat and two vegetables** is a 20th century term with a possible reference to fellatio. **Groceries** is another food term, they are usually carried in a **bag** or **basket**. **Plumbing** is an appropriate functionalist term, and finally, there is the euphemism **ladyware**; in addition to its clothing sense, *ware* also has a sense of care, as is still found in the word *beware*.

Semen is derived from the Latin *serere* meaning to sow (seeds). Likewise **sperm** is Latin for seed and is related to the Greek *speirein*, which also means to sow. Most of the terms for semen, however, are food terms based usually on physical resemblance, though there are some terms which touch on the idea of seeds and sowing. These are **seed** itself, **milt** and **roe**, both acquired from their fishy meaning, **chitty**, which is derived from the Middle English *chithe* meaning sprout or seed (*chitty-faced* in the 18th century meant baby-faced), and Shakespeare's **germen** which is related to *germ*.

The most common food terms are **jelly** and **cream**. **Cream** also gives rise to **face cream**, which Rodgers equates with "a cocksucker's reward." **Cream** also often goes, gastronomically, with **bananas**, which is also an appropriate sexual partnership. **Cream** is joined by other dairy products; we find **melted butter** and **cocoa butter** (for a black man's sperm), **milk** and **hot milk**. Other terms are **honey**, **mayonnaise** and **juice**, which has variants **love juice** and **hot juice**, and the gay **fruit juice**. **French dressing** may make another reference to fellatio, while **pudding**, and the more specific **rice pudding**, add to the other sexual meanings of **pudding**.

Other general food terms are **protein**, **vitamins** and **baby paste**. Terms which also trade on the physical resemblance to semen are **gism** or **jism**, perhaps related to **jazz**, **goo**, **lather**, **letch-water**, which perhaps shows some connection with *letch, lecher* and *lecherous*, **ointment**, which is etymologically related to *anointment*, **starch**, which perhaps relates to the erect penis, **wad**, which may be an abbreviation of *wadge* meaning a lumpy mass, and, finally, **sticky**.

The theme of aggression appears in such Shakespearean terms as **bullets** and **marrow**, which together with **mettle** and **spunk** refer to courage, pluck or spirit. **Spunk** originally meant a spark. Androcentric copulation is brought to mind in **stuff**, from the verb to **stuff**, and **fuck**, also from the verb to **fuck**. **Come**, of course, is derived from its orgasmic meaning, and **spendings**, which is intersexual, emphasizes in males not only the exertion in, but the paying out of semen. There is also the rhyming slang **Victoria Monk**, which rhymes with **spunk**. Partridge states that this comes from a famous character in pornographic fiction, though in fact that character was called Maria Monk. However, it is the surname that is more interesting for it marks yet another reference to religion, especially since religion had the power and determination to control where **spunk** went. Finally, there are informal terms for nocturnal emission; **wet dream** is the most common one, while other terms are **dream whip** and **whipped cream**, which Rodgers calls "the stuff wet dreams are made of."

5. THE LANGUAGE OF
OTHER ASPECTS OF SEXUALITY

This chapter shall examine some of the language of aspects of sexuality not yet covered in chapters 2, 3 and 4. To force some order on the mass of topics I deal first with terms for sexual activities, then terms for people as sexual beings, then the terminology of sexual states, and finally terms for sexual aids or objects. However, there will be some digressions to the terminology of other related sexual phenomena.

Actions

Caressing (Foreplay)

Chapter 2 dealt with the language of sexual intercourse. Intercourse, however, is usually preceded by foreplay. So let us begin by looking at some of the terms that have been generated for this activity, bearing in mind that these activities are often ends in themselves. The English language provides us with many ordinary, standard or normal terms for exhibitions of sexual attentions or affections, such as to **caress**, **cuddle**, **embrace**, **fondle**, **hug**, and so on. Shakespeare used such terms as to **comfort**, **dally**, **handle**, **paddle**, **play**, and **tickle** — and many more. Other terms that show their hand include to **feel someone up**, to **finger**, **fumble**, **grope**, and **read braille**, among others. More obscure terms, also probably related to manual activity, are to **fam** (an obsolete meaning of this is to handle; *famble* was a slang term from the 16th century for the hand, and is possibly related to **fumble**) and to **reef**, which is another term probably derived from its standard nautical sense. Another bodily reference is made in to **neck**.

66

Perhaps the best known term for caressing nowadays is to **pet**; the noun *pet*, besides meaning a favorite domesticated animal, also means a favorite person, a darling. To **spoon** emphasizes the sentimental side of cuddling, while to **firkytoodle** is an obsolete term that hints strongly at what follows foreplay, since **firk** is a euphemism for **fuck**. Many of these terms for caressing can also mean to have sexual intercourse; the boundaries for these terms are not clear. **Canoodle**, a modern variant of **firkytoodle**, may be related to *canny*, meaning either shrewd or, in dialect use, nice or lucky. The suffix in both **canoodle** and **firkytoodle** may be related to *oodles* meaning lots or much. To **dildo** is another term for sexually caressing someone, but I shall deal with this term under its use as a noun, from which the verb is derived, later in this chapter.

Masturbation

Keeping to manual transmission, so to speak, we now turn to words for masturbation. Of all sexual areas, the terminology for this activity is perhaps the most ordered and, more recently perhaps, the most amusing. Most of the terms apply to males, though some are intersexual and a few are for females only. The two basic patterns that dominate, and give an order to, the language of masturbation are the construction of a verb plus the preposition *off*, and a verb plus *the* or *one's* followed by a noun.

Before looking at these patterns and their varied examples we should look at the word **masturbation** itself. The two etymological paths proposed that provide explanation are, firstly (and predominantly) derivation from the Latin *manus* + *stuprare* meaning "to defile with the hand," and secondly (and more speculatively), derivation from the Latin *mas* + *turbare* meaning "to disturb the virile member"; only the former derivation makes for intersexual interpretation. The sense of defilement in relation to masturbation runs through much of the recent history of sexuality in the West, hence the phrase **self-abuse**. Masturbation was regarded, until fairly recently, as a sin and a vice, and all sorts of terrible illnesses were thought to follow an indulgence in this activity. This applied to women as well as men, and clitoridectomies (removal of the clitoris) were sometimes performed in the West, even in the early 20th century, to prevent masturbation. The old beliefs have now, one hopes, disappeared in the Western world and the terminology for masturbation perhaps shows this, for most of the terms are 20th century ones and are generally light-hearted in character.

Since the aim of masturbation is to bring oneself to orgasm or to **relieve oneself**, in euphemistic language, the construction *verb + off* seems appropriate. Examples of these phrasal verbs are to **jack off**, perhaps derived from the Latin *jacere* meaning to throw, to **jerk off**, and to **jeff off**, which sounds like a euphemism for the former two; to **beat off**, **pull off** and to **pump off**, providing further sexual mileage out of **pump**, as does **Portuguese pump**, but more of nationality later, to **toss off**, **whack off** and **wrench off**, and so on. Of these, many terms are intersexual but usually refer to male masturbation.

Verbs alone provide to **churn**, and to **frig**, which could be derived from the Latin *fricare* meaning to rub, or from the Old English *frigan* meaning to love; the first possible derivation supports the masturbatory sense, while the Old English derivation supports the other, now disappearing, sense of sexual intercourse for **frig**. Other solitary verbs are: to **diddle**, which can also refer to sexual intercourse and has overtones of cheating, to **handle**, which can also simply refer to caressing, to **shag** and to **shake**, both also referring to sexual intercourse, and to **wank** or **whank**, which dictionaries, if they list the word at all, state simply "etymology unknown." **Wank** could be related to *whack* and/or *whang*. **Wank** has rhyming slang variations, namely, **barclay** from **Barclays Bank**, **J. Arthur Rank**, and **Jodrell Bank**, and connections between masturbation and banking, the cinema and astronomy respectively are not too difficult to find.

The second grammatical structure that generates many, sometimes hilarious, terms, for masturbation is a *verb + noun* combination. All of these phrases refer to male masturbation usually because of the noun in the phrase. Examples are to **fuck the fist**, which is bluntly literal, to **flog the bishop** and to **flog the donkey** (**donkey** here refers to the penis while **bishop** refers to the glans). Other phrases (that refer to the glans) are to **bash the bishop**, and to **rub one's radish**. Reference to the penis is made in to **pound one's meat**, to **pull one's pudding**, to **pull one's peter**, to **flub the dub** (a *dub* being American slang for a clumsy person), to **pull wire**, to **punish Percy in the palm**, to **gallop the antelope**, to **jerk one's gherkin**, to **paddle one's pickle** and others. Many of these phrases reflect aggression: pounding, punishing, flogging and bashing. The nouns reflect the usual themes: animality, the body, food, cultural artifacts and names. One phrase that refers, instead, to the product of masturbation, is to **make a milkshake**.

The fact that masturbation is often a solitary activity is reflected in such terms as **playing with oneself, playing solitaire** and to **go it alone**, all intersexual. The scarcity of women in the lives of some soldiers gives rise to **soldier's joy** and to **mount the corporal and four fingers**; a variation of this is to **see madame thumb and her four daughters**. Other prepositions besides *off* appear in to **take down**, presumably referring to the eventual detumescence of the penis, and to **shake up** which refers to the semen produced. **Pocket pool** makes a transferred reference to the **balls** or testicles, while **infanticide**, **keeping the census down** and **malthusianism** are all euphemisms for masturbation that rely on the fact that fertilization will not take place. **Hand job** simply states the manual aspect, though *job* can indicate a professional frame of reference.

Terms which are applied only or more usually to female masturbation are to **finger**, and to **digitate** which is a pedantic variation of to **finger**, to **clitorize** which is most explicit, to **make scissors**, to **do the bowling hold** or **hold a bowling ball**. These last three terms refer to multiple simultaneous digital stimulation of the female genitals.

Oral Sex

Oral sexual activity in general is now sometimes referred to as **mouth music**. The technical terms for this activity are **fellatio** and **cunnilingus** for the stimulation of male and female genitals respectively. **Fellatio** comes from the Latin *fellare* meaning to suck, while **cunnilingus** is derived from the Latin *cunnus*, wedge (vulva), and *lingere*, to lick. Many of the terms for **mouth music** are intersexual, though some are clearly for fellatio or for cunnilingus only.

Since the mouth has one obvious primary function, perhaps the most common intersexual term is to **eat**. Related terms are to **gobble** and to **picnic**, while less specific are to **perform** and to **service**, which can also refer to sexual intercourse. Another function of the mouth is to kiss, so to **kiss** or to **kiss it** is also used to refer to oral sex; while kissing or eating, the fellator or cunnilinguist presents her or his head to the genitals, hence the phrase to **give head**. **Gamahuching** or **gamaruching** may reflect euphemistic displacement from the genitals to the legs, since *gam* is slang for leg, though an explanation for the latter part of these terms is missing. Since the genitals are placed halfway down the body, below the head and torso, **going down (on)** and **going south** are euphemisms for oral sex.

On a similar level are the following expressions usually referring to fellatio, all of which have religious overtones: to **worship at the altar**, to **kneel at the altar**, to **say high mass** and to **receive holy communion**. Finally, saying or speaking, which is also an oral activity or function, explains **speaking Low Genitalese**, and another foreign language is utilized in terms for oral sex, namely, French, in **Frenching**, **French job** and **French tricks**, while another method of communicating is to **whistle**, yet another euphemism for oral sex.

Terms for cunnilingus, specifically, are to **dive** and all its variants, to **muff dive**, to **pearl dive** and to **skin dive**, all emphasizing "going down" on, by now, familiar terms for the female genitals. To **growl bite** and to **tip the velvet** are both phrases referring back to **growl** and **velvet**, respectively which both mean the female genitals, while to **lick** and to **tongue**, though intersexual, are usually applied to cunnilingus. **Eating at the Y** is another term based on the shape of the female's open legs during cunnilingus. One obsolete (18th to 19th century) term for cunnilingus is **larking**, which must be related to its playing or sporting sense. The person performing cunnilingus is called a **diver**, a **gash eater**, **lap lover**, **vacuum cleaner**, and so on, all employing familiar female genital terminology, or simply a **linguist**, though this term is intersexual, and adds a significant new flavor to the skills of the lexicographer.

Terms that are specific to fellatio are to **cop a bird**, or **cock**, etc., to **flute**, and the musical to **play the flute**, **horn** or **organ**, to **swallow a sword** and to **polish the knob**. These phrases all make reference to the penis or the glans. One obsolete term from the 19th century is **tittyoggy** or **tittie-oggie**, though the derivation of this is mysterious. References could be found, though with some stretch, to penis (**titbit**) and testicles (*oggs* means stones of fruit and may come from *eggs*) but there is no reference to orality. At first glance this word seems to mean eyeing (ogling) the breasts (titties), the only tenuous connection being that breasts (or nipples) are sucked. General terms that are usually limited to fellatio only, are to **blow** and **blow job**, with all the connotations of *job*, while someone refusing to do a **blow job** is called a **vegetarian**. Other terms are to **suck** or **suck off**, and related to eating, to **whomp it up**, to **yummy it down** and to **scarf up**, from *scarfing* which is black American slang for eating. To **get a facial** refers to the fellator's acquisition.

Rhyming slang also contributes with **plate of ham** which rhymes with **gam**, which is itself slang for fellatio, possibly derived from its slang meaning ("leg") — perhaps a bodily displacement or thought of in relation to **the best leg of three** or **middle leg**? **Plate of ham** has also been shortened in Cockney fashion to **plate**. Another type of slang term is **sally**, which is South African (specifically Cape Town) gay slang for fellatio. That city's variety of slang works on the principle of using female names for things or actions and sometimes matches the first letter of the slang term with the thing specified; **sally** here signifies **suck**.

The most common slang term for a fellator or fellatrix is **cocksucker**, though this is also a derogatory term for a person in general. Two variants on **cocksucker** are **cocklover** and **cockeater**, though Rodgers provides an impressive alternative list of terms many of which are limited to gay slang usage; examples are **acorn picker**, **bone queen**, **come freak**, **flute player**, **jaw queen**, **peter eater**, **protein queen**, **skull pussy** and **worm eater**. These terms all make reference either to terms for the penis (or the glans or semen) or to the mouth, and often refer to both.

Oral sex may occur in many different positions, as does intercourse, but for some reason the activity or position of mutual oral sex has generated a sizeable terminology of its own. The most popular term for this is **soixante-neuf**, French for sixty-nine. That the French word is used is appropriate given the meaning of **Frenching**, while the number **69** is also appropriate since it shows, in simplified outline, or ideographically, two bodies inverted on one another. Other terms for this activity are **loop de loop**, **head over heels**, **alternating flame** (since flames lick?), **linguistic exercise** and **vice versa** which perhaps puns on the *vice* part. The term **boating** is reserved for mutual cunnilingus since **boat** makes reference to the vulva.

Anal Sex

The term **sodomy** comes originally from the biblical city of Sodom in Palestine, while to **bugger** and **buggery** come from medieval Latin *Bulgaris* meaning a Bulgarian who was then regarded as a heretic who engaged in sodomy (buggery includes the possibility of anal sex with animals, which sodomy does not). Since anal intercourse shares the characteristic of penetration with sexual intercourse, many of its terms are simply borrowed — sometimes with qualifications added. Examples are: to **ass fuck** or **arse fuck**, to **butt fuck** or **butt bang**, to **shaft in the bum**, etc.

Many of the verbs from Chapter 2 are also used for anal intercourse — for example: **ram**, **service**, and so on. Reference to the anus or buttocks is made in the following cases: to **part someone's cheeks**, to **split someone's buns**, to **broaden someone's outlook** (the **anus** is also called the **eye**), to **bend someone over**, to **dot the i** (the dot being the anus, the i being the penis), **moonshot**, from **moons** meaning the buttocks, and to **cornhole**, which some say is from the practice in the 1920s in the United States of wiping the rear with dried corncobs. Feces are referred to in such terms as to **stir fudge**, to **stir someone's chocolate**, or to **brown**, while aggression is elicited from to **do a stern job**, though this is also a nautical pun, to **wreck a rectum**, to **burgle** (perhaps associated with rape or with the word **bugger**), and, from animals, come to **wolf** and to **goose**, which we have seen has other related meanings.

Other terms for anal intercourse are **dry hump**, in contrast to the wetness of the vagina, to **ream**, **third way**, which presupposes intercourse and oral sex as the first and second ways, to **perve**, short for *pervert* and to **bless**, a black slang term with very opposite or antithetical connotations. To **greek** comes from the ancient Greeks' practice of male homosexuality, to **oscarize** comes from Oscar Wilde, one of the best known of 19th century male homosexuals, and to **molly** from a female name given to a male homosexual.

The fact that there is no slang terminology for rape has been pointed out by many writers, and the seriousness and outrage of anal rape perhaps also explains the terminological lack in this area. Prison slang, though, contributes some terms for anal rape, such as the literal to **force fuck**, to **break and enter**, with its appropriate criminal overtones, and to **barrel** from the phrase "to have someone over a barrel," meaning to have physical control over someone.

Oral-anal activity is yet another sexual variation. The most common term for it is to **rim**, a rim being a circular border (the anus). Some terms are borrowed from fellatio and cunnilingus terms, sometimes with qualifications. Examples include to **ass blow**, to **clean up the kitchen**, to **play the piano**, an apparent reference to *Rim*ski-Korsakov, **thirty-nine**, since **39** is ideographic, and to **tongue-fuck**.

The Anus and Buttocks

Though I have not provided the terminology for the mouth, the variety and extent of anal terminology perhaps justifies a brief digression. We should remember from Chapter 1 that excretion and copulation are taboos in our society, unlike eating. We should therefore expect, on repressive grounds, more terminology for the excretory region than for the mouth. Terms for the **anus**, **A-hole**, or **ass-hole** show some parallels with the terminology for the female genitals. Gay slang makes use of such words as **eye**, **manhole**, or **mustard pot** to mean anus. **Brown berry** even parallels **cherry** in meaning virgin territory. Defecation is the uppermost thought in **brown**, **crapper**, **dirt road**, **exhaust pipe**, and so on. **Back door** and **wrong door**, **port hole** and **nether throat** rely on position or direction. Place names are found in the rhyming slang terms **Elephant and Castle** (an area and pub name in London, rhyming with asshole, or in British English arsehole), **North Pole** (hole) and **Khyber Pass** which, though it rhymes with **ass** (**arse**), always means anus and is used in such phrases as "kick it up your Khyber Pass."

Terms for the **buttocks** or **ass/arse** show some overlap with terms for the female genitals as well as with terms for the breasts. **Tail** and **prat** can refer to the buttocks or the female genitals, while **fanny** refers to the female genitals in Britian and to the buttocks in America. **Buns** refers mainly to the buttocks, but also to the breasts. The Saxon term **arse** was, until well into the 17th century, a standard term for the buttocks and only thereafter became a vulgarism or true four-letter word. **Neddy**, which also means a donkey, probably acquired its anatomical meaning through the donkey's connection with **ass** which relates through similarity of pronunciation to **arse**. **Bum**, which first appears in the 14th century, is probably not derived from **bottom**, which only appears in the 18th century as a term for the buttocks. **Bumkin** and **bumpkin** are variations on **bum**, *-kin* being a suffix denoting a diminutive.

Buttocks itself is made up from **butt** plus *-ock* which is another suffix denoting a diminutive. **Rump** is derived from Middle Dutch meaning stump. Euphemisms such as **backside**, **behind**, **posteriors** and **fundament** are all self-explanatory. Most of the terms for the buttocks divide into the themes of position or appearance. Like **bottom** and **backside** we also find Shakespeare's **holland**, it being a low-lying country, **flip side**, **south end**, **western end** and such nautically influenced terms as **keel, poop** and **stern**. **Hilltop Drive** and **jutland** probably refer to the shape of the buttocks in relation to the rest of the body, while physical appearance is reflected in: **cakes, rounders, rolls** and **rosy**, or **rosey**, which hints at cheeks.

Miscellaneous

Terms for other forms of sexual activity are briefly reviewed here. **Pit job** and the musical **bagpipe** both refer to fucking the armpits or **coitus in axilla** in medical parlance. **Leggins, rubbins, thighs** and **thigh sandwich** refer to fucking between the thighs or, more technically, **femoral intercourse**. Rubbing against someone to reach a climax is called **frottage**, from the French *frotter* meaning to rub. When specifically a lesbian activity it is called a **flat fuck, bumper to bumper** or **tribadism**, from the Greek *tribein* meaning to rub.

Sexual activity between more than two persons also gives rise to an interesting terminology. Three people engaged in sexual activity is called a **sandwich, cluster fuck, three-way** or **ménage à trois**, from French meaning a household of three, while a threesome lying in bed is called **lying in state** for the odd sex. Group sex is often called an **orgy** from the Latin *orgia*, meaning a nocturnal festival or festivity, though the word is related to **orgasm**; another term for an **orgy** is a **circus** which conjures up a variety of cunning stunts. Other terms are **birthday party, poke party, pig pile**, which usually refers to a male homosexual orgy, and **Roman night** — classical debauchery. Copulatory linkages of many people are referred to as a **daisy chain, floral arrangement, chain gang** or **ring around the rosey**, all quite self-explanatory. Sexual intercourse with someone who has already been had is called **sloppy seconds**, or a **gang bang**, while the person so had is said to have **wet decks**, or is called a **buttered bun**, this term being used as early as the 18th century.

Other sexual activities that have generated some of their own specialist terminologies are in the fields of sadomasochism (or "SM") and bondage and domination (B & D), which are concerned with flagellation, chaining, fetishism (leather, rubber, etc.), urinating or being urinated on, and so on. The terminology of such activities is not part of the purview of this book.

Orgasm

Orgasm can be regarded as the terminus ad quem of all the above activities, which include sexual intercourse of both the heterosexual and homosexual variety, masturbation, oral sex, etc. I shall briefly review the terminology for this experience. Seeing it as an end-point explains the term to **come**, the most common euphemism. Similar expressions are to **bring off** and to **climax**. On the same theme, though considerably more metaphysical or literary, we find to **die**, or **little death** from the French *petite mort*, to **finish**, **loss**, **fading** and to **melt**. All of these terms are, happily, intersexual, and should also remind one of the connection between sex and death, discussed in Chapter 1.

Other terms which are androcentric since they describe ejaculation are to **spend** (with overtones of the value of the seminal fluid or of prostitution), to **shoot** (with aggressive overtones), to **discharge**, to **jet one's juice**, or **give one's gravy**, to **get one's rocks off**, to **shoot one's load**, and so on. Terms for semen have already been discussed in Chapter 4. One phrase for orgasm used of women only, though probably male-created, is to **stand up and cheer** or **stand up and shout**.

Of all these terms, I find the term **orgasm** itself to be the most interesting, for it is derived from the Greek *organ* meaning to swell, and in turn is related to the English words *organ, work* and *energy*, also derived from the related Greek word *ergon*. This cluster of senses shows both the activity or work involved in orgasm as well as the physical condition of the sexual organs in this state. The slang **religious observance** perhaps jokes with the serious side of orgasm while jibing at religion, and a **thrill** is probably its appropriate metaphorical antonym.

People

Having discussed some of the terms for a variety of sexual activities, as well as terminology for the buttocks and anus, we turn now to the terminology for people considered as sexual beings. In *The Slang of Venery*, terms are listed under the headings *man* and *woman* but perhaps not surprisingly there are over three times as many words for women (as sexual beings) than for men, and in general the terms for man are of the **rake**, **ribald**, **whoremonger** variety, while the thousand or more terms for woman emphasize the "woman-as-sex-object," androcentric image and sometimes merge with terms for prostitute. Many of the general terms for woman define her in relation to copulation or the female genitals. The following nouns are good examples of this: **crumpet**, **muslin**, a **bit of jam**, **flat fuck** and so on. **Bit** and **piece** are also used on their own to characterize females and emphasize sexual objectification. The themes of food and clothing are both present in these terms.

Interestingly, a woman is sometimes referred to as a **dish** and endearments like *honey* and *sugar* emphasize this. **Broad** is an American androcentric slang term for a woman or girl that simply relies on the fact that, compared to men, women's hips are broad. **Skirt** is perhaps the best-known clothing term for a woman; **doll** is also something that is dressed up, though it points also to childhood and the treatment of women as children; **wench** comes from Old English meaning a child. The polarization of girl and boy shows in the way *girls* is often used to refer to women while *boys* is less often used in equal contexts. The Australian slang term **brush**, meaning woman, may also have its derivation from grooming, though it could refer to hair which in turn refers to pubic hair, a signifier of woman. The objectification of woman's body can also be witnessed in the use of the term **chassis** applied to a woman though derived from the frame of a motor vehicle. And the discussion of gender in Chapter 1 can be extended to point out that cars, boats and ships are very often given female names or referred to by the pronoun *she*. Only recently, under feminist pressure, were meteorological names for hurricanes broadened to include male names.

The animal world also provides many terms for woman, birds providing **hen**, **chick** as well as **bird** itself; other creatures are **bitch** and **slut**, which is archaic for a female dog, **cow**, **minx**, **sow** and **filly**. **Hussy**, a 19th century term related to *house*wife, which like **slut** has connotations of being loose and easy sexually. Rhyming slang also provides a number of terms, the more interesting ones being **cuddle and kiss**, rhyming with Miss, **ivory pearl**, rhyming with girl and stressing the association of jewelry with women, and **winds do whirl**, perhaps hinting at a flightly characteristic of women, equivalent to the American **floozy** or **floozie**. **Siren** and **femme fatale** both refer to the dangerous woman, while **concubine**, from the Latin *concubina*, meaning to lie down together, like **mistress**, is a **left-handed wife** or a **wife in watercolors**. Terms for males or females considered as sexual partners are simply nouns derived from the verbs for sexual intercourse such as a **fuck**, a **screw**, a **lay**, etc.

Prostitute

Prostitute is derived from the Latin *prostituere* meaning to offer for sale by public exposure, while **whore** is related to the Latin *carus* meaning a dear one, one of the few positively-tainted terms in this section. **Harlot** goes back to Middle English and originally meant a vagabond, but dictionaries give "etymology unknown" for **strumpet**, though, curiously, the word is made up of two parts—**strum** and **pet**—each with sexual meanings. As with terms for women in general, terms for prostitute are sometimes taken from terms for copulation or the genitals; for example: **cocktail**, **tickle tail** and **carrion** (meat, flesh). Animality is also present in **bat**, a creature of the night, and **shrimp**, obsolete since the 18th century, while **cat**, **squirrel** and **hare** all have characteristic fur. Shakespeare even puns on **hare** (**hair**), and **hare** happens to be also close to **harlot**. Food gets a mention in **tart**, which is something tasty.

Some terms for prostitute clearly show the "degenerative" development in the meaning of some words; for example, **trollop** and **trull** are archaic terms for a girl but degenerated around the 17th century into meaning a prostitute. **Doxy** originally meant a female beggar but it too degenerated to mean a prostitute; it may be derived from **dock**, meaning to have sexual intercourse. The marginality of prostitution in English society and the threat that it posed, and still poses, to the central ideological system of society, must go much of the way in explaining the "negative" terminology or the negative connotations of many of the slang terms. (The same argument must also apply to the terminology for homosexuals.) The business side of prostitution is reflected in such terms as **public ledger**, **traffic**, **wholesale**, an Elizabethan pun on **hole**, **streetwalker**, **call girl**, **hooker** and so on; **on the game** is another term for prostitution. **Hedge whore**, according to Grose, is a low beggarly whore who "disposes her favors under a hedge," while **hobby horse** takes advantage of the standard meaning—"a man's favorite amusement" according to Grose—and also plays on the sexual sense of to **horse**. Euphemisms abound in such terms as **a lady of easy virtue**, **sister of the night**, an **unfortunate**, and **scarlet woman**, which has New Testament origins. Religion also features in such terms as **pagan**, and **abbess**, while **aunt**, and **moll** or **molly**, related to the name **Mary**, add status and proper name to themes for terms for prostitute. **Bawd** may be from Old French meaning lively or **gay**, which itself has served as a term for a prostitute; **gay bit** is another variation. **Punk** also meant a whore in the 17th century and is possibly related to **puncture**, meaning to deflower.

Rhyming slang gives rise to **brass nail**, rhyming with **tail**, and the American **mallee root**, rhyming with prostitute; **root** is also Australian slang for sexual intercourse. All the other rhyming slang terms rhyme with **whore**, such as **Jane Shore** or **Jane Shaw**, **Rory O'More**, **early door**, significant in that door could signify the vulva, **boat and oar**, also pointing to the possible genital significance, through shape, of boat, and the numerals **two by four**, **six to four**, and others. The number *two* also appears in the 19th century term **twofer**, though the reason for this is far from clear. It could be, like **twat**, related to the two labia, but could also be related to two-timing, that is, deceiving a lover.

Prostitution terms for males divide up into three sections; firstly there are terms for **pimp**, then there are terms for male prostitutes and finally terms for male homosexual prostitutes, though there is some overlap in the last two categories as well as with the terminology for female prostitutes. **Pimp**, according to the dictionaries, is an etymological mystery, though it sounds close to **pump**, which not only has many sexual meanings but also, as a verb, has a financial nuance, namely of obtaining money from someone. Other terms for pimp are the archaic **bully** and **fancy man** and the more recent **nookie bookie**. Terms for a male prostitute include **gigolo**, which is a back formation from the French *gigolette* meaning a female hired dancer or prostitute; *giguer* is to dance in French — adding to the sexual connotations of dance. **Stud** is another term derived from an Old English term for a stallion kept for breeding. Other terms for a male prostitute — for either heterosexual or homosexual activity — are **cowboy**, usually new to the game, and **hustler**, while terms specifically for male homosexual prostitutes not surprisingly borrow from female terminology, such as **pro**, **hooker**, **cocktail**, **flesh** and so on. Other self-explanatory terms specifically for male homosexual prostitutes are **crack salesman** and **he-whore**.

Homosexual

The term **homosexual** is derived from the Greek *homo* meaning the same, thus **homosexual** refers to people who are attracted to the same sex and so covers lesbianism as well as male homosexuality. Abbreviations of the word are **homo**, and even **mo**, though these apply to males only. Many of the terms for male homosexuals are derived from terms for females, either as sexual beings, sex objects or as prostitutes. We find, for example, **effie**, which is an abbreviation of *effeminate*, **belle**, **daffodil**, **fluff**, **lily**, and other female names such as **Mary**, **Mavis**, **nancy boy**, **pansy**, **powder puff**, **queen** and **twinkle toes**, each reflecting some definitive female quality; the preponderance of flower terms stands out and can only be regarded as paradigmatic of femininity. Examples of prostitute terms are **duchess**, **madame**, and **moll**, also using female names and rank.

Perhaps it is no surprise to find that **faggot** or **fag** was a 15th century pejorative term for a woman, though other suggestions have been provided as to why this term is applied to male homosexuals, such as from the practice of fagging in English public schools (i.e., acting as a personal servant to the older boys) or from the slang term for cigarette, since at one time cigarettes were considered to be effeminate — males smoked cigars. **Punk** is another interesting term that is used for homosexuals, since **punk** can also mean a prostitute. Partridge also gives a slang 19th century use of **punk** to mean a puncture. **Twit** is another derogatory term for a homosexual and shows a resemblance to **twat**, which can also be used derogatively for a person. The passive partner is also referred to as **bum boy**, **bucket boy**, **bender**, **chicken**, and so on. **Fairy** is also applied to the passive partner, though **angel** refers to any male homosexual. Variations on **angel** are **fallen angel**, and **faygeleh**, from Yiddish and German *vogel* meaning a bird. **Angels** and **fairies** all have wings and thus encroach on the common female sexual symbol of a bird.

The active male homosexual partner is referred to as a **bottle opener**, **chuffer**, perhaps related to *chuff* an obsolete term for a fat cheek, or *chuff* meaning a locomotive engine sound, or even *chuff* meaning a boor or churl, and by such terms as **gander**, **miner**, **greek**, **knight**, one of the few flattering terms though now archaic, **turk**, and **wolf**. Older terms are **gut fucker**, **gentleman of the back door** and **backgammon player**, all making reference to sodomy. Then there are general terms for homosexuals, coined by heterosexuals and derogatory without exception. The most common one is **queer**, which also has old slang senses of counterfeit money, an inferior substitute for soot, and a hoax, all dating from the 19th century; others are **deviate**, **misfit**, **perv**, **ponce**, which is also another term for a pimp, thus reinforcing the terminological connection between male homosexuality and (usually female) prostitution, and **pouf** or **poufter** or **pooftah**, which in the 19th century meant a would-be actor and is derived from the French *pouffe* meaning puff, and so is close to **powder puff**.

Further terms are **bent** and **bent wrist**; **bent** perhaps refers to **bending over** and **bender**, but also certainly refers to the condition opposite to **straight**, meaning heterosexual. Think also of **kinky** which refers to any sexual "deviation," derived from *kink* meaning a bend or twist. Another homosexual slang term for a **heterosexual** or **straight** is a **breeder**, which points to the nonprocreative consequences of homosexuality. Not surprisingly, then, homosexuality has been called, by heterosexuals, the **third sex** or **that way inclined**. Denial of one's homosexual leanings or desires has been expressed in such terms as **closet case** or **closet queen**. Such a person is also referred to as **canned fruit**.

We have already seen a number of female names being used to refer to male homosexuals; male names are also used especially as paradigms of the active and passive homosexual type. Active names are **Sam** and **Bill**, while examples of passive ones are **Cecil** and **Seymour**. The term **homosexual** is only a 19th century coinage; names for types of homosexuals, however, go back to Greek; for example, **catamite** refers to a boy who is loved or kept by a mature or older man, and **uranian** is derived from the myth of the male followers of heavenly Aphrodite. **Dilly boy** is derived from Piccadilly Circus, a homosexual meeting, or cruising, place in London. Ageism is an issue also since the age of homosexuals is sometimes expressed in the terminology; we have already seen many terms that refer to the young boy. The old or older homosexual is referred to as **auntie** (which also means an older prostitute), **afghan**, from the shawl that older people wear to keep warm, **aging actress**, and such terms as **old girl** or **old hen**.

Almost all of the above terms for male homosexuals are strictly for male homosexuals; the language of lesbianism is very different, though the term that unites them with their male counterparts is **gay**. Like it or not, the term **gay**, in common parlance and especially among homosexuals themselves, has virtually replaced the term **homosexual**. The term was first used in English in the 13th century to mean merry;

by the 14th century it had come to mean showy and by the 17th century it meant dissipated or promiscuous. By the 19th century a **gay** or a **gay bit** referred to a prostitute, while **gaying it** referred to sexual intercourse. The etymology of **gay**, according to the dictionaries, shows a derivation from the Old French *gai*, though Aman (*Maledicta* III, 2) suggests that it may be derived from the Old English *gal* meaning merry or lascivious and could be related to the Modern German *geil* meaning sexually aroused, which itself is derived from the Old German *geil* meaning strong or merry. If this etymology is correct, both German and English show similar "depreciation" in meaning, from old to modern, with regard to this word. Curiously, homosexuals have recently produced adjectival synonyms for **gay**, namely **jolly** and **happy**. Perhaps partly because of the associations of the word, and partly because of its monosyllabic nature (as opposed to the clumsy **homosexual** which has five syllables), **gay** has been adopted as the most suitable term for compounds such as *gay bar, gaydom*, which refers to gay culture, *gay liberation*, and so on.

The term **lesbian** is derived from the Greek island of Lesbos where the poet Sappho lived. She founded a female literary society and wrote poetry about female homosexuality; Lesbia was one of the names used in her poetry. **Sapphism** is a synonym for lesbianism. There are many variations on lesbian, such as **les, lesbo** and **lizzy**. As male homosexual terminology often refers to the female sex, so lesbian terminology often makes use of male terms or refers to masculinity. Examples are **manny, mason**, since the Masons are a male-only society, **poppa, she-man, slacks**, presumably in contrast to skirts which epitomize women's clothes, **fellow**, and so on. **No-nuts** is a male homosexual slang term for a lesbian, harping on an anatomical fact; male names appear in **tom** and **butch**, referring to the active lesbian partner (**butch** is actually derived by back formation from *butcher*). **Wolf** also refers to the active lesbian partner though it is also used by male homosexuals for the same purpose. Another camp term is **vegetable** which implicitly points to **fruits**, which lesbians are not.

There are also many straightforward terms, such as **lady lover**, **girl kisser**, or **one of the boys**, but perhaps the most common slang term for a lesbian is **dyke**, or **dike**, which can refer to the active or mannish lesbian partner or, often pejoratively, to lesbians in general. **Dyke**, we have already seen, can refer to the female genitals since it means, in standard English, a ditch. However its modern lesbian sense is etymologically mysterious. Flexner and Wentworth as well as

Rodgers suggest that it comes from the *-dite* suffix in the word *her-maphrodite*. The term *hermaphrodite* refers to beings with physical characteristics of both sexes; in Greek mythology Hermaphroditos was the son of Hermes and Aphrodite who merged together with a water nymph, thus acquiring both sexual organs. But how *-dite* became transformed to **dyke** still needs explaining. Perhaps **dyke**'s phonetic resemblance to **dick** is significant? The term *hermaphrodite*, coincidentally, has given rise to terms for a male homosexual also — **mophy** was a late 19th century naval term for an effeminate and well-groomed youth, while **moffie** is a South African term, with the same derivation, meaning a male homosexual. Variations on **dyke** are **bull dyke** and **molly dyke** for the active/passive distinction, and **Dutch girl**, which uses the fact that dykes, that is, embankments, are found in Holland.

Bisexual

Terms for bisexuality, which indicates sexual leanings or desires towards both sexes, as opposed to hermaphroditism, which is a physical condition combining both sets of sex organs, make extensive use of the two-sidedness of this psychological state. **Bi** itself is a common shortened form, while to **wear bifocals**, **bicycle** and to **ride a bicycle** use this prefix. Since heterosexuals are **straight** and homosexuals are **bent**, bisexuals are referred to as **half bent** or **half-and-half**. The tendency to turn one way and then the other explains such terms as **flippy**, **gate swinger**, **swing both ways**, **two-way baby**, **convertible**, **ambidextrous** and **AC-DC**, derived from electrical apparatuses which are adapted to carry both alternating current and direct current; **acey-deucey** is a variant of this. The ambivalence found in bisexuality is expressed in the terms **in between** and **sitting on the fence**. All the above terms apply to both male and female bisexuals, however **gillette blade** refers only to a bisexual female and is explained by the fact that there are double-edged Gillette trademark blades which cut both ways.

The Brothel

Before turning to the terminology of sexual states, another digression is needed to examine the terminology of sexual institutions, in particular the brothel. **Brothel** in the 14th century meant a worthless fellow or person (male or female); by the 15th century it had come to mean a (female) prostitute. Only by the 16th century did it acquire the meaning of a **whorehouse**. Since a brothel is usually a house, *-house* serves as a useful suffix for names for a brothel, often combined with terms for sexual intercourse or terms connected with it. Examples are: **bawdy house** and **leaping house**, from the 16th century, and later, **cathouse**, **joy house**, **meat house**, **naughty house**, **red house** and **sporting house**. *House* is also implied in the rhyming slang term **flea and louse**.

Since brothels are commercial enterprises *-shop* is another useful suffix; we find: **buttocking shop** and **knocking shop** or **knocking joint** as well as **place of sixpenny/sixpence sinfulness**, a 17th century term which must give a fair idea of the ravages of inflation, as well as making reference to sin. Euphemism is found in such terms as **ladies' college** and **academy**, perhaps punning on the implied **knowledge** that is had, while **nunnery**, another 17th century term, makes yet another reference to religion, and perhaps in reaction-formation style, defines something in terms of its perceived polar opposite, though actually the origins of the brothel are probably to be found in religious temples or places of worship.

Another old term for a brothel is a **stew**, which goes as far back as the 14th century. **Stew** must refer to a bathing house or bath, in particular a steam or Turkish bath, where one can stew, that is, sweat and perspire. **Bagnio** is a 16th century term for a brothel and is derived from the Italian for a bath. **Bagnio** and **stew** are now obsolete for though brothels in the past may well have had baths or steam baths, this has ceased to be their defining characteristic. However, we find the bath, usually a Turkish bath, resurrected in the 20th century as a meeting place for male homosexuals. Other gay terms for **baths** are **the tubs**, **skin room**, and the camp **church**, which works in the way the term **nunnery** works for a **brothel**. Finally, **massage parlor**, through an extension of its facilities, has recently become a euphemism for a brothel.

States

Menstruation

The first chapter discussed the significance of marginality or borderline states with regard to sexuality. Puberty, or coming of age, is one such state but there is not much terminology for this. It could be pointed out, though, that the adjective **adult** has recently become a euphemism for *sexual* or *pornographic*, as in *adult movies, adult entertainments*, etc. Varied terminology does exist for menstruation, which is related to puberty. It could be argued that because of the secrecy among women relating to this state and imposed by society, a varied, mainly euphemistic terminology has arisen. **Menstruation** itself comes from Latin and is related to *mensis*, meaning a month, which is roughly its frequency. **Monthlies** is one euphemism, though **period** is a more common term, it being a shortened and euphemistic form of **menstural period**; **turns** is another term which points to cyclic activity and to **be at number one** also takes its sense from counting the days in the cycle.

Nature is a euphemism for any natural bodily process or state and so covers menstruation, as well as "the calls of nature." The natural is joined by its bipolar partner, the cultural, especially in the term **the curse**; this term is perhaps explained by a religious view relating to woman's biblical punishment of suffering in childbearing — **the curse** is also called **Eve's curse**. But given that menstruation is in effect a sign of fertility or of the ability to conceive, which is regarded, even religiously, as a blessing (*blessing* is even etymologically related to *blood*), it is telling how **curse**, with its powerful negative meaning, established itself in our culture as a term for menstruation. In addition to the biblical explanation, the term could be related to the fact that most religions refuse to allow sexual intercourse during menstruation, or more simply it could be related to the inconvenience it may cause.

Women's terms is a more objective or neutral way of looking at the phenomenon, as is reflected in the term **the course**, from which **the curse** would be an altered form. Since blood flows in menstruation one euphemism is to **fly the red flag**; flag perhaps refers to a menstrual or sanitary towel. **The flag is up** is a variation, perhaps also indicating that sexual intercourse cannot yet begin, according at least to biblical taboo. To **be in the saddle** also makes reference to the sanitary towel, as does **OTR**, short for **on the rag**. **Falling off the roof** indicates some medical knowledge of the causes of menstruation especially if the mucous uterine wall is thought of as a roof.

Other typical euphemisms are to **have one's aunt(ie) with one** or to **see one's aunt**. Other family relations enter in **Grandma** (or, **little sister) is here**, **an aunt from Reading** (punning on red), and others. Similar euphemisms are the **captain is home** or the **captain has come** which probably trades on the fact that *captain* was a familiar or jocular form of address in the 18th century. The **cardinal is home** is a variation based on the fact that cardinals' clothing is usually red; *cardinal* was also a slang term for mulled red wine in the 19th century, and furthermore, *cardinal* has been used punningly by writers including Shakespeare to mean *carnal*.

Pregnancy

Pregnancy is the next state to examine from the terminological viewpoint. The etymology of **pregnant** is straightforward, from the Latin *praegnas*; the first syllable means before, while the last syllable is the base of *(g)nasci*, meaning to be born. **Preggers** is a colloquial variation. The wide range of feelings shown toward pregnancy is reflected in terms that are positive, neutral and negative. On the positive emotional side we find **anticipating a happy event**. Neutral terms are **expectant, clucky, in pod, in an interesting condition, not alone,** and to **have a bun in the oven**, another food metaphor. Negative terms include **in trouble, up the spout, up the duff** (*duff* being slang for the buttocks as well as being a kind of flour pudding and a dialect form of *dough*, thus perhaps hinting at the **bun in the oven** idiom), and, finally, **knocked up**, which is based on **knocking**, meaning having sexual intercourse.

Lust

Lust is a term related to the Old High German *lust* meaning desire and to the Old Norse, meaning sexual desire. In the 13th century *lusty* meant joyful and pleasing, and is also related etymologically to **lascivious** via the Latin *lascivus*, meaning wanton, lustful. **Libidinous** comes from **libido**, which in turn is derived from the Latin *libet* meaning "it is pleasing." **Lewd** has obsolete meanings; in the 13th century it meant unlearned, in the 14th century it meant low, and is derived from the Old English *lewde* meaning ignorant; the ignorance, presumably, is of manners and culture and not of the birds and bees. **Licentious** is derived from the Latin *licentia* meaning license, but from the 15th century it came to mean excessive license, before acquiring a specific sexual meaning. I have intentionally grouped together all the words beginning with *l* if only to show how many terms there are in this category; perhaps the *l* sound, the lingual, or more specifically the laminal, is especially appropriate in this context since it hints, however subliminally, at the tongue, which has all sorts of sexual connotations. The etymology of the term **lecherous** brings the tongue to the surface, so to speak, since it is derived from the Old French *lechier* meaning to lick. Licking the lips is also a common human gesture to indicate pleasure.

Of the other terms for *lust* or *lusty* many of them have a respectable literary history. For example, Shakespeare used the following nouns and adjectives: **appetite**, **ardor**, **bawdy**, **blood**, **hot**, **keen**, **salt**, **saucy**, **wanton** and **willing** (among many others). Among these terms certain themes reappear; food and eating, for example, are evident in **appetite**, **salt** and **saucy**, while heat is behind **ardor** (from the Latin *ardere* meaning to burn) and **sweaty**. The other terms reflect the will and or excess, in varying degrees.

Other terms for lust or lusty are **horny**, probably with phallic origins or related to the horns of a cuckold, **steamy**, which fits with the heat-related terms above, **geared up**, **wired up**, **ready** and **in season**, which all emphasize a readiness to begin sexual activity, and **randy** which is related to *rant* and is derived from the Dutch *ranten* meaning to rave; a *raver* is a slang term for someone who is socially or sexually uninhibited. **Raunchy** is a 20th century American slang term for **lecherous**, and could be derived from earlier slang meanings, one of which is being drunk. **Juicy** and **wet** add to the sweaty theme, though they stress lubrication rather than heat; **lubricious** is another term for lewd, though it is rather formal or literary.

Color is an important feature in the terminology of sexuality in general and more specifically with regard to lust and sexual arousal. The color red has already featured in such terms as **red house**, **red lamp**, **red light district**, **scarlet woman** and of course in some of the terms for menstruation. It is referred to again here in **blood** and is hinted at in terms for (sexual) heat. Red, in our culture, is also the color of danger, appropriate, given the status of sexuality in general and of particular forms of it in our society. Blue is also a sexual color in the context of *blue movies* or feeling **blue**. It has been suggested that the reason why blue has been associated with pornography and titillation is because of the blue neon lights that are found at striptease joints, pornographic cinemas, and the like. However, the explanation may be found at a historically much earlier period. Partridge, via Hotten, suggests that the sexual connotation of blue comes from the French *Bibliothèque Bleu* which referred to books of "questionable character." *The Slang of Venery* suggests that blue, in its sexual sense, is derived from the blue dresses that prostitutes wore in Elizabethan times. But whatever the real derivation is, its meaning fits rather uneasily with the informal sense of blue in the phrase *the blues* meaning a state of depression, though *the blues*, meaning a form of music or song originating from black Americans at the turn of this century, is more appropriate to the sexual sense since the blues is a very earthy music and is related to **jazz** with its sexual connotations.

Blueballs refers to aching testicles that are caused by sexual arousal without reaching ejaculation. **Blueballs** are also called **love nuts** and **stoneache**, where **nuts** and **stones** refer to the testicles. **Stoneache** should not be confused with **bone-ache** which was a 16th century term for syphilis. **Blueballs** in males is matched by **green sickness** in females, meaning to suffer from a lack of sexual activity. The color green can imply a lack of experience, though **green meadow** and **green grove** refer to the female genitals by association with the pubic hair. **Having one's greens** also refers to sexual intercourse, though the emphasis here is on food (vegetables) rather than color. In both French and Turkish the color green has definite sexual connotations much like blue or red in English. *Green language* in French refers to vulgar language that includes the French equivalents of English four-letter words.

Erection

Terms for the state of sexual erection are predominantly for males, though some terms have been used of females such as **cunt itch**, **cunt stand** and **hornification**. This last term, however, is also used of males, while to **have a horn** or to **get a horn** is used exclusively of males. **On the honk** could be related to the horn, while **on the bonk** could be related to the 19th century term *bonk* meaning a steep hill, or it could be related to the 20th century term *bonkers* meaning crazy. The firmness of a horn is expressed in such terms for penile erection as **bone, boner, hard-on,** and **stiff.** The *-on* suffix indicates that "all systems go," while the *-off* suffix, which is found in so many terms for masturbation and sexual intercourse, indicates the completion, and usually the satisfaction thereby gained, of the act. To **be up** is a simple term for an erection; other terms are **live wire**, **pulse**, from the throbbing of an erect penis, **putter**, which in standard English is an iron club in golf, **fixed bayonet**, which has aggressive overtones, **upright grand**, which plays on the similarity of a piano to an **organ**, **in one's Sunday clothes** or **in one's Sunday best**, since these clothes used to be starched and were, consequently stiff, and **jack**, which can also simply refer to the penis sans erection. **Half mast** refers to a penis that is half erect, though the implication of **half mast** is that the penis is half limp.

Aids and Objects

Finally, we turn to the terminology for sexual aids, developed either for the purpose of sexual pleasure or for contraception. The development of sex aids clearly shows the cultural side of sex, or the adaption of nature to the technology produced by human culture, and this probably goes as far back in history as does the practice of carving. The **dildo** is the oldest known type of sexual aid. According to Flexner and Wentworth and Grose the word comes from the Italian *diletto*, meaning to delight. Partridge acknowledges this derivation but also suggests that it could be derived from the Old English *dyderian* meaning to cheat or deceive, and thus would be related to **diddle**, which in addition to its sexual meaning also means to cheat. The *Oxford English Dictionary* innocently defines **dildo** as a word used in the refrain of ballads, though the new supplement supplies a maturer definition.

Other terms for the **dildo** are **broomstick** and **broomhandle**, perhaps by association with witchcraft, **lady's friend**, **widow's comforter**, **dingus**, euphemistically based on *thing* (which is *ding*) in German), **potato finger** and **godemiche**, which is the French name, possibly derived from *go* meaning easily or freely in French, and *miché*, a French slang term for a prostitute's customer or **john**. More recently with the aid of battery power, we find **vibrator**. The term for an artificial vagina is **merkin** (discussed in Chapter 3).

The **condom** of **cundum** only appeared in the 17th century and was originally made from dried sheep's gut, though a primitive kind of **condom** probably existed as a result of attempts to artificially increase the size of the penis. The etymology of the **condom** is rather unclear; it is believed to be named after an English colonel, though some say a doctor, by the name of Cundum. Another account gives the French town of Condom the honor for this invention. It could just be that the name was created with jocular intent, for **condom** and **cundum** both show a closeness to **cunt** and the French *con*, while *-dom* is a suffix indicating condition, as in *freedom*, or domain, as in *kingdom*.

Whatever the true origins of **condom**, nations, for a multitude of possible motives, foist responsibility for the **condom** onto foreigners, illustrating Freud's notion of projection on a national level. Thus the English call the **condom** a **French letter**, while the French call it "an English overcoat." We have already seen that **Frenching**, and all its related terms, refers to oral sexual practices, while **Portuguese pump** refers to masturbation, **Dutch girl** to a lesbian (through the association of **dyke**), **greek** and **turk** to male homosexuals, **Irish root** to the penis while **Irish toothache** refers to an erection. The English receive some of their own medicine back; in addition to the **condom**, the French refer to flagellation as the "English vice."

French letter explains a number of other terms for **condom** such as, following the French version, **overcoat** and **raincoat**, and **frogskin** (*frog* being a derogatory slang term for a French person), and **skin**. Even the Australian slang term for a **condom**, namely a **franger**, may be etymologically explained, at least partly, by reference to *French*. Other terms for **condom** are **safe** and **armor**, since condoms were often, and still sometimes are, used not only as a contraceptive but also or primarily as protection against **VD**.

A brief digression is needed here to examine the terminology for venereal disease. Syphilis is often simply abbreviated to **syph**, and so gives sense to the rhyming slang term which is most appropriate with regard to causation, namely, **bang and biff**. The **pox** was standard English for syphilis until the 18th century, but became a vulgar term thereafter, and thus the source of rhyming slang terms for syphilis such as **band in the box**, **coachman on the box** and **jack-in-the-box**. National projection even appears in Shakespeare, who referred to syphilis as the **malady of France**; the disease may initially have spread to Britain from the continent. Gonorrhea is called the **clap** from the Old French *clapoir*, meaning a venereal sore. Some general terms for venereal disease are: **Cupid's itch**, **dose**, and the more recent euphemism, **social disease**. The abbreviation **STD**, which stands for "sexually transmitted diseases," is the current euphemism for any venereal disease, including AIDS, the Acquired Immune Defficiency Syndrome.

Returning to **condom**: other terms for it are **sheath**, which curiously is the Latin meaning of **vagina**, **rubber**, ever since sheep's gut was replaced by rubber, **Durex**, which is a British trademark, and **Trojan**, which is an American trademark, conjuring up the qualities of endurance, and trust and toughness respectively, **glove**, since it ought to fit like one, **johnnie**, which can also refer to the penis and adds a personal touch to the object, **scum bag**, which is based on the slang and derogatory sense of **scum**, meaning semen, and **washer**, which trades on the fact that the male genitals are sometimes referred to as **plumbing**. A vending machine that sells condoms, often found in men's lavatories, is euphemistically called a **bubblegum machine**.

There are not many terms, besides the standard and occasional informal ones, for other contraceptive devices, perhaps because these devices are fairly recent inventions, for example, the *intrauterine device, IUD* for short, or *coil*; the *cap* or *Dutch cap* or *diaphragm*; and the *pill* or *contraceptive pill*. These are all female forms of contraception and may be linguistically regarded as medical devices rather than sexual ones. Dispensing with condoms or other contraceptive devices and relying entirely on the natural ovulation cycle is referred to as the **rhythm method** or **Vatican roulette**, since this is the only form of birth control approved of by the Roman Catholic Church. Copulating without a condom or other contraceptive is called **riding bareback**, which makes use of the term to **ride**, which was a standard English term for sexual intercourse until the 18th century.

GLOSSARY

Key

abbr abbreviation
C century
cf compare
esp especially
ex derived from, explained by
n. noun
sd said
v. verb
= which means
? perhaps
* obsolete

Derog derogatory
Euph euphemism
Fml formal
Infml formal
Joc jocular
Lit literary
Med medical
R.Sl rhyming slang
Sl slang
Std standard

Austr Australian
Br British
Dial dialect
E English
Fr French
Ger German, Germanic
Gr Greek

It Italian
Lat Latin
M middle
O old
SAfr South African
US American
Yid Yiddish

Parenthesized words before the century indicate the theme or themes that are exemplified by the item. They are all straightforward, e.g. aggression, animal, clothing, etc., except for "body," which indicates bodily displacement from the genitals, and "foreign" which indicates a projection to a non–English country or culture.

Parenthesized words following the symbol "R.Sl" indicate the word with which the item rhymes. The symbol "gay Sl" usually refers to male homosexual slang.

A

abbess prostitute or madame in brothel ex head of nunnery cf **nunnery** (religion) C19* Sl

Abraham penis ex Bible, instructed to go forth and multiply (name) C19–20* Joc/Sl

Abraham's bosom   vagina ex **Abraham** C19–20* Joc/Sl

academy   brothel, pun on place for knowledge = learning, sexual intercourse C17–18* Euph

accommodate   copulate sd of women ex take in C17 Lit/Infml

accommodation house   brothel cf **accommodate** C19–20* Sl

AC-DC   bisexual ex equipment functioning on either kind of electric current C20 Sl/Joc

ace of spades   1. dark female pubes ex cards pun on shape of ace and black of spade C19–20* Sl. 2. vagina ex 1. C19–20* Sl

acey-deucey   bisexual ex **AC-DC** C20 Sl

acorn   glans, head of penis ex shape, Lat *glans* = acorn C20 gay Sl

acorn picker   fellator ex **acorn** C20 gay Sl

act of generation   sexual intercourse ex reproduction C16–19* Lit/Euph

Adam's arsenal   male genitals cf **weapon**, **arsenal** (aggression) C18* Lit

addition   sexual intercourse ex adding two individuals together; reproduction C19–20* Euph/Joc

affair   genitals, cf affair = sexual relationship esp short-lived cf **thing** C19–20* Sl/Euph

afghan   elderly male homosexual ex shawl worn by elderly people (clothing) C20 gay Sl

agility   female genitals ex capability cf **snatch** C19* Sl

aging actress   elderly male homosexual ex actress = affected behavior C20 Sl

A-hole   abbr for **arse/ass-hole** C20 Sl

alchemy   sexual intercourse pun on elixir of life, longevity C16–17* Lit/Euph

alternating flame   mutual oral sex ex licking flame cf **lick** C19- Sl

ambidextrous   bisexual ex both hands = both ways C20 Joc

amble   copulate ex leisurely pace cf **ride** C16–17* Infml

angel   male homosexual ex indefinite sexuality of angels cf **fairy** (religion) C20 Sl

anilingus   oral stimulation of the anus C20 Std/Fml

another thing   female genitals ex **thing** = genitals, ?another since male regarded as primary C17* Lit/Euph

anticipating a happy event   pregnant ex pre-birth C20 Infml

antipodes   female genitals ex opposite (of male genitals) C19* Euph

anus   external opening at end of rectum ex Lat = ring C16- Std

appetite   lust ex desire to eat (eating) C16- Lit/Infml

apple dumpling shop   breasts ex **apples, dumplings** C18–19* Sl

apples   1. breasts ex shape (food) C18–19* Sl. 2. testicles ?ex shape (food) C19- Sl

ardor   lust ex fire C16- Lit/Euph

armor   condom ex protection against venereal disease (aggression) C18–19* Sl

around the world, go   lick one's partner all over ex complete journey C20 Sl

arrive at the end of a sentimental journey   copulate ex end page of Sterne's *Sentimental Journey* C19–20* Lit/Sl

arrow   penis cf **target** (aggression) C19* Infml

arse   see **ass**

arsenal   female genitals pun on **weapon** store, **arse** (aggression) C19* Sl

article   1. woman as sex-object cf **piece** C19- Sl. 2. vagina ex 1. cf **thing** C19-
Sl

art of pleasure   sexual intercourse cf **pleasure** C16- Lit

ass/arse   1. buttocks OE -C17 Std C18- Sl/Derog. 2. anus ex 1. OE -C17 Std
C18-Sl. 3. sexual intercourse ex 1. C20 Sl

ass-blow   perform anilingus ex **ass**, **blow** C20 Sl

ass fucking   anal intercourse ex **ass**, **fuck** C20 Sl

asshole   anus ex **ass**, **hole** C18- Sl/Derog

aunt   prostitute ?ex title for unrelated older woman (family) C17–19* Sl

aunt from Reading   menstruation, pun on Reading = redding, reading
(bleeding) cf **aunt with one** C20 Infml

auntie   elderly male homosexual ?ex **aunt** (family) C20 Sl

B

baby maker   penis ex reproduction C19–20* Euph/Joc

baby paste   semen ex reproduction C20 Sl/Euph

back door   anus cf **backside** C20 Sl/Infml

backgammon player   active male homosexual ex back(side), gammon =
game C18–19* Sl

back scuttle   1. copulate from behind ex scuttle = make a hole in C19- Sl.
2. perform anal intercourse ex 1. C20 Sl

backside   buttocks ex position relative to face C16–19 Std C19- Sl/Euph

bag   1. scrotum or male genitals ex container C20 Sl. 2. condom ex container C20 Sl. 3. woman as sex-object C19- Sl/Derog. 4. prostitute ex 3
C19- Sl/Derog. 5. v. copulate ex catch at hunting C20 Sl

baggage   1. prostitute cf **bag** C16–19*. 2. scrotum or male genitals cf **bag**
C20 Sl

bagnio   brothel ex It = bath C16–20* Std/Infml

bag of tricks   male genitals ex **bag** = scrotum, trick = cunning C19–20*
Sl/Joc

bagpipe   1. fellatio ex **flute** (2) (music) C18–20* Sl. 2. copulate in the armpit
ex holding of instrument (music) C18–20* Sl

bags   testicles cf **bag** C20 Sl

bald headed hermit   penis ex no hair ?hermit ex single C19–20* Euph

ball   1. n. testicle (see **balls**). 2. v. copulate pun on enjoyment, testicle
(body, dance) C20 Sl

ballocks   testicles cf **ball** -ock = diminutive, pun on shape, nonsense OE -
C19 Std C19- Sl

ball off   masturbate cf **ball** C20 Sl

balloons   breasts ex shape C20 Sl/Infml

balls   testicles ex shape C16- Sl

balogna/baloney   penis pun on sausage, nonsense (food) C20 Sl

banana   1. penis ex shape (food) C19- Sl. 2. male homosexual esp fellator
(eating) C20 Sl

band in the box   syphilis cf **box** C20 US R.Sl (pox)

bang   copulate, sd of men (aggression, sound) C20 Sl

banger   penis ex kind of sausage cf **bang** (food) C20 Sl

bank and biff   syphilis cf **bang** C20 US R.Sl (syph)

barbettes   breasts ex Std sense = cylinder that covers a turret (aggression) C20 Sl

barclay/Barclay's bank   masturbate ?pun on semen bank, money bank (name) C20 R.Sl (wank)

barrel   forced anal intercourse ex having someone over a barrel cf **bend someone over** C20 US Sl

bash the bishop   masturbate sd of men ex **bishop** (religion) C19- Sl

basket   scrotum cf **bag** C20 Sl

bat   1. prostitute ex night-creature (animal) C17–19* Sl. 2. penis esp large one ex instrument C20 Sl

baths   Turkish baths where homosexual men meet C20 gay Sl

batter   copulate, sd of men cf **bat** (aggression) C20* Sl

bawd   prostitute ex O.Fr = lively C14–16 Std C17–18 Infml C19- Lit

bawdy   lusty ex **bawd** C16- Std/Lit

bawdy house   brothel ex **bawd** C16–18* Std/Infml

bawl   testicle pun on ball, cry? as when hit there C16–17* Lit

bayonet   penis ex dagger cf **sword**, **weapon** (aggression) C19–20* Lit/Sl

bazaar   female genitals ex market cf **merchandise** C19–20* Sl

bazooms   breasts ex **bosoms** ?ex sound like fireworks, knockout C20 Sl

be among the cabbages   copulate sd of men ex **cabbage** = female genitals (food) C19- Infml

beanfeast   sexual intercourse ex enjoyment (eating) C19–20* Infml

bear   copulate from below, sd of women pun on holding up, giving birth C16–17* Lit

beard   female pubes cf **hair** (body) C18–19* Sl

beard-splitter   penis ex **beard** C18–19* Sl

be at number one   menstruate ex menstrual cycle C19–20* Infml

beat off   masturbate sd of men cf **jerk off** (aggression) C20 Sl

beat the meat   masturbate sd of men ex **meat** = penis (aggression) C20 Sl

beaver   female genitals ex **fur** (animal) C20 Sl

bed sports   sexual intercourse ex place, activity C16–17* Lit/Euph

Beecham's pills   testicles ex roundness (name) C19* R.Sl (testicles)

beef   genitals cf **flesh**, **meat** (animal, food) C19- Sl

beef gravy   semen cf **meat**, **juice** (food) C20 Sl

behind   buttocks cf **backside** C18- Infml

belle   male homosexual, ex woman C20* gay Sl

bender   passive male homosexual pun on bending to take penis anally, **bent** C20 gay Sl

bend over   be passive partner in sodomy, cf **bender** C20 gay Sl

bend someone over   be active partner in sodomy cf **bend over** C20 gay Sl

bent   homosexual pun on criminal, loose jointed cf **straight** C20 Sl

bent wrist   passive male homosexual ex affected effeminacy cf **bent** (body) C20 Sl

berk vagina, but esp Derog term ex **Berkeley Hunt** C19- R.Sl (cunt)

Berkeley (Hunt) vagina ex **quarry** cf **venery** (name) C19- R.Sl (cunt)

Berkshire Hunt variant of **Berkeley Hunt**

best vagina ex finest C18–19* Lit/Infml

best leg of three penis ex between two legs (body) C19- Sl/Joc

bi abbr for **bisexual** C20 Infml

bicycle bisexual ex **bi-** same pronunciation in bicycle, bisexual; pun on **ride** C20 Sl/Euph

big pregnant ex size C19- Infml

big brother penis ex individuation of genitals (family) C19–20* Sl

bilbo penis ex Std sense = sword (aggression) C16–17* Lit

Bill masculinity esp among male homosexuals (name) C20 Sl

bint woman as sex object/prostitute ex Arabic C19–20* Sl

bird woman ex feathers = finery (animal) C16- Infml

birds and bees facts of sex ex plant reproduction (animal) C20 Infml/Euph

birthday party orgy ?ex birthday suit = nude C20 Sl

bisexual person sexually attracted to both sexes, bi ex Lat = two C19- Std

bishop 1. condom ?ex largest size (religion) 18* Sl. 2. glans, head of penis ?ex rank, shape of mitre (religion) C19- Sl

bit 1. woman as sex object cf **piece** C19- Sl. 2. sexual intercourse esp in the phrase **have a bit of. . .** ex 1. C20 Sl/Euph

bitch 1. woman esp spiteful one ex female dog (animal) C14–17 Std C18- Sl/Derog. 2. passive male homosexual ex 1. C20 Sl

bite vagina ?ex Sanskrit = split, fork (eating) C17–19* Sl

bit of cauliflower sexual intercourse sd of men ex **cauliflower** = female genitals (food) C18–19* Sl

bit of fish sexual intercourse sd of men ex **fish** = female genitals (food) C19–20* Sl

bit of fluff, have a copulate sd of men ex **fluff** C19- Sl

bit of fun, have a copulate ex enjoyment C19- Infml/Euph

bit of hard for a bit of soft sexual intercourse ex male and female genitals C19–20* Sl

bit of jam 1. sexual intercourse sd of men pun on **jam** = female genitals, squeeze (food) C19- Sl. 2. woman as sex object ex 1. C19- Sl

bit of meat sexual intercourse ex **meat** = genitals (food) C18- Sl

bit of skirt, do/have a copulate sd of men ex **skirt** = woman (clothing) C19- Sl

bit of snug for a bit of stiff sexual intercourse ex female and male genitals C19–20* Sl

bit of stuff woman as sex object ex **stuff** C19- Sl

bit on a fork 1. female genitals ?ex open legs cf **fork** (food) C19- Sl. 2. sexual intercourse ex 1. (food) C19- Sl

black hole vagina ex dark cf **hole** C18–19* Sl

black jack penis of black man cf **Jack** C20 Sl

black joke vagina ?ex **crack** a joke C18–19* Sl/Joc

blackness vagina ex darkness C16–17* Lit

black snake penis of black man ex **snake** (animal) C19–20* Sl

blade 1. penis ?ex *blade = gallant man cf **sword** (aggression) C18–19* Infml. 2. male homosexual ? ex 1. C20 Sl

blanket hornpipe sexual intercourse pun on **pipe**, **horn** (music, bed) C18* Infml

bless perform anal intercourse cf **kneel at the altar** (religion) C20 black gay US Sl

blind alley vagina ex dark passage C19–20* Sl

blind cheeks buttocks ex cheeks behind one (body) C17–20* Sl

blind cupid buttocks ex Cupid = Roman god of love C18–19* Sl

blind entrance vagina ex invisible passage cf **eye** C19* Sl

blind eye 1. anus cf **eye** (body) C18–20* Sl. 2. vagina cf **eye** (body) C18–20* Sl

blinds uncircumcised foreskin ex able to pull it over glans C20 gay Sl

block copulate sd of men ex fit, mount with a block = penis C20 Sl

blood lust ex excitement, passion C16- Lit/Infml

blow fellate ex oral action C20 Sl

blow job fellatio ex **blow**, **job** C20 Sl

blubber breasts ex fatty tissue C18–20* Derog/Sl

blueballs pain in the testicles due to inability to ejaculate ?ex color of veins ?ex blues = depression C20 Sl

blue films/movies pornographic films ex blue = erotic/pornographic ?ex blue neon lights C20 Infml

boat vulva ex shape C18–19* Lit

boat and oar prostitute ex **boat** = vulva, oar = penis C20 US R.Sl (whore)

boating mutual cunnilingus ex **boat** = vulva C20 Sl

bodkin penis ex needle, *dagger cf **sword** C19–20* Sl

bog vagina ex soft wet place C16–17* Lit/Sl

bollocks testicles variant of **ballocks** C19- Sl

bone erect penis ex hardness of bone (body) C19- Sl

bone-ache syphilis ex ache of bones C16–17* Lit/Infml

bone-queen fellator ex **bone**, **queen** C20 Sl

boner erect penis cf **bone** C20 Sl

boobs breasts ?ex boob = blunder cf **bubs** C20 Sl

bookbinder's wife female genitals, pun on manufacture between sheets (reproduction, bed) C18–19* Joc

bore copulate, sd of men, pun on make a hole, make weary (aggression) C20* Sl

bosom breasts ex OE C16- Std

bottle opener active male homosexual ?ex drilling hole in cork (aggression) C20 Sl

bottom buttocks ex lower half of body C18- child's Infml

bottomless pit vagina cf **pit** C17–19* Sl/Infml

bounce copulate ex movement esp on mattress C19- Infml

bowling hold, do the masturbate a woman in scissors fashion with fingers apart ex bowling (sport) C20 US Sl

box vagina ex container pun on box = coffin (death) C20 Sl

box the Jesuit (and get cockroaches)   masturbate sd of men ?ex aggression, **cock**roaches (religion) C18–19* Sl

brace and bits   nipples or breasts C20 US R.Sl (tits)

brakes   female pubes ex Std sense = thickets C16–17* Lit

brass (nail)   prostitute cf **nail** C20* R.Sl (tail)

bread   vagina pun on necessity, bread Sl = money (food) C20* Sl

breadwinner   vagina pun on necessity, bread = money C20 Sl

break and enter   forced anal intercourse ex breaking in, burglary C20 prison Sl

break her leg above the knee   deflower ex breaking hymen (body) C16–17* Lit/Euph

breasts   mammary organs which supply milk to offspring ex OE C16- Std

breeder   heterosexual ex reproduction C20 gay Sl/Derog

bring off   to induce orgasm cf **come** C16- Infml

Bristol City   breast ex football club (name) C20 R.Sl (titty)

bristols   breasts ex **Bristol City** C20 R.Sl (titty)

broad   woman ex women broader in hips than men C20 US Sl

broaden someone's outlook   perform anal intercourse ex widening the **eye** = anus C20 Sl

broody   pregnant ex inclination to breed C19- Infml

broom   female genitals ?ex **hair** ?ex It. *scopare* = sweep, fuck C19–20* Sl

broomhandle/brookstick   1. penis ex **broom** C19–20* Sl. 2. dildo ?ex 1. C19–20* Sl

brothel   house of prostitution ex *worthless fellow, *prostitute C16- Std

brown   1. n. anus ex color of fecal matter C19- Sl. 2. v. perform anal intercourse, also **do a brown (job)** ex 1. C20 Sl

brown berry   virginal anus cf **cherry** C20 gay Sl

Brown Madam   female genitals cf **Miss Brown, madame** ?ex brown *Sl = to deceive, take in ?ex brown = dark C19–20* Sl

brush   woman as sex-object ?ex **hair** C20 Austr Sl

bubbies   breasts ex *bub = drink cf **boobs** C17–18 Std C19- Dial

bubblegum machine   condom vending machine ex coin slot machine C20 Infml/Euph

bubs   breasts ?ex *bub = drink cf **bubbies** C19- Sl

bucket boy   passive male homosexual ex container C20 gay Sl

bud   clitoris ex shape cf **flower** C19* Infml

buds of beauty   nipples ex shape C18* Lit

bugger   practice anal intercourse ex Lat *Bulgaris* ex alleged practice of Bulgarians (name) C16- Std/Derog

buggery   anal intercourse with human or animal cf **bugger** C16- Std/Derog

bugle   penis ex **horn** (music) C16–17* Lit

bulb   glans, head of penis ex shape C20 Sl

bulbs   breasts ex shape C20 Sl/Infml

bull   copulate sd of men pun on cheat, nonsense (animal) C17- Infml

bull dyke   active lesbian cf **dyke, bull**, bull = masculine C20 gay Sl

bullets   semen ex Fr = small ball (aggression) C16- Lit/Sl

bull's eye   1. vagina ex shooting at centre cf **target** C18–19* Lit/Infml
2. anus cf 1. C18–19* Lit/Infml
bully   pimp ex *sweetheart, scoundrel C17–19* Infml
bum   1. n. buttocks C14- Std/Infml/Sl. 2. v. copulate ex 1. C19- Sl
bum boy   passive male homosexual ?ex young servant cf **bum** C19- Sl/Derog
bumkin   buttocks ex **bum**, -kim = diminutive C17* Lit
bumper to bumper   lesbian sexual activity ex rubbing C20 gay Sl/Joc
bumpkin   buttocks pun on **bum**, bump C17* Lit/Joc
bun   1. vagina ?ex sweetness (food) C17–19* Sl. 2. prostitute ex 1. C17–19*
Sl
bung (-hole)   anus ?ex Lat *pungere* = to prick C16- Std/Infml
bun in the oven, have a   pregnant ex preparing food, oven = womb (food)
C19- Infml
bunny   female genitals ex **rabbit, fur** (animal) C18–20* Sl
buns   buttocks ex shape (food) C20 Sl
burgle   perform anal intercourse ?ex **bugger** (aggression) C20 Sl
buried alive   sexual intercourse sd of men pun on penis buried in vagina,
death, cf **die** C17 Joc/Lit
burk   variant of **berk**
burning spot   female genitals ex sexual passion C18* Lit
bury the bone   copulate cf **buried alive**, pun on **bone** = erection (death) C20
Joc
bury the hatchet where it won't rust   copulate cf **buried alive** (aggression,
death) C20 Joc
bush(y)   pubes ex dense cluster cf **hair** C19- Infml
Bushy Park   female pubes ex **bushy** (name) C19 * Infml
business   sexual intercourse pun on commerce, seriousness C17- Euph
bust   breasts ex It = sculpture C17- Std/Fml
butch   active lesbian ex butcher (aggression, name) C20 Sl
butt   buttocks ex ME = strip of land C15–17 Std C18- Infml/Sl
butt bang/fuck   anal intercourse ex **butt, bang, fuck** C20 Sl
buttered bun   1. a woman prepared for renewed intercourse who has just
copulated with another man ex **bun** = vagina, butter = semen C18- Sl.
2. prostitute ex 1. (food) C19–20 * Sl
buttock-ball   sexual intercourse ex **buttocks** pun on **ball** = testicle, dance
(body, dance) C18–19* Infml/Sl
buttocking shop   brothel ex **buttocks** (body) C19* Sl
buttocks   musculature forming the human rump cf **butt** + -ock = diminutive
C13- Std
button   clitoris pun on to be pressed, fingered C19- Sl/Joc
buttons   nipples ex shape C20 Sl

C

cabbage   female genitals ?ex shape of cut cabbage cf **greens** (food) C19–20* Sl
cabbage garden/patch   female genitals ex **cabbage, garden** C19–20* Sl

cake   female genitals ex sweetness, roundness (food) C20 black Sl
cakes   buttocks ex roundness (food) C20 Sl
call girl   prostitute ex telephone request C20 Sl/Infml
canary   1. penis ex *codpiece cf **cuckoo** (animal) C17–19* Sl. 2. mistress ex kept **bird** C18–19* Sl
candle   penis, ex shape, melting when lit C20 Sl
canned fruit   homosexual who denies his homosexuality ex canned = closed, fruit C20 gay Sl/Joc
canoodle   caress cf **firkytoodle** C19- Infml
cans   1. buttocks ex shape C20 Sl. 2. breasts ex shape C20 Sl
Cape Horn   female genitals ex **horn** (name) C18–19* naval Sl/Joc
Cape of Good Hope   female genitals ex male's hope to **dock** (name) C18–19* naval Sl/Joc
captain has come/captain is home   menstruation ex captain = familiar term of address C18–19* Sl/Infml
cardinal is home   variant of **captain is home** ex cardinal = deep red color
caress   to touch, fondle sexually ex Lat *carus* = dear C17- Std
carnal knowledge   sexual intercourse ex Bible, knowledge of the flesh cf **knowledge** C16- legal and Fml
carnal part/stump   penis ex carnal = **flesh, stump** C17* Lit
carrion   prostitute ex body, **flesh** C18–19* Sl
carrot   penis ex shape (food) C19- Sl
carrying all before one   pregnant pun on approval, large stomach C20 Joc
case   1. n. vagina ex container C18–20* Lit/Infml. 2. v. copulate sd of men ex 1. C20 Sl
cat   1. prostitute ?ex catching mice (animal) C16–19* Sl. 2. female genitals ?ex 1. **fur**, cf **puss** (animal) C16–19* Sl
catamite   homosexual boy ex Ganymede, Gr myth of youth abducted by Zeus (name) C16- Std/Fml
cat and kitties   breasts cf **cat** (animal) C20 US R.Sl (titties)
catheads   breasts ex shape C18–19* naval Sl
cathouse   brothel ex **cat**, house (animal) C20 Sl
cattle(truck)   copulate ?ex **cat** in cattle (animal) C20 R.Sl (fuck)
cauliflower   female genitals ?ex **flower, greens** (food) C18–19* Sl
Cecil   femininity esp in male homosexuals ex sissy, sound (name) C20 heterosexual Sl/Joc
center of attraction/bliss   female genitals pun on central concern, joy C18–19* Infml
central furrow   female genitals ex groove in center C18* Lit
central office   female genitals ex center, commerce C19* Sl
chain gang   male homosexual orgy cf **daisy chain** C20 gay Sl
chamber combat   sexual intercourse ex place, war (aggression) C16–17* Euph/Lit
chamber work   sexual intercourse ex place, labor C16–17* Euph/Lit
charge   copulate sd of men ex rush in, (aggression) C16–17* Infml
Charley/Charlie (Hunt)   vagina, but esp Derog term (name) C20* R.Sl (cunt)

Charleys/Charlies 1. breasts ?ex **Charley** (name) C19- Sl. 2. testicles (name) C19- Sl

charms breasts ex spell they cast C18- Infml

chassis woman as sex object ex vehicle structure ?pun on **ride** C20 Sl

chat female genitals ex Fr = cat (animal) C19-20* Sl

cheeks buttocks ex similarity to facial cheeks (body) C18- Infml

cherry virginity, hymen pun on cherry = young girl and fruit with red juice = blood (food) C20 Sl

cherry pie 1. girl cf **cherry** (food) C19- Infml. 2. virginity cf **cherry** (food) C20 Sl

chestnuts 1. breasts ex chest (food) C20 Sl/Infml. 2. testicles ex shape cf **nuts** (food) C20 Infml

chick young woman cf **bird** (animal) C20 Infml

chicken 1. boy unfamiliar with homosexuality cf **chick** (animal) C20 gay Sl. 2. passive homosexual ex 1. C20 gay Sl

chink female genitals pun on money, prison, crack C18-20* Sl

chitty semen ex ME *chithe* = seed C18-19* Sl/Infml

chuffer active male homosexual ?ex sound of locomotive engine, boor C19-20* Sl

church Turkish baths ?ex regular attendance (religion) C20 gay Sl/Joc

churn masturbate ex movement, agitation C19-20* Sl

circle vagina ex shape C16-17* Lit

circus orgy ?ex stunning acts, performances C20 Sl/Joc

civet female genitals cf **cat** (2), **puss** (animal) C18-19* Sl

clap gonorrhea ex Fr C16-19 Std C19- Infml/Sl

clasp caress ex hold C16-17* Lit

clean up the kitchen anilingus ?ex clean the mess C20 Sl

cleft female genitals ex shape C17- Sl

clicket sexual intercourse ex Std sense sd of foxes (animal) C17-18* Sl

cliff breasts ex outline against body C16-17* Lit

climax orgasm ex Gr = ladder C17- Std/Infml

clipped in the ring deflowered ex **hit** in the **ring** = vagina C16* Lit

clit abbr of **clitoris** C20 Infml

clitoris part of female genitals homologous with penis ex Gr C17- Std

clitorize masturbate sd of women ex **clitoris** C18-19* Infml

closet case/queen homosexual who denies his homosexuality ex closet = locked away cf **queen** C20 Sl

cloth female pubes (clothing) C18* Lit

club penis cf **hit** (aggression) C19* Sl

clucky pregnant ex sound of hen with chicks C20 Austr Sl

cluster fuck threesome sexual arrangement ex closeness C20 Sl

cluster fuck party orgy ex close together cf **cluster fuck** C20 Sl

coachman on the box syphilis cf **box** C19-20* R.Sl (pox)

cobblers (awls) also **cobs**, abbr testicles ex tools C19- R.Sl (balls)

cock 1. penis pun on upright, tap/faucet (animal) C16-18 Std C19- Sl. 2. female genitals ?ex **cockles** (animal) C19- US Dial Sl

cockeater fellator esp male homosexual ex **cock**, **eat** C20 Sl

Cock Inn vagina ex **cock**, inn cf **hotel** C19–20* Joc/SL

cockles female genitals esp labia (animal, food) C18–20* Sl

cocklover fellator, ex **cock** C20 Sl

cockstand erection ex **cock**, **stand** C18- Sl

cocksucker fellator but esp Derog term ex **cock**, **suck** C19- Sl

cocktail 1. prostitute pun on **cock**, **tail**, alcoholic drink C19–20* Sl. 2. male homosexual prostitute ex 1. C20 Sl

cocoa butter semen of black man ex cocoa = dark, butter = semen (food) C20 Sl

coconuts 1. breasts ex milk, shape (food) C20 Sl. 2. testicles ex shape cf **nuts** (food) C20 Sl

cod scrotum ex ME = seed C16–18 Std C19- Sl

codpiece 1. bag in clothing covering male genitals ex **cod** C16- Std. 2. Penis ex 1. C17–19* Sl

cods testicles ex **cod** C16- Infml

coffee house/shop vagina ex wide public appeal; come in, go out (eating) C18–19* Sl

coinslot vagina cf **money**, **slit** C20 Sl

coit 1. v. copulate ex Lat = go together C18-Fml. 2. n. buttocks ?ex quoit C20 Austr Sl

coitus in axilla sexual intercourse in the armpit ex Lat C18- Fml/Med

coitus interruptus sexual intercourse with withdrawal before ejaculation ex Lat C18- Fml/Med

Colonel Puck copulate (name) C20* R.Sl (fuck)

come 1. v. experience orgasm ex reach, get to C19- Infml/Euph. 2. n. semen ex v. C19- Infml

comefreak fellator esp male homosexual cf **come** C20 Sl

comfort caress C16- Infml

commerce sexual intercourse cf **business**, **trading** C16–17* Lit/Euph

commodity female genitals cf **thing** C16–19* Lit/Euph

conceive become pregnant ex Lat cf **know** = copulate, have conception C13- Std

concern genitals ex interest in C19* Infml/Euph

concubine mistress ex Lat = lie together C13- Std/Fml

condom sheath worn on penis during sexual intercourse ?ex name C18-Std

congress sexual intercourse ex meeting cf **union** C16- Fml

constable female genitals ex sound of first syllable pun on policing C16–17* Lit/Joc

continental shots pornographic photographs of female genitals ex European porn (foreign) C20 Sl/Infml

controlling part vagina ex ruling, regulating man's lust C18* Lit/Joc

converse copulate ex communication C16–17* Lit/Euph

convertible bisexual ex both ways C20 Sl

convulsion of bliss orgasm ex ecstatic spasms C19- Fml/Lit

cooch vagina ?ex hootchy-kootchy = sexy dance C20 Sl

cookie female genitals cf **cake** (food) C20 Sl

cop a bird/dock/doodle/joint fellate ex terms for penis, cop Sl = seize C20 Sl

cop a cherry   deflower ex **cherry** = hymen, virginity, cop Sl = seize C20 Sl
copper stick   penis ex police truncheon (aggression) C19–20* Sl
copulate   have sexual intercourse ex Lat *copulare* = to join together C17- Std
coral branch   penis ex shape C17* Lit
corner   female genitals cf **cranny** C16–17* Lit
cornhole   1. anus ex **hole**, use of dried corn cobs to clean anus (food) C20
   Sl. 2. v. perform anal intercourse ex 1. C20 Sl
cottage   public lavatory for male homosexual cruising ex OE *cot* = hut C20
   Sl/Euph
couch rugby   sexual intercourse pun on tackle, scrum (sport) C20 Infml/Joc
couple(d) with, (be)   copulate ex joining C15- Infml
coupling-bat   penis ex join, **bat** C18–19* Sl
coupling-house   brothel ex joining place C18–19* Sl
course   menstruation ex cycle C19- Infml
cow   1. woman ?ex milk (animal) C18- Sl/Derog. 2. prostitute ex 1. (animal)
   C19–20* Sl
cowboy   male prostitute ex **cow** C20 Sl
coyote   female genitals pun on coy, wild (animal) C19* Sl
crack   1. female genitals pun on shape, excellent C16- Sl. 2. prostitute ex 1.
   C17–19* Sl
crack a judy/pitcher/teacup   deflower, pun on **crack** = female genitals
   (judy = Sl = woman; pitcher, teacup both containers) C19–20* Sl
crack salesman   male homosexual prostitute ex **crack** between buttocks C20
   Sl
cranny   female genitals cf **crack, cleft** C19–20* Sl
cranny hunter   penis ex **cranny** C19–20* Sl
crapper   anus ex crap = excrement C20 Sl
cream   1. n. semen ex appearance (food) C19- Sl/Infml. 2. v. to ejaculate ex
   1. C19- Sl
cream-catcher   vagina ex **cream** C19–20* Sl
cream-stick   penis ex **cream, stick** C19- Sl
crease   female genitals ex shape cf **cranny** C19–20* Sl
crevice   female genitals cf **cranny** C19–20* Sl
crown   glans, head of penis ex crown on head C20 Infml
crown jewels   male genitals esp testicles ex valuable cf **family jewels** C20
   Joc/Infml
crumpet   1. woman as sex object ex OE = bent ?ex **muff** in muffin ?ex **buttered bun** (food) C19- Sl. 2. sexual intercourse sd of women ex 1. (food)
   C19- Sl
cuckoo   penis ex cuckoo = cuckold cf **cuckoo's nest** C19–20* Infml
cuckoo's nest   vagina ?ex cuckoo = cuckold (animal) C19–20* Infml
cucumber   penis ex shape (food) C20 Sl/Infml
cuddle   1. caress C18- Std. 2. copulate ex 1. C19- Euph
cuddle and kiss   girl ex caressing C20 R.Sl (miss)
cullions   testicles ex Fr, Lat = testicle C14–17* Std/Infml
culls   testicles abbr of **cullions** C16–17* Infml
cundum   variant of **condom**

cunnilingus oral stimulation of the female genitals ex Lat *cunnus* = vulva, *lingere* = lick C19- Std

cunning female genitals pun on sound of first syllable, shrewd C16–17* Lit/Joc

cunny female genitals ?ex Lat *cunnus* = vulva ex cony = rabbit (animal) C17-Sl

cunt 1. vagina ex OE Ger ?Lat 13–16 Std 16- Sl. 2. woman as sex object ex 1. C19- Derog/Sl. 3. buttocks C20 male homosexual Sl

cunt curtain female pubes ex **cunt** C19–20* Sl

cunt itch/stand sexual arousal in women cf **itch**, **stand** C18- Sl

Cupid's Arms vagina cf **Cock Inn**, Cupid = Roman god of love (name) C19–20* Joc/Sl

Cupid's Hotel vagina cf **hotel** (name) C19–20* Joc/Sl

Cupid's itch venereal diseas cf **itch**, Cupid = Roman god of love (name) C20 Sl

cure the horn copulate sd of women ex **horn** = erection C19–20* Sl

curlies/curls pubes ex usually curled C20 Infml

curse, the menstruation ?ex Eve's curse ?ex **course** C19- Infml

curtains uncircumcised foreskin ex drawn over glans C20 gay Sl

cushion buttocks ex sat upon C20 Sl

cut 1. n. female genitals cf **gash**, **wound** C19- Sl. 2. (of penis) circumcised ex surgery C20 Infml

Cyclops penis pun on one-eyed, monster cf **Polyphemus** (name) 19* Lit

D

daffodil passive male homosexual ?ex **flower** cf **lily** C20 Sl

dairy (arrangements) breasts ex milk C18- Joc

daisy female genitals ex OE = day's **eye** cf **flower** C19–20* Sl

daisy chain male homosexual orgy, men linked penis to anus ex interlinking chain C20 gay Sl

dally caress ex O.Fr C16- Lit/Infml

damsons testicles ex shape (food) C16–17* Lit

dance the beginning of the world copulate ex reproduction (dance) C16–17* Lit

dance the goat's jig/matrimonial polka copulate, matrimonial = missionary (dance, animal) C19* Sl

dance the mattress jig copulate ex movement, place cf **jig** (dance, bed) C18–19* Sl

dance the sheets copulate ex movement, place (dance, bed) C17* Lit/Euph

danglers testicles ex hanging down C19- Sl

dark meat genitals of black person cf **light meat**, **white meat**, **meat** (food) C20 Sl

dart (of love) penis cf **prick** (aggression) C16–17* Lit/Euph

dash one's doodle masturbate sd of men ex **doodle** C20 Sl/Infml

deflower deprive of virginity ex **flower** C14- Std

delicate glutton female genitals ex appetite (eating) C18* Lit

delight sexual intercourse ex enjoyment C18–19* Lit/Euph

den   vagina ex secluded place C16–17* Lit

desire   lust ex OFr C13- Std

deviate   homosexual ex deviation from norm C20 heterosexual Sl/Derog

devil   penis ex putting devil in **hell** = vagina (Boccaccio) (religion) C18–20* Lit/Joc

diamonds   testicles pun on valuable, **stones**, cf **jewels** C20 gay Sl

dick   penis ?ex familiar name cf **jack, johnnie** C19- Sl

dickory dock   penis cf **dick, dock** C20 R.Sl (cock)

diddle   1. copulate pun on shake, swindle C19–20* Infml. 2. masturbate ex 1. C19–20* Infml

die   experience orgasm ex coming to an end cf **fading** (death) C16–17* Lit

digitate   masturbate sd of women ex **finger** C18* Lit/Fml

dike   variant of **dyke**

dildo   1. n. object substituted for erect penis ?ex It = delight ?ex OE *dyderian* = cheat C16- Std. 2. v. caress or arouse with a dildo ex n. C18–19* Lit

Dilly boy   male homosexual ex Piccadilly, London, a cruising place (name) C20 Sl

ding-dong   penis ?ex sound ?ex dangling C20 Infml

ding-dongs   testicles ?ex sound ?ex dangling C20 Infml

dingle-dangle   penis ex hanging down C19- Sl/Infml

dingus   1. penis ex Ger *ding* = thing C20 Sl. 2. dildo ex 1. C20 Sl

dinners   nipples ex feeding (eating) C20 Sl

dipstick   penis ex **stick** that dips C20 Joc

dirk   penis esp erect one, ex Std sense = dagger (aggression) C18- Infml

dirt road   anus ex excremental passage C20 Sl

dirty old man   1. lecherous old man ex dirty = sexually arousing C20 Infml. 2. elderly male homosexual ex 1. C20 Sl. 3. male heterosexual who chases lesbians ex 1. C20 lesbian Sl

discharge   ejaculate cf **shoot** C16–17* Lit

discourse   sexual intercourse, ex communication C16–17* Lit/Euph

dish   sexually attractive woman ex tasty, edible (food) C20 Infml/Sl

ditch   vagina cf **drain** C19- Derog/Sl

dive   perform cunnilingus ex **go down** C20 Sl

diver   cunnilinguist ex **dive** C20 Sl

dock   copulate sd of men ex v. = moor, link; pun on n. = tail C16–19 * Sl

Doctor Johnson   penis cf **John Thomas, johnnie** (name) C18–19* Lit

dog   copulate on all fours ex canine fashion (animal) C19- Infml

dog's rig   sexual intercourse in casual manner ex **dog**, rig = naval preparation C18–19* Sl

do it   copulate ex action, agency cf **it** C18- Euph

doll   attractive woman ex dolled up = made up, dream doll C20 Infml

do miracles   copulate ex wonderful, extraordinary C16–17* Lit

dong   penis ?ex sound ?ex dangling C20 Sl

donkey   large penis ?ex **dong** (animal) C19- Sl

doodle   penis ?ex **cock**-a-doodle-doo C18- Infml

do over   copulate pun on repeat, beat up (aggression) C19–20* Infml

dose venereal disease ex medical use for quantity, something unpleasant C19- Sl

dot 1. clitoris cf **button** C19–20 Sl. 2. anus ex roundness C20* Sl

dot the i anal intercourse ex **dot** 2., i = penis C20 Sl

double fire payment two ejaculations during sexual intercourse cf **fire, spendings** C18* Lit/Infml

dove elderly lesbian ?ex bird ?ex past tense of **dive** (animal) C20 lesbian Sl

downy bit 1. young woman as sex object cf **bit** C19* Sl. 2. female genitals ex 1., **hair** C19* Sl

doxy prostitute ?ex **dock** = copulate C16–20* Sl

drain vagina pun on passage, exhaust C19–20* Derog/Sl

drapes uncircumcised foreskin ex pull over cf **blinds** C20 gay Sl

draw the blinds pull back foreskin C20 Sl/Joc

dream whip nocturnal emission of semen ex **whipped cream** (food) C20 Sl

droopers breasts ex hanging down C20 Sl

drumstick penis ex shape cf **hit** (music) C19- Sl

dry bob sexual intercourse without ejaculation ex bob = movement, dry = no semen C18–19* Infml

dry hump anal intercourse ex no vaginal lubrication C20 gay Sl

dry run 1. variant of **dry bob**. 2. sexual intercourse using male contraceptive ex no contact with female lubrication C20 Sl

duchess 1. woman having sexual intercourse while wearing shoes ?ex status C18–19* Sl. 2. passive male homosexual ex 1. C20 prison Sl

duff buttocks ?ex inferior ?ex dough C19- Infml/Euph

dugs 1. nipples C16–19 Std C19- Sl. 2. breasts ex 1. C16–19 Std C19- Derog/Sl

dumb glutton female genitals ex appetite (eating) C18–19* Sl

dumb oracle female genitals cf **oracle** unlike mouth C19–20* Infml/Euph

dumplings breasts ex shape (food) C18- Sl

dumpling shop breasts cf **dumplings** C18–20* Sl

Durex condom ex brand trademark ?ex durable C20 Br Std

Dutch girl lesbian ex **dykes** in Holland (foreign) C20 Sl/Euph

dyke 1. lesbian ?ex hermaphro*dite* C20 Sl. 2. female genitals ex dyke = **ditch** C19–20* Sl

E

ear copulate sd of men ex Std sense = **plough** (body) C16–17* Lit

early door prostitute ex paying extra for admission to Music Hall before everyone else (music) C19–20* R.Sl (whore)

east and west breast ex both sides C20 US R.Sl (breast)

eat perform fellatio or cunnilingus ex mouth activity C20 Sl

eat at the Y perform cunnilingus ex **eat**, Y = open legs C20 Sl

eat poundcake perform anilingus ex **poundcakes** C20* Sl

effie passive male homosexual ex abbr of effeminate C20 heterosexual Sl/Derog

eggs   testicles ex shape (food, reproduction) C20 Sl

Elephant & Castle   anus ex name of British pub (name) C19- R.Sl (arse-hole)

embrace   caress ex O.Fr C16- Std/Fml

enjoy   copulate ex **pleasure** C16- Euph

etcetera   female genitals cf **thing** C16–17* Lit/Euph

Eve's curse   menstruation ex Bible woman's curse of childbearing C19- Infml

Eve's custom house   vagina ex Bible, where Adam made his first entry, C18–19* Joc

exchange DNA   copulate ex genetic exchange (reproduction) C20 Joc

exhaust pipe   anus ex motor vehicle exhaust, also at back C20 Sl

expectant   pregnant ex Lat C16- Std

eye   1. vagina ex similarity-lids, moisture, surrounding hair, etc (body) C16–17* Lit. 2. anus ex roundness (body) C20* Sl

eye-opener   penis pun on opening of **eye** = vagina or anus, remarkable thing C19–20* Sl

F

face cream   semen ex fellatio, **cream** = semen C20 gay Sl

fading   orgasm ex feeling cf **die** (death) C16–17* Lit

fag   male homosexual ?ex fag Sl = cigarette — once considered effeminate or abbr of **faggot** C20 Sl/Derog

faggot   male homosexual ?ex *pejorative term for woman, ?ex **fag**, C20 Sl/Derog

faigele   variant of **faygeleh**

fail in the furrow   copulate without ejaculation ex furrow = vagina C19–20* Sl

fairy   male homosexual, esp. passive one, cf **angel** C20 Sl/Derog

fallen angel   male homosexual ex sin, cf **angel** (religion) C20 Sl

fallen star   elderly male homosexual cf **aging actress** C20 Sl

falling off the roof   menstruation ?ex mucous uterine wall falling ?ex tiles being red C20 Infml

fam   caress ex *famble = hand C19–20* Sl

family jewels   testicles ex precious **stones** C20 Sl/Infml

fancy man   pimp ex *fancy = woman, ex sweetheart C19–20* Sl

fancy woman   1. mistress ?ex decorative C19–20* Sl. 2. prostitute ex 1. C20 Sl

fanny   1. vagina ?ex Cleland's *Memoirs of Fanny Hill* (name) C18- Br Sl. 2. buttocks ?ex fan n. = shape v. = to beat ?ex fantail (name) C20 US Sl

faygeleh   male homosexual ex Yid = bird cf **fairy**, having wings (animal) C20 Sl

feather(s)   female pubes ex bird (animal) C18–19* Infml/Euph

feed one's pussy   copulate sd of women ex **pussy** (eating) C20 Sl

feed someone's monkey   copulate sd of men ex **monkey** = vagina (animal, eating) C20 Sl

feel someone up   caress C18- Infml

feet for children's shoes/stockings, make   copulate (body, reproduction) C18–19* Euph

feigeleh variant of **faygeleh**

fellatio oral stimulation of the penis ex Lat *fellare* = suck C19- Std

fellow lesbian ex male ascription C20 Sl

femme fatale woman as sex object ex Fr C19- Infml

femoral intercourse intercourse between the thighs ex femur = thighbone C19- Std/Fml

ferret copulate pun on hunt, search out, cheat (animal) C19–20* Infml

fiddle 1. v. copulate sd of men pun on instrument, cheating (music) C19–20* Sl. 2. n. female genitals cf **strum** = copulate (music) C19–20* Sl

fiddle bow/stick penis ex **fiddle** (music) C19–20* Sl

fig female genitals ?ex insulting gesture, fleshy fruit (food) C19–20* Lit/Sl

figleaf female pubes ex genital covering in fine art C19* Infml

filly young woman ex young mare (animal) C17- Infml

finger 1. caress ex use of fingers C16- Sl/Infml. 2. masturbate ex use of fingers esp sd of women C20 Sl/Infml

fire ejaculate pun on passion, **shoot** (aggression) C20 Infml

fireworks orgasm pun on great display, explosion C20 Infml/Joc

firk copulate ?ex **dirk** and **fuck** C16-19* Euph for **fuck**

firkytoodle caress ?ex **firk** C17–19* Sl/Infml

first game ever played sexual intercourse ex primacy of sexual "game" (sport) C19–20* Infml/Joc

first leg of three penis cf **best leg of three** (body) C19–20* Sl/Joc

fish female genitals ?ex odor, wetness (animal, food) C19–20* Sl

fist fuck 1. masturbate cf **finger** C-19 Sl. 2. insert entire fist in rectum C-20 gay Sl

fit end to end (or fit ends) copulate ex compatible union C19–20* Infml

fixed bayonet erect penis cf **dirk** (aggression) C19–20* Sl

flag is up menstruation ex stop signal for fertilization, copulation C19- Sl/Joc

flapdoodle penis ?ex **cock**-a-doodle cf **doodle** C17–18* Sl

flapper penis ?ex **flapdoodle** or flapper = hand (body) C19* Sl

flash in the pan sexual intercourse without ejaculation ex idiomatic sense = short lived C18- Infml/Joc

flat-cock woman ex no penis C18–19* Joc/Sl

flat fuck 1. lesbian sexual activity ex no penile intromission C20 lesbian Sl. 2. woman as sex object ?ex 1. C20 Sl

flea and louse brothel ?ex fleapit (animal) C19–20* R.Sl (whorehouse)

fleece 1. female pubes pun on swindle, **hair** C18- Sl. 2. female genitals ex 1. C18- Sl

flesh 1. n. genitals ex carnal cf **meat**, **beef** C16- Lit. 2. v. copulate ex n. C16–20* Infml

flesh it copulate ex **flesh** C16–20*Infml

flesh peddler 1. pimp ex seller of **flesh** C19- Sl. 2. prostitute ex. 1. C19- Sl

fleshy excrescence clitoris ex appearance C18* Lit

flier/flyer hasty sexual intercourse C18- Sl

flip-flap penis ex dangling C17–19* Lit/Infml

flip it off masturbate sd of men cf **finger** C20 Sl

flippy   bisexual ex flip from one sex to the other C20 Sl

flipside   buttocks ex phonograph record ex rear side C20 Sl/Joc

flog the bishop   masturbate sd of men ex **bishop** = glans (aggression, religion) C19- Sl

flog the donkey   masturbate sd of men ex **donkey** = penis (aggression, animal) C19- Sl

floods   menstruation ex flow C20 Infml

floozie/y   1. woman as sex object ?ex loose C20 Sl. 2. prostitute ex 1. C20 Sl

floral arrangement   male homosexual orgy, men linked penis to anus cf **daisy chain** C20 gay Sl

flourish   hasty sexual intercourse cf **flier** C18- Sl

flower   1. female genitals ?ex shape, flow of blood C16-20* Lit. 2. virginity? ex bloom C18- Lit/Infml

flower of chivalry   female genitals ex **flower** 1 and 2 C19-20* Lit

flowers   menstruation ex flow C19- Sl/Joc

flowers and frolics   testicles cf **ball** C20 R.Sl (bollocks)

flub the dub   masturbate sd of men ex evade, spoil, fail C20 Sl

fluff   1. female pubes ex **hair** C19- Sl. 2. young woman ex 1. C20 esp Austr Sl. 3. male homosexual ex 2. C20 Sl/Infml

flute   1. n. penis ex shape (music) C19- Sl. 2. v. fellate ex n. C20 Sl

flute player   fellator ex **flute** (music) C20 Sl

fly the red flag   menstruate ex red = blood flag = sanitary towel C19- Sl

fly trap/cage   vagina ex entrapment (animal) C19* Derog/Sl

fondle   1. caress ex fond C17- Std. 2. copulate ex 1. C17- Euph

foot   copulate ex Fr *foutre* = fuck (body) C16-17* Lit/Euph

foraminate   1. deflower ex foramen = opening C19* Fml. 2. copulate ex 1. C19* Fml

force fuck   forced anal intercourse cf **fuck** C20 prison Sl

forebuttocks   breasts ex front, similarity to buttocks (body) C18-19* Sl

forecastle/forecourt/forehatch   vagina ex front quarters C19-20* naval Sl

foreplay   sexual stimulation before sexual intercourse cf **play** C20 Std/Fml

foreskin hunter   prostitute ex search for men C19-20* Sl/Joc

forest   female pubes cf **bush** C16-18* Infml

fork   1. copulate, sd of men (aggression, eating) C19- Sl. 2. female genitals ex open legs cf **bit on a fork** ex 1. C19-20* Sl

fornicate   copulate ex Lat *fornix* = arch C16- Std/Fml

fornicator   penis ex **fornicate** C19* Sl

Fornicator's Hall   vagina ex **fornicate** C19* Sl

forty four   prostitute C20 US R.Sl (whore)

fountain   breasts ex of milk C16-17* Lit

four-legged frolic   sexual intercourse ex four legs involved (body) C19* Infml

foutering   sexual intercourse ex Fr *foutre* C16-17* Euph for **fucking**

franger   condom ?ex French letter C20 Austr Sl

French dressing   semen ex appearance cf **Frenching** (foreign, food) C20 Sl

Frenching   perform fellatio or cunnilingus ex French = oral sex (foreign) C20 Sl

French job   perform fellatio or cunnilingus cf **Frenching** (foreign) C20 Sl
French letter   condom ex envelope (foreign) C19- Infml
French tricks   perform fellatio or cunnilingus cf **Frenching** (foreign) C19- Sl
Friar Tuck   copulate (religion, name) C19–20* R.Sl (fuck)
frig   1. masturbate ex Lat *fricare* = to rub or ?ex OE *frigan* = to love C16- Sl.
   2. copulate ex 1. C19–20* Euph for **fuck**
frogskin   condom ex frog Sl = French (letter), **skin** C20 Sl
front attic/door/room/window   female genitals ex front aperture, space
   C19–20* Sl
front door mat   female pubes cf **mat**, pun on home, **hair**, welcome C19–20*
   Sl
front gut   female genitals ex front (body) C19–20* Sl
froth   semen ex appearance C18* Lit
frottage   1. lesbian sexual activity ex Fr *frotter* = rub C19- Std. 2. rubbing
   against someone to orgasm ex 1. C19- Std
fruit   male homosexual ?ex fruit Sl = crazy (food) C20 Sl
fruitful vine   female genitals ex reproduction C19–20* Sl
fruit juice   semen cf **fruit**, **juice** (food) C20 gay Sl
fuck   1. v. copulate ex ME, Ger = strike (aggression) C16- Sl. 2. n. act of
   copulation ex v. C18- Sl. 3. n. person esp female, as sex partner ex 2. C19-
   Sl. 4. n. semen ex 1. C19- Sl
fuck hole   vagina cf **fuck**, **hole** C19–20* Sl
fuck the fist   masturbate sd of men ex **fuck**, cf **hand job** C20 Sl
fucus   copulate ex similarity of sound C16–17* Euph for **fuck**
fumble   caress sd of men ex *fumbling = impotent C16–20* Infml
fun and frolics   testicles cf **ball** C20 R.Sl (bollocks)
fundament   1. buttocks ex base C13- Std/Euph. 2. anus ex base C13-
   Std/Euph
funny bit   female genitals cf **bit**, **black joke** C19–20* Euph/Sl
fur   female pubes cf **hair** C18- Sl
furbelow   female pubes pun on **fur**, below C17–19* Sl/Joc
furburger   female genitals ex **fur** cf **meat** (food) C20 Sl
furrow   female genitals ex groove C19–20* Sl
furze (-bush)   female pubes ex **bush(y)** C19–20* Sl
futter   copulate ?ex Fr *foutre* C16–17 * Euph for **fuck**
futz   copulate C19- Euph for **fuck**
fuzz   female pubes cf **hair** C17- Sl

G

gadget   penis ex **tool**, instrument C20 Sl/Infml
gallop the antelope/maggot   masturbate sd of men ?ex antelope having
   horn ?ex maggot = whim (animal) C19–20* Sl
gam   fellate ?ex gam Sl = leg ?ex **gamahuching** C19- Sl
gamahuching/gamaruching   perform fellatio or cunnilingus ?ex gam = leg,
   It or Fr C19–20* Sl
game, the   prostitution ex the pastime, hunt (sport) C17- Sl

gander   active male homosexual ?ex **goose** (animal) C20 gay Sl

gang bang   several men successively copulating with one woman cf **bang** C20 Sl

gap   female genitals cf **hole** C18–20* Sl

garden   female genitals ex **garden of Eden**, pun on **green(s)** ?ex Covent Garden — red light district of London C16–20* Euph/Lit

garden gate   vagina ex **garden**, opening C19–20* Sl

garden hedge   female pubes ex **garden, hedge** C19–20* Sl

garden of Eden   female genitals ex Bible, the beginning of sex C16–20* Lit/Euph

gash   vulva ex shape cf **wound** C18– Sl

gash eater   cunnilinguist ex **gash, eat** C20 Sl

gasp and grunt   copulate ex sound C20 R.Sl (cunt)

gate swinger   bisexual pun on swinger = lively, both directions C20 Sl

gay   1. prostitute ?ex merry C19* Sl. 2. homosexual ?ex 1. C20 Sl/Infml

gay bit   prostitute cf **gay, bit** C19* Sl

gaying it   copulate ex gay = merry cf **do it** C19–20* Infml

gear   genitals ex equipment C16–19 Std C19– Infml

geared (up)   lusty ex **gear** C20 Sl

genitals   male or female organs of reproduction ex Lat = relating to birth C14– Std

gentleman of the back door   active male homosexual **back door** = anus C18–20* Infml/Euph

German helmet   glans, head of penis ex shape (foreign) C20 Sl

germen   semen ex germ C16–17* Lit

get a facial   fellate ex **face cream** = semen C20 Sl

get into her pants   copulate sd of men ex entry (clothing) C18– Sl

get one's ashes hauled   copulate sd of men pun on heat cf **fire** C20 Sl

get one's balls/rocks off   reach orgasm sd of men ex **balls, rocks** C20 Sl

get one's oats   copulate sd of men ex necessity (food) C16– Std/Infml

get there   copulate sd of men ex success C19– Infml

get the sugar stick   copulate sd of women ex **sugar stick** = penis (food) C18–20* Sl

giblets   genitals (body) C18–20* Sl

gillette blade   bisexual woman ex double-edged blade cut both ways (name) C20 lesbian Sl

gig(g)   female genitals ?ex gig Sl = nose ?ex **jig** C17–19* Sl

gigolo   male prostitute ex Fr *giguer* = dance C20 Std

girl kisser   lesbian ex male activity C20 Sl

girl-shop   brothel ex trade in girls C19* Sl

gism   semen ?ex Lat *jacere* = throw C20 Sl

give head   perform fellatio or cunnilingus, when fellatio pun on head = glans, fellator's head C20 Sl

give juice for jelly   copulate sd of women ex **juice** 2., **jelly** C19–20* Sl

give oneself   copulate sd of women ex offering to man C17– Infml

give one's gravy   reach orgasm esp sd of men ex **gravy** = semen (food) C19–20* Sl

give standing room for one   copulate sd of women, pun on **stand** = erection, place, ex allow one male entry C19- Joc/Infml

glands   1. testicles ex anatomical sense (body) C20 Euph. 2. breasts ex anatomical sense (body) C20 Euph

glans   head of penis ex Lat = acorn, because of its shape C17- Std

globes   1. breasts ex roundness C18- Infml. 2. testicles ex roundness C18-19* Lit

glove   condom ex fit C19- Infml

goat   1. lecher ex **horns** (animal) C17- Infml. 2. penis ex 1. C17-20* Sl

goat-milker   1. prostitute ex **goat**, **milk** (animal) C19* Sl. 2. vagina ex 1. (animal) C19* Sl

gobble   perform fellatio or cunnilingus ex **eat** with haste C20 Sl

gobbler   fellator ex **gobble** C20 Sl

godemiche   dildo ex Fr ?ex *miche* = prostitute's customer C19- Lit/Fml

go down/south   perform fellatio or cunnilingus cf **dive** C19- Sl

go it alone   masturbate ex solitary activity C20 Sl/Infml

golden shower   urination in sexual activity ex color of urine C20 Sl

gongs   testicles ?ex sound, dangling cf **ding-dongs** C20 Infml

goo   semen ex appearance C20 Sl/Infml

goolies   testicles ?ex **marbles** cf **stones** C19- Sl

goose   1. v. copulate sd of men ?ex goose's neck = penis ?ex **goose and duck** pun on goose Sl = spoil (animal) C19- Sl. 2. v. prod in the anus C20 Sl. 3. perform anal intercourse ex 2. C20 Sl. 4. n. woman as sex object ex 1. C19- Sl

goose and duck   copulate (animal) C19- R.Sl (fuck)

gooseberries   testicles ex shape cf **goose** (food) C18-19* Sl

goose's neck   penis ex phallic shape (animal, body) C19-20* Sl

gorilla salad   thick pubes ex hairy (animal, food) C20 Sl

go to bed with   copulate ex place (bed) C16- Infml/Euph

go tromboning   compulate sd of men pun on **bone** = erection, sliding in and out of trombone (music) C19-20* Sl

goytoy   uncircumcised penis ex Yid *goy* = gentile ex Jewish practice of circumcision C20 Sl

grafting   sexual intercourse pun on joining, uniting C17* Euph

grandma with one, have one's   menstruate cf **have one's aunt with one** (family) C19- Infml/Euph

grant the favor   copulate sd of women ex generosity C18-19* Infml

grasp and grunt   copulate ex sound and hold C20 R.Sl (cunt)

gravy   semen ex appearance cf **meat** (food) C18-20* Sl

gravy-maker   penis ex **gravy** C19-20* Sl

grease the wheel   copulate sd of men ex lubricate the **wheel** = vulva C19-20* Sl

greek   1. n. active male homosexual ex practice in ancient Greece (foreign) C20 Sl. 2. v. perform anal intercourse ex 1. C20 Sl

green goose   prostitute cf **goose**, **greens** (animal) C19-20* Sl

green grove/meadow   1. female genitals cf **garden** C19-20* Sl/Infml. 2. female pubes ex 1. C19-20* Sl/Infml

greens (get, give, have) sexual intercourse ex **garden (of Eden)**, green vegetables esp **cabbage** or ex O.Scots *grene* = to pine for (food) C18- Sl

green sickness celibacy sd of women ex green = inexperienced C18-19* Sl

grin female genitals ex* flash the upright grin = nude; pun on mouth, smile (body) 19* Sl/Euph

grind copulate pun on friction, hard work C16- Infml

gristle penis ex sinew (body) C17-20* Lit/Sl

groan and grunt copulate ex sound C20 R.Sl (cunt)

groceries male genitals cf **basket** (food) C20 Sl

groove copulate pun on canal = vagina, music, enjoy C20 Sl

grope caress ex feel about C20 Sl

ground rations sexual intercourse ex necessity (food) C19-20* Sl

growl (and grunt) female genitals ex sound C20 R.Sl (cunt)

growlbite perform cunnilingus ex **growl, bite** C19- Sl

grumble and grunt copulate ex sound C20 R.Sl (cunt)

gully (hole) female genitals ex gully = passage, **hole** C19-20* Sl

gun 1. penis cf **shoot, weapon** (aggression) C20 Sl. 2. gonorrhea ex abbr C19-20* Sl

gusset female genitals ex piece of material in garment (clothing) C17-19* Sl

gut entrance female genitals cf **front gut** (body) C19* Sl

gutfucker active male homosexual ex gut = bowels, **fuck** (body) C19-20* Sl

gutstick penis cf **gut entrance** (body) C19-20* Sl

gutter vagina pun on canal, lowness C19-20* Sl

gymnasium vagina ex Gr = naked exercise C19* Joc

H

hair 1. female pubes C16- Lit/Sl. 2. woman as sex object ex 1. C19-20* Sl

hairburger/pie female genitals ex **hair** 1. cf **meat** (food) C20 Sl

hair-divider/splitter penis ex **hair** 1. C19-20* Sl

hairy oracle female genitals cf **oracle, hair** C19-20* Sl/Infml

hairy wheel female genitals cf **wheel, hair** C19- Austr Sl

half and half bisexual ex divided attentions C20 Sl/Infml

half bent bisexual ex divided attentions C20 Sl/Infml

half mast half-erect penis ex lowering of flag esp in mourning C20 Sl/Joc

hammer penis cf **hit** (aggression) C20 Sl

Hampton Wick penis (name) C19- R.Sl (prick)

hand job masturbation ex done by hand C20 Sl

handle 1. v. caress ex hand C16-17* Lit. 2. v. masturbate ex hand C20 Sl. 3. n. penis pun on hand, part of utensil, etc. C20 Sl

handstaff penis ex rod, held by hand C19-20* Infml

happy homosexual ex **gay** C20 gay Sl/Joc

hard-on erect penis ex firmness C19- Sl

hare prostitute pun on **hair, rabbit** (animal) C16-17* Lit

harlot prostitute ex ME = vagabond C13- Std

hat 1. female genitals ?ex old hat ?ex hat often felt (clothing) C18-19* Sl. 2. prostitute ex 1. C18-19* Sl

have possess sexually C16- Infml/Euph

have it (off) copulate ex possess C19- Infml

have one's aunt(ie)/a friend with one menstruate ex busy, occupied C19-Infml/Euph

have one's banana peeled copulate sd of men ex **banana** (food) C19-20* Sl

have one's nuts cracked copulate sd of men ex **nuts** (food) C20* Sl

have sex copulate C16- Infml/Euph

head 1. glans of penis ex top part (body) C20 Sl/Infml. 2. hymen ex abbr of **maidenhead** (body) C17- Infml/Euph

head over heels mutual oral sex pun on position, extremely (body) C20 Sl

heaven vagina cf **hell** (religion) C19-20* Joc/Euph

heavers breasts ex move up and down with effort C17-19* Joc/Infml

hedge female pubes cf **bush** C18* Lit/Infml

hedgewhore beggarly prostitute ex **whore** working under hedge C17-18* Sl

hell vagina ex put the **devil** = penis into hell (Boccaccio) cf **heaven** (religion) C18-20* Lit/Joc

hemispheres breasts ex shape C19-20* Lit/Infml

hen woman cf **chick**, **cock** (animal) C17- Infml

heterosexual person sexually attracted to opposite sex ex Gr *heteros* = other C19- Std

he-whore male prostitute pun on male **whore**, **donkey** C20 Sl

Hilltop Drive upturned buttocks ex appearance (name) C20 gay Sl

hit copulate, sd of men (aggression) C16-17* Sl

hive female genitals ex **honey** = semen C19-20* Sl

hive it copulate ex **hive** C19-20* Sl

hobby horse prostitute, pun on horse, favorite (animal) C16-17* Infml

hoist in, do/have a copulate esp sd of men ex raise up, naval sense C19* Infml

hold a bowling ball masturbate a woman with fingers in scissors-fashion ex bowling (sport) C20 Sl

hole 1. n. vagina ex orifice C16- Infml/Sl. 2. v. copulate sd of men ex n. C19- Sl. 3. n. anus ex **ass-hole** C14- Sl/Infml

hole in one sexual intercourse ex **hole**, golfing (sport) C19- Infml

hole of content/holes vagina ex orifice C16-19* Euph/Infml

holland buttocks ex low country (name, foreign) C16-17* Lit/Joc

Holloway vagina ex hollow, way (name) C19* Joc

homo homosexual esp male ex abbr C20 Sl

homosexual person sexually attracted to same sex ex Gr *homos* = same C19-Std

honey semen ex stickiness (food) C18-20* Sl

honeyfuck copulate ex **honey**, **fuck** (food) C19-20* Sl

honeypot vagina ex container, **honey** (food) C18-20* Sl

hooker prostitute ex hook = catch C19- Sl

hoop vulva ex **circle** C19-20* Sl

horizontalize copulate ex laying flat C19* Infml/Joc

horizontal refreshment sexual intercourse ex lying down C19* Infml/Joc

horn (have, get a)   erect penis ex hardness, shape, cuckoldry (animal, music) C16- Sl

hornification   erect penis or clitoris ex **horn** C18-20* Sl

horny   lusty ex **horn** C19- Sl

horse   copulate sd of men cf **ride** (animal) C17- Infml

hot   lusty ex sexual heat C17- Lit/Infml

hot-assed/arsed   lusty sd of women cf **hot, ass/arse** C17-20* Infml/Sl

hot beef/meat/mutton 1. prostitute cf **hot, mutton** (food) C19* Sl. 2. female genitals cf **hot, meat** (food) C19* Sl

hot dog   penis ex shape, sausage = penis (food, animal) C20 Sl

hotel   vagina ex provide lodging cf **lodge** C19-20* Euph

hot juice   semen ex **hot, juice** C20 Sl

hot lips   female genitals ex labia, passion (body) C19-20* Sl

hot milk   semen ex **hot, milk** (food) C19- Sl

hot pudding for supper sexual intercourse sd of women ex **pudding** = penis, **supper** = female genitals (eating) C19-20* Sl

hot roll with cream   sexual intercourse pun on **roll** = copulate, penis; **cream** = semen (food) C19-20* Sl

house of ill repute/fame/pleasure   brothel cf **whorehouse, cathouse,** etc. C18- Infml/Euph

house under the hill   vagina cf **thatched house under the hill** C19-20* Sl/Joc

huddle   copulate ex closeness C18-20* Infml/Euph

hug   caress ex closeness C17- Lit/Infml

hump   copulate ex forming a hump C18- Sl

hunger   lust cf **appetite** (eating) C16- Fml/Lit

husbandry   sexual intercourse sd of men ex farming cf **tillage** pun on husband C16-17* Lit

hussy   woman ex housewife C19- Infml

hustle   copulate ex push, obtain through force C19-20* Sl

hustler   (male) prostitute ex **hustle** C20 Sl

hymen   membrane at entrance to vagina ex Gr = membrane C17- Std/Fml

I

idol   penis ex worship (religion) C18* Lit

impale   copulate, sd of men cf **fork** (aggression) C19* Infml

impudence   penis ex Lat = without shame (esp sd by women) C18-19* Infml

in-and-in (play at)   sexual intercourse sd of men ex thrusting C17-19 * Infml

in-and-out (play at)   sexual intercourse, sd of men ex thrusting C17-20* Sl/Infml

in an interesting condition   pregnant C18- Infml/Euph

in between   bisexual ex between choosing either sex C20 Infml

in Cock Alley   sexual intercourse sd of men ex **cock,** alley = vagina C18-20* Infml

incognita   prostitute ex Lat = not recognized C18-19* Sl/Infml

in Cupid's Alley sexual intercourse sd of men ex Cupid's Alley = vagina C19–20* Infml

ineffable female genitals cf **monosyllable** C19* Euph/Infml

infanticide masturbation sd of men ex no conception possible (death) C19–20* Sl/Joc

in full fig with erect penis ?ex dressed cf **fig** = (female) genitals C19* Sl

in love lane sexual intercourse sd of men ex love lane = vagina C19–20* Infml/Euph

in one's Sunday best/clothes with erect penis ex starched clothes = stiff (religion) C19* Infml/Joc

in pod pregnant ex plant reproduction C19–20* Sl

in season lusty ex on heat C19 Infml/Euph

inside worry, do an copulate sd of men ex internal agitation C19–20* Sl

intemperance lust, ex extreme desire C17- Lit/Fml

intercourse abbr of sexual intercourse ex Lat *intercursus* = running between C15- Std/Euph

in the club pregnant ex join new group C20 Infml

in the familiar way pregnant pun on familiar, family way C19- Joc

in the family way pregnant ex reproduction C19- Infml

in the saddle, be menstruate ex saddle = sanitary towel cf **saddle** C19- Sl

intimacy sexual intercourse ex closeness C17- Euph

intimate with, be copulate ex closeness C17- Euph/Fml

introduce Charley/Charlie copulate sd of men cf **Charley** (name) C19–20* Infml

in trouble pregnant C19- Infml/Euph

invade copulate sd of men cf **charge** (aggression) C17* Lit

Irish root penis ex **root** (foreign) C19–20* Sl/Joc

Irish toothache erect penis ex **Irish root** (foreign, body) C19–20* Sl/Joc

it 1. sexual intercourse cf **do it** C15- Euph. 2. genitals ex 1. C15- Euph

itch lust C17- Sl/Infml

itcher female genitals ex **itch** C19–20* Sl

itching Jenny female genitals ex **itch**, Jenny = female (name) C19–20* Sl

ivory pearl woman ex value C20* R.Sl (girl)

J

Jack penis or erect penis ?ex common male name, ?ex lifting device (name) C19–20* Sl

jack in a/the box 1. penis ex **jack** springing up = erection C19–20* Sl. 2. syphilis pun on **jack** = penis, **box** = vagina, sudden shock C20* R.Sl (pox)

jack off masturbate, sd of men ex **jack** or Lat *jacere* = throw C20 Sl

Jack Robinson penis ex swiftness — before one can say — cf **John Thomas** (name) C19–20* Sl

Jacob penis cf **Jack** (name) C19* Sl

Jacob's ladder   vagina ex **Jacob**, **ladder** which leads to **heaven** (name, religion) C19* Sl

jam   female genitals pun on sweetness, squeeze (food) C19–20* Sl

jam pot   vagina ex container, **jam** (food) C19–20* Sl

Jane Shaw/Shore   prostitute ?ex jane = woman, shore — if naval origin (name) C19–20* R.Sl (whore)

janey   1. lesbian woman ex jane = woman (name) C20 Sl. 2. vagina ?ex 1. or abbr of **vagina** (name) C20 lesbian Sl

J. Arthur Rank   masturbate ex film producer (name) C20 R.Sl (wank)

jaw queen   fellator ex mouth, **queen** C20 gay Sl

jazz   sexual intercourse ?ex jasm = **gism** (music) C19–20* Sl

jeff off   masturbate sd of men (name) C20 Sl/Euph (for **jerk/jack off**)

jelly   semen ex appearance (food) C17- Sl

jelly bag   1. vagina ex container, **jelly** C17–20* Sl. 2. scrotum ex container, **jelly** C17- Sl

jerk off   masturbate ex movement C18- Sl

jerk one's gherkin   masturbate sd of men ex jerk, gherkin = penis (food) C20 Sl

Jersey City   breast (name) C20 US R.Sl (titty)

jet one's juice   ejaculate sd of men ex **juice** C19- Sl

jewel   virginity, hymen ex value C18–20* Lit/Infml

jewel case   vagina ex value, container cf **jewel**, **case** C18–20* Lit/Infml

jewels   male genitals esp testicles cf **family jewels**, **jewel**, C20 Infml

jezebel   penis ex Bible (name) C19* Sl

jig(-jig)   copulate ex movement (dance) C19–20* Sl/Euph

jiggle   1. copulate ex move jerkily C19- Infml. 2. actively display breasts ex jiggle-shows (television) C20 Infml

jism   variant of **gism**

job   copulate ex Std senses = work, take advantage or ex jab C16–20* Infml

Jock   penis ex common Scottish name cf **Jack** (name) C18- Sl

Jodrell Bank   masturbate ex astronomical observatory (name) C20 R.Sl (wank)

Joe Hunt   vagina, but esp Derog term (name) C20* R.Sl (cunt)

jog   copulate ex jerky movement C16- Sl

john   prostitute's customer ex john = man (name) C20 Sl

johnnie   1. penis ex john = man (name) C19–20* Infml. 2. condom ?ex 1. (name) C20 Infml

Johnny Rollicks   testicles (name) C19- R.Sl (bollocks)

johnson   penis ex john = man ?ex Dr. Johnson (name) C20 Sl

John Thomas   penis ex john = man (name) C19–20* Sl

join giblets   copulate ex **giblets** (body) C18–20* Sl/Euph

joint   1. brothel ex place C18- Sl. 2. penis ?ex joined on, joining C20 Sl

jointess   clitoris ex **joint**-ess = feminine form C20 Sl/Joc

jolly   homosexual ex **gay** C20 gay Sl/Joc

joy   copulate cf **enjoy** C17* Infml

joy house   brothel ex **joy** C20 Sl
joystick   penis ex **joy, stick** C20 Sl
jubes   breasts ?ex jujubes = sucking sweets C20 ?R.Sl (boobs)
juggle   copulate ex Lat = to jest C16–17* Lit
jugs   breasts ex containers cf **dugs** similar sounding C20 Sl
juice   1. semen ex secretion C19- Sl. 2. vaginal fluid cf **wet** C19- Sl
juicy   lusty esp of women ex **juice** C19- Sl/Infml
jump   copulate ex movement (aggression) C17–20* Infml
jungle meat   penis of black man cf **meat** (food) C20 Sl/Derog
jutland   buttocks ex jut out (name) C18–19* Sl/Joc

K

keel   buttocks ex naval sense = bottom of ship C19–20* Infml
keen   lusty ?ex ken = knowledge C16- Lit/Infml
keep the census down   masturbate sd of men ex population control cf **infanticide** C19–20* Joc
keister   buttocks ex Ger *kiste* = box C20 Sl/Infml
kettle   vagina pun on heat, container C18–20* Infml/Sl
kettledrums   breasts ex roundness (music) C18–19* Sl
key   penis pun on **lock**, chastity of women C18–20* Sl/Infml
keyhole   vagina ex **key, hole** C18–20* Sl/Infml
Khyber Pass   anus ex narrow path between Pakinstan and Afghanistan
(name) C19- R.Sl (arse)
kindness   sexual intercourse ex generosity, favor C18–19* Euph/Infml
kinky   considered sexually deviant ex kink = bend C20 Sl/Infml
kiss (it)   perform fellatio or cunnilingus ex mouth, lips C20 Sl
kit   male genitals cf **gear, tool** (clothing) C19–20* Sl
kitten's ear   female pubes ex soft, triangular cf **puss** (animal, body) C19*
Sl
kitty   female genitals cf **cat, puss** (animal) C19–20* Sl
knackers   testicles ?ex knackered = exhausted ?ex knack = trick C19-
Sl/Infml
kneel at the altar   fellate ex performing on one's knees (religion) C20 gay
Sl
knee-trembler   sexual intercourse while standing ex sensation of weakness
in knees (body) C19* Infml/Joc
knick-knack   female genitals ex trifle, ornament C19- Sl/Infml
knight   male homosexual cf **sword** (aggression) C20 Sl
knish   vagina ex Yid = dumpling (food) C20 Sl
knob   1. glans, head of penis ex shape C20 Sl. 2. penis ex 1. C20 Sl
knob-polisher   fellator ex **knob** C20 gay Sl
knobs   nipples ex shape C20 Sl
knock   copulate sd of men cf **nock, hit** (aggression) C16- Sl/Infml

knocked up   pregnant ex **knock** C19- Sl
knocker   penis ex **knock** C17* Sl
knockers   breasts pun on handling, entering cf **knock** C20 Sl
knocking joint/shop   brothel ex **knock** C19-20* Sl
knot   glans, head of penis ex shape C20 Sl
know (a woman)   copulate sd of men ex Bible knowledge = carnal knowledge C13- Fml
knowledge   sexual intercourse ex Bible cf **carnal knowledge** C13- Fml
kosher dill/meat   circumcised penis ex Jewish dietary laws (food) C20 Infml
KS   perform anilingus ex abbr for kiss shit C20 Sl/Euph
kwela   sexual intercourse ex African = mount (music) C20 SAfr Sl

L

lace (curtains)   uncircumcised foreskin cf **blinds, drapes** C20 gay Sl
ladder   vagina ex climbing up C16-20* Sl
ladies' college   brothel pun on school/**knowledge** cf **academy** C18-19* Sl
ladies' tailoring   sexual intercourse cf **stitch** (clothing) C19-20* Sl
Lady Jane   female genitals ex Jane = woman (name) C19* Sl
lady lover   lesbian ex male activity C20 Sl
lady of easy virtue   prostitute ex loose morals C18-20* Infml/Euph
lady's delight/lollipop/treasure   penis ex enjoyment for women C19* Infml
lady's friend   dildo cf **widow's comforter** C19- Euph/Infml
ladyware   male genitals ex goods for a lady C16-17* Lit
lame duck   sexual intercourse, irony in lame = ?post coital C20 R.Sl (fuck)
lance   penis cf **sword** (aggression) C16-17* Lit
lap   female genitals pun on lick, upper thigh (body, eating) C16- Lit/Infml
Lapland   female genitals cf **lap** (name, body, eating) C19* Joc/Infml
laplover   cunnilinguist ex **lap** C20 Sl
larking   cunnilingus ex Std sense = frolic C18-20* Sl
lascivious   lustful ex Lat C15- Std
last act/liberties   sexual intercourse ex last = ultimate cf **die** (death) C18-19* Lit/Euph
lather   1. vaginal fluid pun on worked up, appearance C19-20* Sl. 2. semen pun on worked up, appearance C19-20* Sl
lay   1. v. (also passive **get laid**) copulate ex Std sense = cause to lie down C20 Sl. 2. n. person as sex partner ex v. C20 Sl
leap   copulate cf **jump** C16-20* Lit/Infml
leaping house   brothel ex **leap**, house C16-17* Infml
leather   female genitals ex skin (body, animal) C16-20* Sl
leather-lane   vagina ex **leather** C18-20* Sl
leather-stretcher   penis ex **leather** C18-20* Sl
lecher   lewd man ex O.Fr *lecher* = lick C14- Std
lecherous   lustful, smutty ex O.Fr *lecher* = lick C14- Std
left-handed wife   mistress ex left = inferior C18-19* Infml

leg business   sexual intercourse ex work, involvement of legs (body) C19–20* Infml/Euph

leggins   intercourse between the thighs ex use of legs C20 Sl

les   abbr of **lesbian** C20 Infml/Sl

lesbian   female homosexual ex Lesbos, place where Greek poetess Sappho wrote C19- Std

lesbo   variant fo **lesbian** C20 Sl

letchwater   1. vaginal fluid ?ex **lecher** C18–20* Sl. 2. semen ?ex **lecher** C18–20* Sl

let in   copulate sd of women ex allow intromission C16- Lit/Infml

lewd   obscene, lusty ex OE = ignorant C14- Std

Lewis & Witties   breasts ex department store (name) C20* Austr R.Sl (titties)

lezz   variant of **les** abbr of **lesbian**

libidinous   lustful ex Lat *libido* = desire C20 Std

libido   lust ex Lat = desire C20 Std/Fml

licentious   lusty ex Lat = license C16- Std/Fml

lick   perform cunnilingus or fellatio ex tonguing C20 Sl

lie in state   copulate in bed with two women sd of men ?ex great status C18–20* Joc/Sl

lie with   copulate pun on fib cf **lay** C16- Euph

life preserver   penis ex reproduction C19* Sl/Joc

lift leg, play at   copulate cf **mount** (body) C18–20* Lit/Infml

light meat   genitals of white person cf **white meat**, **dark meat**, **meat** (food) C20 Sl

light the lamp   copulate pun on heat, ignition C19–20* Lit

lily   passive male homosexual ex flower (name) C20 Sl

limp-wrist   passive male homosexual cf **bent wrist** (body) C20 Sl

ling   1. vagina ex type of fish (animal, food) C19–20* Sl. 2. female pubes ex ling Scottish = heather C16–17* Lit

lingam   penis ex Sanskrit cf **yoni** C18- Lit

linguist   fellator or cunnilinguist ex Lat *lingua* = tongue cf **tongue** C20 Joc/Sl

linguistic exercise   mutual oral sex ex **linguist** C20 Joc/Sl

lipstick   penis pun on **stick** emerging from container, sticking between lips, C20 Joc/Sl

lipwork   sexual intercourse, ex kissing (body) C19–20* Infml/Euph

little boy in the boat   clitoris ex **boat** = vulva, boy = male part C19–20* Infml

little brother   penis cf **big brother** (family) C19–20* Sl

little death   orgasm ex Fr *petite mort* cf **die** C19* Lit/Fml

little ploughman   clitoris ex object in furrow, masculine C19* Lit

little shame tongue   clitoris ex Ger cf **tongue**, **pudenda** C19* Lit

little sister   female genitals cf **little brother** (family) C19–20* Sl

little sister is here   menstruation cf **little sister** (family) C19- Infml/Euph

live in sin   live together and have sexual intercourse without being married (religion) C16- Infml

live rabbit   penis cf **rabbit** (animal) C19–20* Sl

live wire   erect penis ex wire = penis, live = having electricity ?ex shock (aggression) C20 Sl
lizard   penis ex shape (animal) C20 Sl
lizzy   variant of **lesbian** (name) C20 Sl
load   semen ex amount C20 Sl
lob   penis ex Ger = dangling C18–19* Sl
lobster   1. penis ex **lob** (animal, food) C18–19* Sl. 2. vagina ?ex **lob** = penis, -ster = female suffix (animal, food) C18–19* Sl
lobster pot   vagina ex container cf **lobster** C18–19* Sl
lock/locker   vagina pun on chastity, cf **key** C18–20* Sl
lodge   vagina pun on container, implant, house C16–17* Lit
loins   genitals ex O.Fr C14- Std/Fml
lollipop   penis, pun on stick, sucking, sticky C20 Sl/Infml
long eye   female genitals ex longways **eye** (body) C19* Sl
loopdeloop   mutual oral sex cf **head over heels** C20 Joc/Sl
Lord knows what   female genitals cf **thing** (religion) C18–20* Euph
lose the match and pocket the stakes   copulate sd of women pun on being taken, but taking stakes = penis, semen; pocket = vagina (sport) C19–20* Sl
loss   orgasm sd of mean ex loss of semen cf **die** (death) C16–17* Lit
love apples   testicles cf **apples** (food) C19–20* Sl
love juice   1. semen cf **juice** C19- Sl/Infml. 2. vaginal fluid cf **juice** C19- Sl/Infml
love nuts   pain in the testicles due to inability to ejaculate ex **nuts** = testicles cf **blueballs** C20 Sl
lovers' knot   sexual intercourse ex joining together C19–20* Infml
love work   sexual intercourse ex labor C13- Euph
lowlands   female genitals pun on geography, lowness C18–19* Joc/Sl
lubricate   copulate ex make slippery C18–19* Lit/Euph
lubricious   lusty ex Lat = slippery C16- Std/Fml
lullaby   penis ?ex copulation before sleep (music) C19–20* Joc/Sl
lust   sexual desire ex OE C15- Std
lute   female genitals ex fingering (music) C18* Lit

M

machine   1. penis ex Fr cf **tool** (instrument) C19–20* Sl. 2. female genitals ?ex 1. C19–20* Sl. 3. condom ex instrument C19* Sl
madame   1. female brothel keeper ex woman in charge C19- Sl/Infml. 2. elderly male homosexual ex 1. C20 gay Sl
Madge   1. female genitals ex common Scottish name for woman (name) C18–19* Sl. 2. male homosexual ex 1. (name) C20 gay Sl
mad Mick   penis cf **stormy Dick** (name) C20 R.Sl (prick)
Mae West   breast ex buxom film star C20* R.Sl (breast)
magazines   testicles ex cartridge of firearm cf **bullets** (aggression) C19* Sl
magnet   female genitals ex attraction C18–20* Sl
magpie's nest   vagina ?ex bird (animal) C18–20* Sl

maidenhead 1. hymen, virginity ex maiden + hood C13- Std. 2. anus ex 1. C18- gay Sl

main avenue vagina pun on **ride**, passage C18–20* Infml

make a milkshake masturbate sd of men ex **milk** (food) C20 Sl

make babies copulate (reproduction) C20 Euph/Joc

make ends meet copulate pun on joining, surviving C19–20* Joc

make faces copulate (body, reproduction) C18–19* Euph

make love copulate C16- Euph/Infml

make piggies copulate (animal reproduction) C20 Sl/Joc

make scissors (of someone) masturbate a woman with fingers apart as scissors C20 Sl

make the scene/it copulate ex success C20 Infml

make whoopee copulate ex Std sense = excitement, fun (sound) C19- Infml

malady of France syphilis ?ex came from France to England (foreign) C16–17* Lit

male catcher female genitals cf **mantrap** C18–20* Sl/Joc

malkin female genitals ex Scottish = cat, hare (animal) C16–19* Sl

mallee root prostitute ex mallee bush in Australia cf **root** C20 Austr, US R.Sl (prostitute)

malthusianism 1. masturbation ex theory of sexual constraint for population control C19* Lit/Joc. 2. sodomy ex 1. C19* Lit/Joc

mammets breasts ex Lat C16–17* Lit

man copulate sd of men ex n. C16–20* Lit/Infml

Manchester City breast ex football club cf **Bristol City** (name) C20 R.Sl (titty)

manhole 1. vagina pun on **man**, **hole**, danger C19- Sl. 2. anus pun on **man**, **hole** C20 gay Sl

manhood penis ex maleness C19- Euph

man in the boat clitoris ex **boat** = vulva, man = male part C19–20* Sl

manny lesbian ex man (name) C20 Sl

man oil semen ex male liquid C20 Sl

mantrap 1. vagina ex trap for men (aggression) C18–19* Infml. 2. prostitute ?ex 1. C19- Sl/Infml

maracas breasts ex pair, shape (music) C20 Sl

marbles testicles ex round objects C19- Sl/Infml

mark (of the beast) female genitals cf **gash**, **slit** (animal) C18–19* Lit/Sl

marrow semen ex appearance, from **bone** (body) C16–17* Lit

marrowbone penis ex **marrow**, **bone** (body) C19–20* Sl

Mary male homosexual ex female name (name) C20 Sl

Mary Jane female genitals ex jane = woman (name) C19* Sl/Euph

mason lesbian ?ex builder = masculine ?ex male only member C20 Sl

massage parlor brothel ex body massage C20 Euph

masterpiece 1. female genitals pun on master, piece, outstanding work/thing C18–20* Joc. 2. penis pun on master's piece, outstanding work/thing C18–20* Joc

masturbation manual stimulation of genitals ex Lat ?*manu-stuprare* = defile with the hand C19- Std

mat   female pubes cf **front door mat** C19- Sl

Mata Hari   female pubes ex hairy mat, seductive female spy C20 Sl/Joc

matinee   sexual activity in the afternoon ex afternoon performance C20 Sl

Mavis   passive male homosexual ex female name cf **moffie** (name) C20 SAfr gay Sl

mayonnaise   semen ex appearance (food) C20 gay Sl

meat   1. genitals cf **flesh** (food) C16- Infml/Sl. 2. sexual intercourse ex 1. cf **bit of meat** C16- Infml/Sl

meat and two vegetables   male genitals ex penis and two testicles cf **meat** (food) C20 Joc/Infml

meat-house   brothel ex **meat**, house C19-20* Sl

meat-market   1. breasts ex **flesh** (food) C19-20* Sl. 2. female genitals ex **flesh** (food) C19-20* Sl

meddle   copulate ex involvement C14- Euph/Infml

medicine   sexual intercourse pun on medicine = something that is good for one, must be taken C19-20* Infml/Joc

meggs   testicles ?ex **nutmegs**, *meggs = coins C19-20* Sl

melons   breasts ex shape (food) C20 Sl

melt   reach orgasm pun on sexual fire, heat C16-20* Lit/Infml

melted butter   semen ex appearance cf **melt** (food) C18-20* Sl

melting pot   vagina cf **pot**, **melt** C19* Infml

member   penis ex ME *limb, organ ex Lat C13- Std/Fml

member for Cockshire   penis pun on **member**, **cock**, male member (of British parliament) C19* Joc

memories   breasts pun on mammary = of the breast, something remembered C20 Joc

ménage à trois   threesome sexual arrangement ex Fr = household of three C20 Std/Lit

menstruation/menstrual period   monthly discharge from the uterus of non-pregnant women ex Lat *mensis* = month C16- Std

merchandise   1. female genitals cf **commodity** C20 Sl. 2. male prostitute ex 1. C20 Sl

merkin   1. artificial pubic hair ?ex Fr *mere* = mother, -kin = diminutive C19- Std. 2. artifical vagina ex 1. C19-20* Std. 3. vagina ex 1. and 2. C19-20* Sl

merry bout   sexual intercourse ex jolly C18-19* Euph

merryland   vagina ex **merry bout** C19* Sl/Euph

merrymaker   penis ex **merry bout** C19* Sl/Euph

mettle   semen ex courage, character C17-20* Lit/Infml

mickey   penis cf **mouse** (name) C19- Sl

Mickey Mouse   1. penis cf **mickey**, **mouse** (name, animal) C20 Infml. 2. female genitals ?ex fur (name, animal) C20 Infml

middle finger/leg   penis ex central (body) C19- Sl

midlands   female genitals pun on geography, midriff C19* Joc/Sl

milk   1. n. semen or vaginal fluid ex appearance (food) C17- Sl/Infml. 2. v. to cause ejaculation ex 1. C17- Sl/Infml

milker   1. female genitals ex **milk** C19-20* Sl. 2. masturbator ex **milk** C19-20* Sl

milk jug   vagina ex container, **milk** C18–20* Sl
milkman   1. masturbator ex **milk** C19–20* Sl. 2. penis ex **milk** C19–20* Sl
milk pan   vagina ex container, **milk** C18–20* Sl
milkshakes   breasts ex milk C19– Sl
milk shop   breasts ex milk C19–20* Sl/Joc
milky way   breasts pun on milk, **heaven** C17–20* Lit/Sl
milliner's shop   female genitals (clothing) C19* Sl
milt   semen ex semen or testes of fish (animal) C19* Sl/Infml
mine of pleasure   vagina ex tunnel cf **quarry, pleasure** C17–19* Lit/Infml
miner   active male homosexual ex drilling C20 gay Sl
minx   1. woman as sex object ex *Sl = woman (animal) C16– Sl. 2. prostitute ex 1. C16– Sl
misfit   homosexual ex deviation C20 heterosexual Sl/Derog
Miss Brown   female genitals cf **Brown Madam** (name) C18–19* Sl
Miss Horner   female genitals ex **horn** = erection (name) C19–20* Sl
missionary('s) position   sexual intercourse with man on top of woman (religion) C19– Joc
Miss Laycock   female genitals pun on **lay, cock** (name) C18–19* Joc/Sl
mistress   woman having extramarital relationship with man ex Fr C14– Std
mo   homosexual esp male ex abbr C20 Infml/Euph
model   prostitute, male or female ex attractive C20 Sl/Euph
moffie   male homosexual esp effeminate one ?ex her*maph*rodite cf **mophy** C20 SAfr Sl/Derog
mole   penis ex burrowing (animal) C19–20* Sl
mole-catcher   vagina ex **mole** C19–20* Sl
moll(y)   1. prostitute ex mary (name) C17–20* Sl. 2. woman (name) C18– Sl/Infml. 3. male homosexual (name) C18–20* Sl. 4. v. perform anal intercourse ex 3. C20 Sl
mollies   breasts ex **molly** C20 gay Sl
molly dyke   passive lesbian ?ex **mollies** cf **bull dyke** C20 Sl
money   female genitals ?ex showing one's money C18–19* child's Infml
monkey   vagina ?ex monkey business ?ex **hair** (animal) C19– Sl
monosyllable   vagina ex **cunt** being a monosyllabic word C18–19* Euph/Lit
mons pubis/veneris   fleshy cushion over pubic bone in women ex Lat = hill of pubes/Venus C17– Fml
monthlies   menstrual periods C19– Infml/Euph
moons   buttocks ex roundness C20 Sl
moonshot   anal intercourse ex **moons** C20 Sl
mophy   effeminate young male ?ex her*maph*rodite C19–20* Sl
mort   1. prostitute ex mort = woman, pun on death (death) C16–19* Sl. 2. vagina ex 1. C16–19* Sl
mortar   vagina pun on mortar = cannon and cf **pestle** = penis (aggression) C19–20* Sl
moss   female pubes ex appearance C18* Lit
mot(te)   1. vagina ex **mort** ?ex Fr = word, i.e. the word = **cunt** C18–19* Sl. 2. prostitute ex 1., ex **mort** C18–19* Sl
mother of all saints/souls   female genitals (religion, reproduction) C18–19* Sl

mount copulate esp sd of men ex climbing onto cf **ride** (animal) C16- Std/Fml

mount pleasant female genitals cf **mons pubis** (name) C19* Joc

mount the corporal and four fingers masturbate sd of men ex army cf **finger**, **mount** C18–20* Sl

mouse 1. penis ?ex shape, burrowing (animal) C19–20* Sl. 2. female genitals cf **mouser** (animal) C19–20* Sl

mouser vagina ex **mouse** cf **cat** C19–20* Sl

mouth music fellatio and/or cunnilingus ex mouth (music) C20 Sl

mouth thankless vagina ex orifice (body) C16–17* Scottish Sl/Lit

muff female genitals ex softness of hair C17- Sl

muff dive perform cunnilingus ex **muff**, **dive** C20 Sl

multiplication sexual intercourse ex reproduction cf **addition** C19–20* Euph

muscle penis ex **stiff** (body) C20 Sl

mushroom female genitals ?ex mush/room (food) C19* Sl

muslin 1. woman as sex object (clothing) C19–20* Sl. 2. female genitals ex 1. C19–20* Sl

mustard pot 1. vagina ex container, spicy C19–20* Sl 2. anus ex mustard = feces C20 Sl

mute vagina ?ex silent mouth C20 gay Sl

mutton 1. prostitute(s) cf **meat** (food) C16- Sl. 2. female genitals ex 1. C17- Sl. 3. sexual intercourse ex 2. C17- Sl

mysteries of love/Venus sexual intercourse ex wonder, Venus = Roman goddess of love C18–19* Lit/Euph

N

naf(f) vagina ex back slang of fan, abbr of **fanny** C19* Sl

nag penis ex horse cf **horse** (animal) C19* Sl

nail copulate sd of men cf **screw** (aggression) C20 Infml

naked seeing self female genitals cf **eye** C16–17* Lit

nance/y (boy) passive male homosexual ex female name (name) C19- Sl

national indoor game sexual intercourse ex popularity (sport) C19–20* Infml/Joc

natural prostitute ex **nature** C17–19* Sl

nature 1. genitals ex inherent, fundamental C16- Euph. 2. menstruation ex 1. C19- Euph

naughty, the 1. female genitals pun on indecent, naught = **nothing** C19–20* Sl/Euph. 2. sexual intercourse ?ex 1. C20 Austr Sl

naughty house brothel ex **naughty**, house C16–20* Lit/Infml

nautch vagina ex Sanskrit = dance C18–20* Sl

Nebuchadnezzar penis ex Bible cf **take Nebuchadnezzar out to grass** (name) C19–20* Sl

neck 1. n. breasts ex proximity (body) C16–17* Lit./Euph 2. v. caress ex twining of necks C20 Infml

neddy buttocks ex neddy = ass (name) C17- Infml

needle penis cf **prick**, **pin** C18–19* Infml

needle case vagina ex container cf **needle**, **case** C18–19* Infml

nether end/eye/mouth   vagina ex below, beneath (body) C14–18* Lit
Netherlands, the   genitals ex low country (name, foreign) C16–20* Lit/Sl
nether throat   anus ex below (body) C20 Sl
nibble, have a   copulate cf **taste**, **bite** (eating) C19–20* Sl
nick   1. n. female genitals ex **crack** C18–20* Sl. 2. v. copulate ex n. C18–20* Sl
night physic   sexual intercourse ex physic = medicine C16–18* Euph/Joc
night stick   penis ex **stick** C19–20* Sl
night work   sexual intercourse pun on labor C16–18* Euph/Joc
Nimrod   penis ex hunter, pun on **rod** (name) C19–20* Sl
ninnies   nipples ex ninny = simpleton cf **boob** C20 gay Sl/Derog
nipped in the bud   infant circumcision pun on cut while very young, in outgrowth = penis C20 Infml
nipples   outlet for milk in center of breast ex nib = point C16– Std
nips   abbr of **nipples** C20 Infml
nock   1. n. female genitals ?ex notch, pun on **knock** C16–18* Sl. 2. v. copulate ex n. C16–18* Sl
no-nuts   lesbian ex **nuts** = testicles C20 Joc/Sl
nookie/nooky   1. sexual intercourse ?ex **nug**, **nick** = copulate, female genitals C19– Sl. 2. vagina ex 1. C20 Sl
nookie bookie   pimp ex **nooky**, bookmaker ex accepts money C20 Sl/Joc
noose   vagina pun on circle, trap (aggression) C20 Sl
North Pole   anus ex geographical point (name) C19–20* R.Sl (hole)
nose   penis ?ex protuberance, emitting mucus (body) C16–17* Lit
not alone   pregnant ex with child C20 Joc/Euph
notch   female genitals ex **nick**, pun on **score** C18–20* Sl
nothing   female genitals ex shape (O), **thing** = genitals C17* Lit
novelty, the   female genitals ex interesting C18–20 Joc/Euph
nudge, nudge (wink, wink)   copulate ex push, hint C20 Euph/Joc
nug   copulate ?ex nudge C17–19* Sl
nums   nipples ex num num = eat, appetite (food) C20 Sl
nunnery   brothel ex place for women cf **abbess** (religion) C16–20* Lit/Sl
nursery   female genitals (reproduction) C19–20* Sl
nutmegs   testicles ex shape cf **nuts** (food) C17–20* Sl
nuts   testicles ex shape (food) C18– Sl/Infml

O

O   female genitals ex shape cf **nothing** C17* Lit
occupy   copulate sd of men cf **take** C16– Sl/Infml
odd   homosexual ex unusual C19–20* Euph/Infml
ointment   semen ex appearance, medicinal value C18–20* Sl
old Adam   penis ex first man, sin (name) C19–20* Infml
old girl/hen   elderly male homosexual ex girl, hen C20 gay Sl
old horny/Hornington   penis ex **horn** C18–20* Sl
old thing   female genitals cf **thing** C18–20* Sl

one in the box   pregnant ex **box** C19–20* Infml
one of the boys   lesbian C20 Infml
onion   1. glans, head of penis ex onion, Sl = head (food) C20 Sl. 2. woman engaging in a **gang bang** ?ex onion having many *lay*ers, C20 Austr Sl
onion skin   foreskin ex **onion** C20 Sl
on the bonk/honk   having an erection ?ex honk = **horn** C20 Infml
on the game   engaged in prostitution ex **game** C19- Sl
on the rag   menstruate ex rag = sanitary towel C20 Sl
open up the arse/ass   perform anal intercourse cf **ass** C20 gay Sl
oracle   female genitals ex Lat *orare* = request (religion) C19–20* Infml/Euph
orange   female genitals ?ex juiciness (food) C17* Lit
orbs   1. breasts ex shape C18–19* Infml. 2. testicles ex shape C20 Infml
orchard   female genitals ex reproduction, fruit C16–20* Lit/Sl
orchestra (stalls)   testicles cf **orchids** (music) C19- R.Sl (balls)
orchids   testicles ex Gr *orchis* = testicle C19* Lit/Infml
organ   penis ex Gr = tool C18- Euph
orgasm   peak of sexual excitement ex Gr = swell C17- Std
orgy   group sexual activity ex Gr C16- Std
orifice   female genitals ex **hole** C16- Std/Infml
ornaments   testicles ex decoration C19* Sl
oscarize   perform anal intercourse ex Oscar Wilde, famous homosexual (name) C20 Sl
OTR   menstruate ex abbr for **on the rag** C20 Sl
oven   vagina pun on heat, container (eating) C18–20* Infml
overcoat   condom ex sheath (clothing) C20 Sl/Joc
oyster   1. female genitals ex appearance, texture, delicacy (animal, food) C19–20* Sl. 2. semen ex Sl sense = gob of phlegm C18–19* Sl

P

paddle   caress cf **handle** C16–17* Lit
paddle one's pickle   masturbate sd of men cf **paddle, pickle** (food) C20 Sl
padlock   vagina pun on chastity cf **lock, key** C18–20* Sl
pagan   1. n. prostitute ex practice in pagan Greece (religion) C16–17* Lit. 2. sexual intercourse other than **missionary position** (religion) C20 Sl
pancake   woman cf **cake** (food) C20 Sl
pansy   male homosexual esp. passive ex flower C20 Sl
panters   breasts ex deep breathing C19–20* Infml/Joc
pantry shelves   breasts ex containing food (eating) C19* Infml
papaya   vagina ?ex juiciness cf **paps** (food) C20 Sl
paps   nipples ex Lat C12- Std/Fml
parley   copulate ex communicate C16–17* Lit/Euph
parlor room   vagina cf **front room** C19–20* Sl
parsley   female pubes ex cluster (food) C18–20* Sl
parsley bed   vagina ex **parsley** (food, bed) C17–20* Sl
part someone's cheeks   perform anal intercourse ex **cheeks** = buttocks (body) C20 Sl

passion   lust C16- Lit/Fml

Pat and Mick   penis (name) C19–20* R.Sl (prick)

patch   female genitals ex pubic patch C19–20* Sl

patha-patha   sexual intercourse ex African = touch-touch (music) C20 SAfr Sl

pearl dive   perform cunnilingus ex **oyster** = female genitals, **dive**, C20 Sl

pebbles   testicles cf **stones** C19–20* Sl

pecker   penis pun on appetite, **cock**, courage C19- Sl

peculiar river   vagina ex *peculiar = mistress C17–20* Lit/Sl

peepee   penis ex pee = urine C19- child's Infml

peeping sentinel   clitoris ex peeping out of vulva, pun on pee C19* Sl/ Infml

pen   1. penis ex Lat *penna* = feather, quill C16–20* Sl. 2. vagina ex enclosure C19–20* Sl

pencil   penis ex shape, esp in phrase **lead in one's pencil** = erection C19- Sl

pendulum   penis ex hanging C19–20* Sl

penis   male copulatory organ ex Lat = tail C17- Std

penis muliebris   clitoris ex Lat = woman's penis C17- Med/Fml

perform   1. copulate cf **do it** C19- Sl. 2. perform fellatio or cunnilingus ex 1. C20 Sl

period   menstrual period ex abbr C19- Infml

periwinkle   female genitals ?ex **winkle** = penis, peri- = around (animal) C19–20* Sl

perpendicular, do a   copulate while standing cf **upright** C19* Infml/Joc

perv(e)   1. n. male homosexual ex pervert C20 heterosexual Sl/Derog. 2. v. to perform anal intercourse ex 1. C20 heterosexual Sl

pestle   1. n. penis cf **mortar** vagina (aggression) C19–20* Sl. 2. v. copulate sd of men ex n. C19–20* Sl

pet   caress ex fondness, favorite C20 Infml

petal   passive male homosexual ex flower C20 Sl

peter   penis ex Gr = rock (name) C19- Infml

peter eater   fellator ex **peter**, **eat** C20 Sl

petticoat   women cf **skirt** (clothing) C17- Infml

pickle   penis ex cucumber esp in phrases **paddle/pump one's pickle**, cf **prickle** (food) C20 Sl

picklock   penis ex opening **lock** cf **key** C18* Lit

pick the lock   deflower ex undo **lock**, pun on vagina, chastity belt C16* Lit

picnic   1. n. orgy (eating) C20 Sl. 2. v. perform fellatio or cunnilingus (eating) C20 Sl

piece   woman as sex object cf **bit** C14- Sl

piece of ass   vagina ex **piece**, **ass** C20 Sl

piggies   1. breasts ex fleshiness (animal) C20 Sl. 2. nipples ex 1. (animal) C20 Sl

pig pile   homosexual orgy (animal) C20 gay Sl

pike   penis cf **weapon** (aggression) C16–17* Lit

pile-driver   penis ex repeated hammering (aggression) C19- Sl

pillow-mate   wife, mistress or prostitute ex bed partner (bed) C19- Infml

pills testicles abbr of **Beecham's pills**, pill = roundness C19–20* R.Sl (testicles)

pimp male procurer ?ex O.Fr C17- Std

pin penis cf **prick** C17–20* Sl/Infml

pipe 1. vagina pun on tube, **smoke** C19–20* Sl. 2. penis pun on length, **smoke** C19- Sl

pipkin female genitals ex small seeds (reproduction) C17–19* Infml

pistol penis cf **gun, weapon** (aggression) C16–20* Lit/Infml

piston (rod) penis ex movement, pis(s), **rod** C20 Sl

pit vagina pun on deep cavity C17–19* Sl/Infml

pitcher vagina ex container cf **crack a pitcher** C17–20* Infml/Sl

pit job sexual intercourse in the armpit cf **blow job, hand job** C20 Sl

pit of darkness vagina ex **pit**, darkness C17–19* Sl/Infml

pizzle penis ex bull's penis (animal) C17–20* Std/Sl

place of sixpence/penny sinfulness brothel ex price for sin C17* Lit/Infml/Euph

placket 1. woman as sex object (clothing) C17* Sl/Infml 2. vagina cf slit (clothing) C17–18* Sl

plank penis pun on length cf **pole** C20 Sl/Infml

plate (of ham) fellate (food) C20 R.Sl (gam)

play caress cf **foreplay, sport** (sport) C16- Infml

play hanky panky copulate pun on foolishness, cheating C19- Infml

play one's ace copulate sd of women ex ace = female genitals pun on ace = winning move C19–20* Sl

play solitaire masturbate ex game played alone C19* Euph/Joc

play the flute/horn/organ fellate ex terms for penis, blowing instruments (music) C20 Sl

play the national indoor game copulate ex popularity, game (sport) C20 Infml/Joc

play the piano perform anilingus ex *Rim*ski-Korsakov Russian pianist cf play the **organ** (music) C20 Sl/Joc

play the trombone copulate sd of men pun on **bone** = erection, sliding of trombone (music) C19–20* Sl

play with oneself masturbate ex occupy, amuse oneself C19- Infml/Euph

pleasure 1. orgasm ex feeling C16- Euph/Infml. 2. sexual intercourse ex 1. C16- Euph/Infml

pleasure boat female genitals ex **pleasure, boat** = vulva C19–20* Sl

pleasure garden female genitals ex **pleasure, garden** C17–19* Infml

plough copulate sd of men, pun on work in groove, sow seeds C17- Lit

plug copulate sd of men ex Std sense = insert and fill C18- Sl

plug tail penis ex **plug, tail** C18* Sl

plum(-tree) female genitals ?ex juiciness, ?ex groove on side (food) C16–17* Lit/Euph

plumbing male genitals ex waterworks C20 Infml/Euph

plush female pubes ex soft pile C19–20* Sl

pocket vagina ex container C19* Sl

pocket pool   masturbation esp of testicles through trouser pocket ex game, pun on **balls** (sport) C20 Sl

pointer   penis ex long rod, measuring stock C19–20* Infml

poke   1. v. copulate, sd of men ex Std sense = jab, make a hole (aggression) C19- Infml/Sl. 2. n. act of copulation ex v. C19- Infml/Sl. 3. n. woman as sex object ex v. C19- Infml/Sl

poke hole   vagina ex **poke**, **hole** C19–20* Sl

poke party   male homosexual orgy ex **poke** C20 gay Infml/Sl

poker   penis ex **poke** (aggression) C19- Sl

pole   erect penis ex shape C19- Sl

polish one's ass on the top sheet   copulate sd of men ex man on top of woman, under sheet (bed) C19–20* Sl/Joc

polish the knob   fellate ex **knob** C20 Sl

Polyphemus   penis ex one-eyed creature in Greek myth cf **Cyclops** (name) C19* Lit

pompoms   breasts ?ex gun ?ex fluffy balls (aggression) C20 Sl

ponce   1. pimp ?ex pounce C19- Sl/Infml. 2. male homosexual ?ex 1. C20 Sl

pond   vagina ex container, wet C16–17* Lit

pony   penis ex **horse** cf **nag** (animal) C19* Sl

pooftah/ter   passive male homosexual ex Fr *pouffe* = puff C20 heterosexual Sl/Derog

poontang   1. sexual intercourse ?ex Fr *putain* = prostitute C19- Sl. 2. vagina ex 1. C19- Sl

poonts   breasts ?ex **poontang** ?ex points C19- Sl

poop   1. n. buttocks ex back of ship C17–20* Sl. 2. v. copulate ex n. C17–18* Sl

poop-hole   anus ex **poop** 1. C17- Sl

poppa   lesbian ex father (family) C20 lesbian Sl

pork   copulate (food, animal) C19- Sl/Infml

porthole   1. anus ex small round **hole** C17- Sl. 2. vagina cf **hole** C17–20* Sl

Portuguese pump   masturbation cf **pump off** (foreign) C19–20* Sl

possess someone   copulate esp sd of men cf **take**, **occupy** C15- Fml

posteriors   buttocks ex position C17- Std/Fml

pot   lesbian ?ex cooking pot or *pot = woman C20 Sl

potato finger   1. penis ex shape (food, body) C17–18* Sl. 2. dildo ex 1. (food) C17- Sl

pouf(ter)   variant of **poof(ter)**

poundcakes   buttocks cf **cakes** (food) C20 Sl

pounders   testicles ex weight C17–18* Lit/Infml

pound one's meat   masturbate sd of men ex **meat** (aggression) C20 Sl

pouter   vagina ex lips C19–20* Sl

powder puff   passive male homosexual ex Sl = sissy C20 Sl

pox   syphilis ex plural of pock C16–18 Std C19- Sl

prat   1. buttocks ?ex *prate = idleness, prattle C16- Sl. 2. vagina ?ex 1. C19- Sl

preggers   variant of **pregnant** C20 Infml

pregnant   carrying a fetus in the womb ex Lat C16- Std
premises   vagina ex house cf **occupy** C19–20* Sl/Euph
pretty   young boy unfamiliar with homosexuality C20 gay Sl
prick   penis ex v. = pierce C16–17 Std C18- Sl
prickle   penis cf **prick** C16–20* Std/Lit
prick pride   erection ex **prick**, pride = upright, erect C16–20* Sl
private parts/privates   genitals ex usually clothed, covered C16- Euph
private property   genitals ex private, ownership C19–20* Infml
prize   sexual intercourse ex success pun on prize = force open C16–17 Lit
pro   prostitute ex abbr for professional C20 Sl/Infml
prod   copulate sd of men cf **poke** C19–20* Sl
promised land   female genitals ex Bible cf **garden of Eden** C19* Joc/
   Infml
prostitute   person, esp woman, offering sex for money ex Lat C16- Std
protein   semen ex necessity for life (food) C20 Sl
protein queen   male homosexual fellator ex **protein, queen** C20 Sl
pubes   pubic hair ex Lat *puber* = adult C16- Std
public ledger   prostitute ex open to all C18–20* Sl
pud   penis ex abbr of **pudding** or **pudenda** C20 Sl
pudding   1. penis ex sausage-shaped pudding (food) C17- Sl. 2. sexual intercourse ex 1. (food) C17–20* Sl. 3. semen ex 1. cf **rice pudding** (food) C17- Sl
pudenda   genitals, esp female ex Lat *pudere* = to be ashamed C17- Fml
pudendum   singular of **pudenda**
pull off   masturbate sd of men ex movement cf **jerk off** C19- Sl
pull one's peter/pudding   masturbate sd of men ex **peter, pudding** C19- Sl
pull wire   masturbate sd of men ex **wire** C20 Sl
pulpit   female genitals ex container (religion) C17* Lit
pulse   1. vagina ?ex throbbing, feeling C19–20* Sl. 2. erect penis ex throbbing of blood C20 Sl
pump   1. v. copulate sd of men ex action C18- Sl. 2. n. vagina ex container
   C17- Sl. 3. n. penis ex handle of pump C18- Sl
pump off   masturbate ex movement cf **jerk off** C19- Sl
pump one's pickle   masturbate cf **pump off, pickle** C20 Sl
punch   deflower ex Std sense = hit, * = stab (aggression) C18–19* Infml
puncture   deflower ex make a hole C19- Sl/Infml
punish Percy in the palm   masturbate sd of men cf **self-abuse, hand job**
   (name) C20 Sl/Joc
punk   1. prostitute ?ex **puncture** C18–19* Sl. 2. male homosexual ?ex 1.
   C19- Sl
punse   female genitals ex Yid = punch C19- Sl
puppies   nipples cf **paps** (animal) C20 gay Sl
purse   vagina ex container cf **money** C17–20* Sl
puss   female genitals ex pussy-**cat** (animal) C17- Sl
pussy   1. female genitals ex pussy-**cat** (animal) C17- Sl. 2. anus ex 1. C20
   male homosexual Sl
put four corners on the spit   copulate ex spread out ?ex *spit = deflower cf
   meat C19* Sl

putter erect penis ex golf stick pun on putting = hitting, placing (sport) C20 Sl

putz penis ex Yid = ornament cf **schmuck** C19- Sl/Derog

Q

quagmire vagina ex wet soft place C16–17* Lit/Joc

quail prostitute ex bird, hunted, amorous (animal) C17–19* Sl

quaint female genitals, version of **cunt** ex O.Fr = pleasant C14–16 Sl C17- Dial

quarry vagina, pun on mine, prey C18–19* Infml/Euph

queen (originally **quean**) male homosexual ex *quean = prostitute C19- Sl

queen of holes vagina ex most important **hole** C17* Lit

queer male homosexual ex criminal, counterfeit, weird C20 hetersoexual Sl/Derog

quiff 1. copulate ex Std senses = success, hair C18–20* Infml. 2. female genitals ex 1. cf **quim** C18- Sl

quim female genitals ?ex Celtic = womb C16- Sl

quim bush/whiskers/wig female pubes ex **quim** C19- Sl

quiver vagina pun on case for **arrows**, **shake** C17* Lit

R

rabbit copulate ex propensity for frequent copulation, breeding (animal) C19- Dial/Infml

rabbit pie prostitute cf **rabbit** (animal, food) C19–20* Sl

radish glans, head of penis ex shape (food) C20 Sl

raincoat condom ex protection C20 Sl/Joc

rake sexually promiscuous man ex rakehell cf **rake out** C17- Std/Infml

rake out copulate sd of men ex movement, pun on rake C19–20* Sl

Ralph femininity esp in male homosexuals (name) C20 heterosexual Sl/Joc

ram 1. copulate, sd of men (aggression, animal) C19- Sl. 2. perform anal intercourse ex 1. C20 Sl

rammer penis ex **ram** C19–20* Sl

randy lustful ex rand = rave, rant C18- Infml

ranger penis ?ex rover = promiscuity C18–20* Sl

rasp 1. n. female genitals ex rubbing C19–20* Sl. 2. v. copulate ex rubbing C19–20* Sl

raunchy smutty ?ex raucous, **randy** C20 Infml

raw meat penis cf **meat** (food) C18–20* Sl

read braille caress ex fingering C20 Infml/Joc

ready sexually willing ex prepared C19- Infml

real thing vagina ex **thing**, pun on genuine C19- Sl/Euph

ream perform anilingus ex widening a hole C20 Sl

receive holy communion   fellate ex kneeling, receiving semen (religion) C20 Sl

receiver general   prostitute ex take anyone C19* Sl/Joc

rector of the females   penis pun on erection (religion) C17–20* Lit

red ace   reddish female pubes ex **ace of spades** C19–20* Sl

red house/lamp/light   brothel ex color red signifying prostitution C19- Infml

red light district   area containing brothels ex **red light** C19- Infml

reef   caress ex naval sense = gathering in a sail C20 gay Sl

regulator   female genitals ex regulator of sex cf **controlling part** C18–19* Joc

relieve   1. copulate ex relief from desire C19* Infml/Euph. 2. ejaculate ex relief from desire C19* Infml/Euph

relieve oneself   masturbate ex relief C19- Infml/Euph

religious observances   orgasm pun on seriousness, ritual, keeping C20 Joc

relish   sexual intercourse pun on appetizer, enjoyment (food) C19* Sl

rest and be thankful   female genitals ?ex after copulation C19–20* Euph/Joc

returning naked to the womb   incest, of a male with his mother, pun on birth, copulation C16* Joc

reverse western   sexual intercourse with woman on top of man ex contrary to western custom C20 prostitute Sl

rhubarb   penis ex shape (food) C19–20* Infml

rhythm method   natural contraception based on menstrual cycle C20 Std

ribald   1. n. sexually promiscuous man ex *rascal cf **bawd** C14–19* Std. 2. lusty ex n. C16- Std

rice pudding   semen ex appearance (food) C20 Sl

ride   copulate ex sitting atop (animal) ME-C18 Std C19- Infml

ride a bicycle   bisexual ex **bi** in bicycle, cf **ride** C20 Sl

ride bareback   copulate without a condom ex no saddle = contraception cf **ride** C20 Sl

ride St George or **ride the dragon upon St George**   sexual intercourse with woman on top of man ex Fletcher's *Mad Lover* (animal) C17–19* Joc/Lit

rifle   copulate sd of men ex Ger = groove (aggression) C18* Lit

rim   perform anilingus ex widening a hole C20 Sl

ring   vagina pun on circle, wedding ring C16–20* Infml

ring around the rosey   male homosexual orgy, men linked penis to anus cf **rosey**, **daisy chain** C20 gay Sl

rip off   copulate pun on exploit (aggression) C20 ?prostitute Sl

rocks   testicles cf **stones**, **pebbles** C20 Sl

rod   penis ex shape cf **handstaff** C18–20* Infml

roe   semen ex semen and testes of fish (animal) C19–20* Sl/Infml

roger   1. n. penis ex Ger = spear (name) C17- Sl. 2. v. copulate sd of men ex n. ?ex expression of agreement (name) C18- Sl

roll (in the hay)   copulate ex movement cf **bounce** C20 Infml

rolls   buttocks ex shape (food) C20 Infml

roly-poly   penis ex jam pudding cf **jam**, **pudding**, **roll** (food) C19–20* Sl

Roman night   male homosexual orgy ex practice of Roman orgies (foreign) C20 gay Sl

rooster 1. penis ex **cock** (animal) C19–20* Euph. 2. female genitals ?ex where **cock** roosts ?ex **cock** 2. (animal) C19–20* Euph

root 1. n. penis pun on shape, origin C19- Sl. 2. v. copulate ex n. C20 Austr Sl

Rory O'More prostitute (name) C19–20* R.Sl (whore)

rose 1. female genitals ex shape cf **flower** C18–20* Lit. 2. virginity ex 1. C18–20* Lit

rosebud anus ex shape C20 gay Sl

rosebuds nipples ex shape cf **rose, buds of beauty** C20 Sl

rosey/rosy buttocks ex red **cheeks** C20 Sl

rounders buttocks ex shape C20 Sl

rubber condom ex material from which it is made C20 Infml

rubbins intercourse between the thighs ex rubbing C20 Sl

rubigo penis ex Lat *ruber* = red ex rubbing C16–17* Scot Sl

rub off 1. copulate ex friction C17–19* Infml. 2. masturbate ex friction C19- Sl

rub one's radish masturbate ex **radish** C20 Sl

rug pubes cf **mat** C20 Infml

rule of three male genitals ex penis and two testicles, pun on rule = control, measuring stick C18–20* Sl/Joc

rummage copulate ex hastiness C19–20* Infml

rump 1. n. buttocks ex M. Dutch = stump C15- Std. 2. v. copulate ex n. C18–20* Sl

rump splitter penis ex **rump** C17–19* Sl

rump work sexual intercourse ex **rump** C19–20* Sl

Russian duck copulate (animal, foreign) C20 R.Sl (fuck)

rut copulate ex deer (animal) C17- Sl/Infml

S

saddle female genitals ex shape cf **ride** C17–20* Infml

safe condom ex protection against conception C19 Infml

saint's delight vagina cf **delight, heaven** (religion) C19- Infml

salami penis ex sausage shape cf **meat** (food) C20 Sl

sally fellatio ex sally = suck (name) C20 SAfr Sl

salt 1. copulate pun on necessary substance, experienced sailor, flavoring (food) C17–18* Sl. 2. lust ex 1. cf **saucy** C16- Lit/Infml

salt-cellar vagina ex container, **salt** C19* Sl

Sam masculinity esp among homosexuals (name) C20 Sl

sample copulate cf **taste** (eating) C19- Infml

sampler female genitals ex **sample** C19–20* Sl

sandwich threesome sexual arrangement ex *lay*ers (food) C19- Sl

Sapphism lesbianism ex Sappho, Greek poetess (name) C19- Std/Lit/Fml

sard copulate ?ex Lat = fish (animal, food) C10–17* Infml/Sl

saucy lusty cf **juicy** C16- Lit/Infml

say high mass fellate ex kneeling cf **kneel at the altar** (religion) C20 gay Sl

scale copulate sd of men cf **jump, leap** C17–20* Infml/Lit

scarf up   perform fellatio or cunnilingus ex scarf Sl = eat C20 Sl

scarlet woman   prostitute ex Bible, scarlet = red C16- Std/Fml

schlong   penis ex Yid/Ger = snake (animal) C19- Sl

schmuck   penis ex Yid = ornament C19- Sl/Derog

schwantz   penis ex Yid/Ger = tail (animal) C19- Sl

score   copulate ex success (sport) C20 Infml

scratch   female genitals ?ex **cut, itch** C20 Sl

screw   1. v. copulate ex Std sense = rotate into (aggression) C18- Sl. 2. n. person as sex partner ex v. C19- Sl

screwdriver   penis ex **screw** C20* Sl

screw some ass   1. copulate cf **screw, ass** C20 Sl. 2. perform anal inter-course cf **screw, ass** C20 Sl

scrotum   sac containing testicles ex Lat *scrautum* = sheath for arrows C16- Std

scum   semen ex matter in liquid C20 Sl/Derog

scum bag   condom ex **scum, bag** C20 Sl

scut   1. female pubes ex **rabbit's tail, fur** (animal) C16–20* Sl. 2. female genitals ex 1. (animal) C16–20* Sl

scuttle   deflower ex Std nautical sense = make a hole in C19–20* Infml

seal   make pregnant cf **sew up** C19–20* Sl

seals   testicles ex **seal** C19–20* Infml

seed   semen ex OE C13- Std/Fml

seed plot   vagina ex **seed** (reproduction) C19–20* Infml

see madame thumb and her four daughters   masturbate sd of men ex use of fingers cf **mount the corporal and four fingers** C19–20* Sl/Joc

see one's aunt(ie)/friend   menstruation ex busy, occupied (family) C19- Infml/Euph

see stars lying on one's back   copulate sd of women pun on looking upward, being knocked out C19–20* Infml/Joc

self-abuse   masturbation ex opinion that it is unhealthy, sinful C19- Fml/Joc

semen   testicular liquid containing sperm ex Lat *serere* = sow C14- Std

semiglobes   breasts ex shape cf **globes, hemispheres** C19- Infml

sensitive spot   clitoris ex excitatory organ C19* Infml

service   1. copulate ex serving, prostitution C20 Sl/Euph. 2. perform fellatio or cunnlingus ex 1. C20 gay Sl. 3. perform anal intercourse ex 1. C20 gay Sl

services   sexual intercourse pun on commerce, religion C17- Euph

settlement in tail, make a   copulate sd of men ex **tail** = genitals C19–20* Joc

sew up   1. copulate cf **stitch** (clothing) C19–20* Sl. 2. make pregnant ex. 1. (clothing) C19–20* Sl

sexual intercourse   copulation ex Lat C17- Std/Fml

sexual science   sexual intercourse cf **art of pleasure, knowledge** C19* Joc/Infml

Seymour   femininity in male homosexuals ex sissy sounding (name) C20 heterosexual Sl/Joc

shaft in the bum   perform anal intercourse ex **bum** C20 Sl

shag   1. copulate ?ex sense of exhaustion, hair or *shake C18- Infml. 2. masturbate ex 1. C18–20* Infml

shag bag 1. woman as sex object, originally = lowly fellow ex **shag, bag** C19-Derog/Sl. 2. vagina ex **shag, bag** C20 Sl

shake 1. copulate ex movement C16–20* Sl. 2. masturbate sd of men ex 1. C16–20* Sl

shake bag vagina ex **shake, bag** C19–20* Sl

shake up masturbate ex **shake** C19–20* Sl

shape vagina ex *the* shape cf **monosyllable** C18* Euph

sharp and blunt vagina cf **cut** C19- R.Sl (cunt)

shaving brush female pubes ex **bushy** C19* Sl

sheath 1. vagina ex Lat *vagina* = sheath C18* Euph. 2. condom ex shape C19- Infml

shell female genitals pun on container, egg C19–20 Infml

she-male/she-man lesbian C20 heterosexual Sl

shitter anus ex shit = feces C20 Sl

shoot ejaculate ex Std sense = eject, discharge cf **fire** (aggression) C19- Infml

Shooter's hill female genitals pun on **shoot**, mons pubis (name) C19–20* Joc

shoot in the bush/over the stubble ejaculation before insertion of penis ex **bush, stubble** C19- Infml

shoot in the tail 1. copulate sd of men cf **shoot, tail** 2. C19- Sl. 2. perform anal intercourse cf **tail** 1. C19- Sl

shoot one's load ejaculate ex **shoot, load** C20 Sl

short and curlies pubes ex short curly hair C20 Infml

short-arm penis ex short-arm = general inspection in army (body) C20 Sl

shove copulate sd of men ex Std sense = push with force C17–20* Infml

shrimp 1. prostitute (animal, food) C17* Lit. 2. penis esp small one ex shrivelled (animal, food) C20 Sl

shrine of love vagina ex adoration (religion) C19* Lit/Euph

shrubbery female pubes cf **bush** C19- Infml

shtup copulate sd of men ex Yid = push cf **shove** C19- Sl

silent beard female pubes cf **beard** C17–19* Joc/Infml

silent flute penis cf **flute** (music) C18–19* Sl/Infml

simple infanticide masturbation cf **infanticide** (death) C19–20* Joc

siren seductive woman ex Gr myth of nymphs who lured sailors and their ships onto rocks C14- Std/Lit

sister of the night prostitute ex night employment (family) C19* Euph

sit on the fence bisexual ex between choosing either sex, undecided C20 Sl/Infml

six to four prostitute C20 R.Sl (whore)

sixty nine (69) mutual oral sex ex ideograph-69 C19- Infml

skin 1. female genitals cf **flesh** (body) C17- Sl/Euph. 2. condom ex sheath C19- Sl/Infml

skin-coat female genitals ex **skin** (body, clothing) C17–18* Infml

skin dive perform cunnilingus ex **skin, dive** C20 Sl

skin room Turkish bath, meeting place for male homosexuals ex naked bodies C20 Sl

skirt woman ex what is worn (clothing) C16–19 Std C19- Sl/Infml

skull pussy fellator ex skull = head, mouth; **pussy** C20 gay Sl

slacks lesbian ex pants = male fashion cf **skirt** (clothing) C20* Sl

slap and tickle sexual intercourse ex foreplay C20 Sl/Infml

sleep with copulate ex lie in bed with C16- Euph

slip (a length) copulate sd of men ex move smoothly, length of **yard** C19- Sl

slit vulva ex shape C17- Infml/Euph

sloppy seconds second man to copulate with woman/man already had ex wetness, second turn C20 Sl/Joc

sluice vagina ex channel C17–20* Sl/Infml

slut sexually promiscuous woman C14- Std/Derog

smoke copulate ex heat generated cf **fire** C17–19* Sl

snake penis pun on shape, in grass = pubes (animal) C20 Sl

snatch 1. hasty sexual intercourse C17–20* Sl. 2. vagina ex 1. pun on seizure C19- Sl

snippet vagina ?ex **cut** C19–20* Sl

snog caress cf **nug**, C20 Infml

snug copulate cf **nug** C19–20* Infml

social disease venereal disease pun on social = of people, friendly C20 Infml/Joc

sodomite man who commits **sodomy** C14- Std/Fml

sodomy anal intercourse with man or woman ex Bible, Sodom = evil town (name) C13- Std

soixante neuf mutual oral sex ex Fr = sixty nine, 69 ideographically C19- Infml/Lit

soldier's joy masturbation sd of men ex no/few women in army cf **joy** C19–20* Sl

south-end buttocks ex direction C20 Sl

sow 1. woman (animal) C19- Sl/Derog. 2. male homosexual esp fat one (animal) C20 Sl

sow one's (wild) oats copulate sd of young men pun on **plough** C16- Std/Infml

speak low Genitalese perform fellatio or cunnilingus ex language, oral activity C20 gay Sl/Joc

spend ejaculate ex payment C16- Sl

spender vagina ex container of **spendings** C18–19* Sl

spendings semen or vaginal fluid ex payment, passing of time C16- Sl

sperm male reproductive cells (also **spermatozoa**) ex Gr C14- Std

spindle penis ex **rod** C19–20* Sl/Infml

split copulate sd of men ex Std sense = divide, break C18- Sl

split mutton 1. penis ex **split**, **mutton** (food) C17–19* Sl. 2. woman as sex object ex 1. (food) C18–20* Sl

split someone's buns perform anal intercourse ex **buns** C20 Sl

spoil a woman's shape make pregnant, pun on **shape** C17- Infml

spoon caress sentimentally ?ex n. = *fool C19- Infml

sporran pubes ex **fur** pouch C19–20* Sl

sport 1. sexual intercourse pun on pastime, **game** C19–20* Sl. 2. male prostitute ?ex 1. C20 Sl

sporting house brothel ex **sport**, house C19–20* Sl

sport of Cupid's archery/Venus vagina ex **sport**, gods of love, archery, cf **shoot**, **arrow** C18* Lit/Euph

spunk semen ex courage cf **mettle** C19- Infml

squirrel 1. prostitute ex **fur** (animal) C18–19* Sl. 2. female genitals ex 1. C19- Sl

stab in the thigh copulate sd of men (aggression, body) C19–20* Infml/ Euph

stalk penis cf **root** C16–17* Lit

stand erection ex erect C16- Infml

standup and cheer/shout orgasm sd of females pun on applause, reaching end C20 Sl/Joc

starch semen, ex appearance pun on stiffness = erection C19- Sl

star-gazer erect penis ex facing up C18–20* Sl

steamy lusty cf **sweaty** C20 Infml

stem penis ex shape cf **root**, **stalk** C19* Sl

stern buttocks ex rear of ship C16- Joc/Infml

stern job, do a perform anal intercourse, pun on rear, austere C20 Sl/Joc

stew(s) brothel ex bath C14–20* Std/Infml

stick 1. n. penis ex shape C17- Sl. 2. v. copulate sd of men pun on n., jam, stand C19–20* Sl

sticky semen pun on **stick**, texture C20 Sl

stiff erect penis ex hardness C17- Sl

sting penis cf **prick** (aggression) C19–20 Sl

stir caress C16- Lit/Infml

stir fudge/someone's chocolate perform anal intercourse ex fudge, chocolate = feces (food) C20 Sl

stitch copulate sd of men cf **prick** (clothing) C18–20* Sl

stoneache pain in the testicles due to inability to ejaculate ex **stones** cf **blueballs** C20 Sl

stones testicles ex shape C12–19 Std C19- Sl/Infml

storked pregnant ex symbol of stork deliverying baby (animal) C20 Infml

stormy Dick penis ex stormy, **dick** (name) C20 US R.Sl (prick)

straight heterosexual cf **bent** C19- Infml

strawberries nipples pun on color, shape (food) C20 Sl

strawberry patch red pubes ex red patch C20 Sl

streetwalker prostitute ex soliciting C19- Infml

stretch leather copulate ex result of **leather** = female genitals C18–20* Sl

strum copulate sd of men ex fingering (music) C18–20* Sl

strumpet prostitute C14- Std/Fml

stubble female pubes cf **hair** C18- Infml

stud virile man esp male prostitute ex male animal used for breeding C20 Sl/Infml

study astronomy copulate esp sd of women ex looking up cf **see stars lying on one's back** C20 Euph/Infml

stuff 1. v. copulate sd of men ex Std sense = cram, fill. 2. n. semen ex 1. C19- Sl

stump   penis ex shape cf **root, stem** C17- Sl
suck   perform fellatio or cunnilingus ex oral activity cf **eat** C19- Sl
suck and swallow   vagina ex suck penis, swallow semen (eating) C19–20* Sl
suck ass(hole)   perform anilingus ex **suck, ass(hole)** C20 Sl
sugar basin   vagina ex container, sweetness C19–20* Sl
sugar stick   penis ex sweetness, shape (food) C19–20* Sl
supper   female genitals pun on evening meal (eating) C19–20* Sl
swallow a sword   fellate ex **sword, eat** C20 Sl
sweaty   lusty ex sweat cf **wet** C18- Infml
sweet agony/death   sexual intercourse cf **die** C18* Lit
swing both ways/swingy   bisexual ex both ways = both sexes C20 Sl
swinge   copulate sd of men ex *beat (aggression) C16–18* Sl
swive   copulate ex OE = swivel, revolve C14–16 Std C17–18* Infml
sword   penis cf **weapon** (aggression) C16- Lit/Infml
syph/siph/siff   abbr for syphilis C19- Infml

T

tail   1. n. buttocks ex position in animal (body, animal) Std C14–18 C18-
   Infml/Sl. 2. n. female genitals ex 1. Std C14 —18 C18- Infml/Sl. 3. n. penis
   ex shape Std C14–18 C18- Infml/Sl. 4. v. copulate ex n. C18–20* Sl. 5. n.
   prostitute ex 2. C18–19* Sl
tail feathers   female pubes ex **tail** 2   C17–19* Infml
tail gap/gate/hole   see **tail** 2
tail juice   semen ex **tail** 3   C17–19* Infml
tail pike/pin/pipe/tackle   see **tail** 3
tail tickling/wagging/work   sexual intercourse ex **tail** 2, 3, & 4   C18–19*
   Infml/Sl
take (someone)   copulate sd of men cf **occupy** C16- Lit/Fml
take a slice   copulate sd of men cf **cake** (food) C17–20* Lit/Joc
take a trip to the moon   perform anilingus ex **moon** = buttocks C20 Sl
take down   masturbate sd of men ?ex ridding an erection C20 Sl
take in beef/cream   copulate sd of women ex beef = penis, **cream** = semen
   (food) C19–20 Sl
take Nebuchadnezzar out to grass   copulate sd of men ex **Nebuchadnezzar,**
   grass = green(s) = sexual intercourse, pubes (name) C19–20* Sl
take the starch out of   copulate sd of women ex **starch** = semen C19–20* Sl
tale of two cities   breasts ex Dickens Lit title C20 R.Sl (titties)
talk   copulate ex communicate C16–17* Lit/Euph
tallywag   penis ?ex Lat = cutting, ?score, label; wag? = hang C18–20* Infml
tallywags   testicles ?ex **tallywag**, ?hanging C18–20* Infml
tantrum   penis ex rage, fit C17–19* Lit
target   vagina cf **arrow, shoot, bull's eye** C19* Infml
tart   1. sexually promiscuous woman ex woman in general ex sweet pastry
   (food) C19- Std/Infml. 2. prostitute ex 1. C20 Infml/Sl
tassel   penis, esp small one ex hanging sense C20 Sl

taste copulate ex undergo, try cf **sample** (eating) C16–17* Lit/Euph

tasty sexually inviting (eating) C19- Infml

teahouse/room public lavatory for male homosexual cruising cf **cottage** C20 Euph

teats nipples ex O.Fr and Ger C13- Std/Fml

teazle vagina ex teasel = plant, pun on tease C19–20* Sl

tender agony sexual intercourse cf **sweet agony** C18* Lit

tenuc female genitals ex back slang of **cun(e)t** C19–20* Sl

testicles two male reproductive glands in scrotum ex Lat *testiculus*, diminutive of *testis* = witness (of virility) C15- Std

thatch female pubes ex **hair** C18–19* Infml/Sl

thatched house vagina ex container, **thatch** C18–19* Sl

thatched house under the hill vagina ex **thatched house, mons pubis** C18–19* Lit/Sl

that there sexual intercourse cf **it** C19- Br Dial/Euph

that way (inclined) homosexual C20 heterosexual Euph

thighs/thigh sandwich intercourse between the thighs close together (food) C20 Sl

thing genitals cf **it** C17- Sl/Euph

thingstable female genitals ex **thing**, *con*stable C17* Joc/Lit

thingumbobs testicles ex **thing**, bobs = hanging pun on unnamed things C18–19* Sl/Euph

third sex homosexuality ex first and second sex C20 Infml

third way anal intercourse ex first and second way = intercourse, oral sex C20 gay Sl

thirty-nine (39) anilingus ex ideograph 3 = buttocks cf **69** C20 Sl

Thomas penis cf **tom, John Thomas** (name) C17- Sl

thorn penis cf **prick** (aggression) C16–17* Lit

thousand pities breasts C19–20* R.Sl (titties)

thread the needle copulate sd of men ex thread entering **eye** of needle (clothing) C19–20* Sl

threepenny bits breasts ex roundness C20 R.Sl (tits)

three way threesome sexual arrangement C20 Infml

thrill orgasm ex OE *thyrlian* = to pierce ex excitement C20 Infml/Sl

throw a leg over copulate esp sd of men cf **mount** (body) C19–20* Infml

throw up ejaculate ex of semen C19–20* Sl

thrum copulate sd of men ex fingering (music) C17–19* Sl

thump copulate, sd of men (aggression, sound) C17–20* Infml

tickle caress ex Lat = titillate C14- Infml

tickle-tail 1. penis ex **tickle, tail** C17–20* Sl. 2. prostitute ex **tickle, tail** C18–20* Sl

tickle–Thomas vagina ex **tickle, Thomas** = penis (name) C19–20* Sl

tickle-toby penis ex **tickle, toby** (name) C17–19* Sl

tickle your fancy male homosexual cf **tickle, fancy piece** C20 R.Sl (nancy = female name)

tick-tack sexual intercourse ?ex aggression, sport, or sound C16- Infml

tidbit/titbit female genitals ex tasty piece of food C17–18* Sl/Infml

till   female genitals ex **money, box** C19- Sl

tillage   sexual intercourse sd of men ex sowing crops C16–17* Lit

tilting   sexual intercourse sd of men ex thrust of pole (sport) C16–17* Lit

tip the velvet   perform cunnilingus pun on **velvet** = tongue, vagina C17–20*
Sl

tit   1. nipple ex teat C17- Sl/Dial. 2. breast ex 1. C18- Sl. 3. prostitute
C19–20*   Sl. 4. female genitals ?ex 3. or tit = horse, girl C18–20* Sl

titmouse   female genitals ?ex **tit** 4. ?ex smallness (animal) C17–18* Sl

tits   breasts ex **tit** 2. C19- Sl

tittie-oggie/titty-oggy   fellatio ex **tit** implying sucking C19–20* Sl

titty   1. breast ex **tit** 2. C19- Sl/Infml 2. heterosexual intercourse ex female
partner (body) C20 gay Sl

tiv(v)y   female genitals ex activity C19–20* Sl

toby   1. buttocks (name) C17- Sl/Infml. 2. female genitals (name) C17–20*
Sl

tom   1.v copulate sd of men ex male of certain animals (animal) C19–20*
Infml. 2. lesbian ex male name (name) C20 Sl

Tommy Rollicks   testicles (name) C19- R.Sl (bollocks)

tongue   perform cunnilingus or fellatio ex **lick** C20 Infml

tongue fuck   perform anilingus ex **tongue, fuck** C20 gay Sl

tool   penis ex instrument C16–18 Std C19- Infml

top ballocks   breasts ex round like ballocks but at top part of torso (body)
C19–20* Sl

top buttocks   breasts cf **top ballocks** (body) C19–20* Sl

toss off   masturbate sd of men ex movement cf **jerk off** C18- Sl

touch up   1. caress ex fingering C18- Infml. 2. copulate sd of men ex 1.
C18–19* Infml. 3. masturbate ex 1. C19–20* Infml.

toupee   1. female pubes ex **hair** C18–20* Joc. 2. merkin 1. artificial hair
C18–19* Joc

towns and cities   breasts C20* R.Sl (titties)

toy   1. n. vagina cf **play, game** C14- Lit/Sl. 2. v. caress cf **play** C16-
Lit/Infml

tracy bits   breasts ?ex tracy = three cf **threepenny bits** C20 Austr R.Sl (tits)

trading   sexual intercourse cf **commerce** C16–17* Lit/Euph

traffic   1. prostitute ex circulation C16–17* Lit/Infml. 2. sexual intercourse
?ex 1. C16- Lit/Infml

trapstick   penis, ex **stick** that traps C17–19* Lit/Infml

tray bits   breasts ?ex tray = three cf **threepenny bits** C20* Aust. R.Sl (tits)

treason   sexual intercourse ex adultery C17–19* Lit/Joc

treasury   vagina ex value cf **jewel case** C16–17* Lit/Joc

tree of life/love   penis cf **stem** (reproduction) C19* Lit/Fml

tribadism   lesbianism ex Gr *tribein* = rub C17- Std/Fml

trick   1. n. prostitute's customer ex deceit C20 Sl. 2. v. copulate sd of
women ex n. C20 Sl

Trojan   condom ex brand trademark ?ex trustworthy C20 Infml/Euph

trollop   1. sexually promiscuous women ?ex Ger *trolle* = prostitute C17- Std.
2. prostitute ex 1. C18- Infml

trombone   penis ex shape, sliding in and out, **bone** (music) C19* Sl

trout   vagina ?ex **peculiar river** cf **fish** (food, animal) 17* Lit

trull   prostitute ex Ger *trolle* = prostitute C16–19* Infml

tubs   baths esp Turkish bath where homosexual men meet ex tub = bath C20 Sl

tumble   copulate ex Std sense = toss about C16- Lit/Infml

turk   active male homosexual ?ex Turkish soldiers practicing sodomy in 19th century (foreign) C20 Sl

turn   copulation esp in phrases **to take a turn in** ... C19- Infml

turnip   glans, head of penis ex shape (food) C20 Sl

turn on   sexually arouse ex switch on C19- Infml

turnpike   vagina pun on gate, passage, **pike** C18–19* Infml

turns   menstruation ex cycle C19- Infml

turrets   breasts ex towers, guns C16–17* Lit

tush(y)   buttocks ex Yid *tochis* C19- Sl/Infml

twang   copulate ex sound of plucked string cf **thrum** (sound) C17–18* Sl

twat   female genitals ex OE = passage ?ex two (labia) C17- Derog/Sl

twatchel/twachel   variants of **twat** C17–19* Sl

twat rug   female pubes ex **twat** C20* Sl

twinkle toes   passive male homosexual cf **angel, fairy** C20 Sl

twit   passive male homosexual ex fool C20 heterosexual Sl/Derog

twixt wind and water   vagina ex between anus and urethral opening (body) C17–20* Lit/Joc

two-backed beast, do the   copulate ex Rabelais, forming two backs (animal) C16–19* Lit/Infml

two by four   prostitute C20 US R.Sl (whore)

twofer   prostitute ?ex two cf **twat** ?ex two-timing = deceiving C19–20* Sl

two-way baby   bisexual ex two ways = male and female C20 Sl

U

udders   breasts ex animal teats C18- Derog/Sl/Joc

uncle   1. penis cf **big brother** (family) C19–20* Sl. 2. elderly male homosexual (family) C20 Sl

uncle Dick   penis cf **dick** (name, family) C20 R.Sl (prick)

undergo   copulate esp sd of women pun on experience, go under C16–17* Joc/Lit

underpetticoating, go   copulate sd of men ex underclothes (clothing) C17–19* Sl

understand   copulate sd of women pun on under**stand** = erection and understand = **know** C16–17* Joc/Lit

undertake   copulate esp sd of women pun on take from under, commit to do C16–17* Joc/Lit

undertaker   vagina ex **undertake** (death) C18–19* Joc/Infml

unfortunate   prostitute ex unfortunate circumstances C18–19* Euph

union   sexual intercourse ex joining cf **congress** C15- Fml/Euph

unit   penis pun on one, equipment C20 Sl

unsliced bologna   uncircumcised penis ex bologna = sausage (food) C20 Sl

up   1. erect penis cf **stand, stiff** C19- Infml. 2. sexual intercourse sd of men ex having it up a woman C19- Sl

upper works   breasts cf lower parts = genitals C19* Joc/Infml

upright   sexual intercourse in standing position cf **perpendicular** C18- Sl

upright grand   erect penis, pun on piano = organ, upright = erect C20 Sl/Joc

upright grin/wink   female genitals cf **grin, eye** C19* Sl/Joc

up the duff/spout   pregnant ex spoilt C20 Sl/Infml

uranian   male homosexual ex Gr = heavenly C20 Lit/Fml

V

vacuum   vagina ?ex **nothing, hole** C18–19* Infml

vacuum cleaner   cunnilinguist ex **vacuum** suction C20 Sl

vagina   female copulatory organ ex Lat = sheath C17- Std

valve   female genitals ?ex **vulva** C19–20* Sl

Vatican roulette   natural contraception based on menstrual cycles ex Vatican = catholic practice, roulette = gamble C20 Infml/Joc

vault   copulate sd of men cf **jump, scale** C16–17* Lit/Infml

VD   abbr for venereal disease C20 Infml

vegetable   lesbian ex parallel with **fruit** = male homosexual (food) C20 gay Sl

vegetarian   male homosexual who will not fellate, ex limited diet C20 gay Sl

velvet (sheath)   vagina ex smoothness cf **sheath** C17–19* Sl

venery   sexual sport, pun on hunting, game (aggression) C15- Fml/Lit

venture   copulate pun on try, adventure C17* Lit

Venus's glove   vagina ex glove = tight fit, Venus = Roman goddess of love (clothing, name) C16–17* Lit

Venus's highway   vagina ex Roman goddess of love, passage cf **main avenue** C18–19* Fml

Venus's mark   female genitals cf **mark** (name) C19–20* Infml

vibrator   vibrating dildo ex battery power C20 Std

vice   vagina pun on grip, sin C16–17* Lit

vice versa   mutual oral sex ex both ways cf **vice** C20 Sl

Victoria Monk   semen (name, religion) C19–20* R.Sl (spunk)

virgin   person esp a woman never having had sexual intercourse ex Lat C13- Std

vitals   genitals ex importance, essence C19- Euph

vitamins   semen ex life-giving quality (food) C20 Sl

voluptuous   sexually arousing ex Lat = pleasure C14- Std

vulva   external female genitals ex Lat = womb C16- Std/Med

W

wad   semen ?ex wadge = lumpy mass C20 Sl

wallet   vagina ex container, **money** cf **purse** C18–20* Sl

wand   penis pun on shape, magic cf **fairy** C20 gay Sl

wang   penis ?ex whang = thong, strike (sound, aggression) C20 Sl

wank (off)   masturbate ?ex whang = strike C19- Sl

wanton   lusty ex desire C13- Std/Fml

ware   female genitals cf **commodity, merchandise** C18–19* Sl

warren   brothel ex **rabbit** = **cunny** colony C17–19* Joc/Sl

washer   condom ex **plumbing** C20 Sl/Infml

waste pipe   vagina ex passage C18–19* Derog/Sl

water engine/works   penis or urethral opening in women ex urine C19- Infml

water sports   urination in sexual activity ex urine, **sport** C20 Sl

weapon   penis (aggression) C16- Lit/Sl

wear bifocals   bisexual ex two focuses cf **bi** C20 Sl/Euph

weewee   penis or urethral opening in female, ex wee = urine C19- child's Infml

wench   young woman ex OE = child, weak C13- Std/Infml

western end   buttocks ex direction C19–20* Sl

wet   lusty esp sd of women ex genital arousal cf **juicy** C18- Sl/Infml

wet bottom, do a   copulate sd of women ex lubrication (body) C19–20* Sl

wet decks   sd of women having just copulated cf **buttered bun** C18- Sl

wet dream   nocturnal emission of semen ex wetness C19- Infml

whack off   masturbate ?ex whack = strike C20 Sl

whang   variant of **wang**

whank   variant of **wank**

wheel   vulva ex circle C16–17* Lit

whelk   female genitals cf **oyster** (animal) C19–20* Joc/Sl

whim   female genitals ex impulsive thought C18–20* Lit/Joc

whim-wham   female genitals cf **whim** C18–20* Lit/Joc

whipped cream   nocturnal emission of semen cf **cream** (food) C20 Sl/Infml

whirlygigs   testicles ex toy, top, whirl C17–19* Infml

whistle   1. penis cf **flute** (music) C19- Infml. 2. fellate cf **blow** C20 gay Sl

white meat   genitals of white man or woman, cf **meat** (food) C20 Sl

whole   vagina pun on **hole**, complete C16–17* Lit/Joc

wholesale   prostitution pun on **hole**, sale C16–17* Lit/Joc

whole voyage   sexual intercourse pun on going all the way C16–17* Lit/Euph

whomp it up   fellate ex sound (eating) C20 Sl

whore   prostitute ex Lat *carus* = dear OE- Std

whorehouse   brothel ex **whore**, house C16- Std/Sl

whoremonger   sexually promiscuous man ex **whore** C16- Std/Fml

whore-pipe   penis ex **whore, pipe** 2. C18–19* Sl

whore's milk   semen cf **milk, whore** C20 Sl

wicket   female genitals ex casement ?pun on wicked C18–19* Infml

wide open beaver   pornographic photographs of female genitals ex **beaver** = female genitals (animal) C20 Sl

widow's comforter   dildo ex **comfort** cf **lady's friend** C19- Euph/Infml

wiener   penis, ex wiener sausage pun on wee = urine, small (food) C20 Sl

wife in watercolors   mistress pun on "dissolving" wife, not permanent C18-19* Infml/Joc

wig   female pubes cf **hair, toupee** C18-19* Joc

willing   sexually available C14- Std

willy   1. penis cf **weewee** (name) C20 child's Infml. 2. passive male homosexual ?ex 1. (name) C20 heterosexual Sl

win   copulate ex success C16-17* Lit

winds do whirl   woman ?ex flightly C19-20* R.Sl (girl)

wind up the cock   copulate ?ex *Tristram Shandy* pun on habit, keep going C18-19* Lit/Joc

winkle   penis cf **weewee** C19-20* child's Infml

wire   penis ex length cf **pull wire** C20 Sl

wired up   sexually willing, lusty ex electrically connected C20 Sl

wolf   1. n. active lesbian ex seduction (animal) C20 gay Sl. 2. v. perform anal intercourse (aggression, animal) C20 gay Sl. 3. male homosexual ex male flirt (animal) C20 Sl

woman's terms   menstruation cf **Eve's curse** C16-17* Lit

woollies   pubes ex wool cf **plush** C20 Sl

wop   penis ?ex sound, whopper = large one C20 Sl

work it off   masturbate cf **jerk off** C20 Sl

workshop   female genitals ex place in which to work cf **gymnasium** C18-19* Sl

work up   copulate sd of men pun on penetrating, laboring C19- Infml

world   breast ex sphere C16-17* Lit

world's smallest hotel   vagina, ex leaving **bags** = testicles outside cf **hotel** C20 Joc

worm   penis ex shape cf **snake** (animal) C20 Sl

wormeater   fellator ex **worm, eat** C20 Sl

worship at the altar   fellate ex kneeling cf **kneel at the altar** (religion) C20 gay Sl

wound   female genitals cf **gash**, pun on appearance, bleeding C16-19* Lit

wounded in the thigh   deflowered ex piercing (body) C16-17* Lit/Euph

wreck a rectum   perform anal intercourse ex harm to rectum C20 Sl

wrench off   masturbate sd of men cf **jerk off, plumbing** C20 Sl

wriggle navels   copulate ex movement (body) C18-20* Infml/Euph

wrinkle   female genitals ex **furrow** (body) C20* Sl

wrong door   anus cf **back door** C18* Lit/Joc

Y

yard   penis ex measure, *measuring rod C14-19* Lit/Euph

yawn   vagina ex open mouth C20 Sl

yentz   copulate ex Yid = that (thing), cheat C19- Sl
yoni   female genitals ex Sanskrit cf **lingam** C18- Lit
yummy it down   fellate ex eating with relish (food) C20 Sl
yum-yum   genitals ex delicious, tasty (eating) C20 Sl

Z

zigzig   copulate ex movement cf **jig-jig** (dance) C19–20* Sl/Euph

BIBLIOGRAPHY

Below is a selection of books, dictionaries and articles consulted while writing this book.

Abelman, P. *The Mouth and Oral Sex*. Runningman Press, 1969.

Aman, R. "On the Etymology of Gay." *Maledicta*, III, 2, 1979.

Ash, M. "The Vulva: a Psycholinguistic Problem." *Maledicta*, IV, 2, 1980.

Ashley, L.R.N. "Kinks and Queens." *Maledicta*, III, 2, 1979.

_____. "Lovely, Blooming, Fresh and Gay." *Maledicta*, IV, 2, 1980.

Bailey, N. *Universal Etymological Dictionary*. 1721.

Barltrop, R., and Wolveridge, J. *The Muvver Tongue*. Journeyman, 1980.

Barnhart, C.L. *A Dictionary of New English*. 1973.

_____. *The Second Barnhart Dictionary of New English*. 1980.

Bataille, G. *Eroticism*. City Lights, 1986.

Beigel, H.G. *Sex from A to Z*. Panther, 1961.

Berger, P.L., and Luckmann, T. *The Social Construction of Reality*. Doubleday, 1966.

Branford, J. *Dictionary of South African English*. Oxford University Press, 1980.

Bristo, A. *The Sex Life of Plants*. Barrie & Jenkins, 1978.

Chambers 20th Century Dictionary. 1983.

Charney, M. *Sexual Fiction*. Methuen, 1981.

Claire, E. *Dangerous English*. Eardley Publications, 1980.

Collins Dictionary of the English Language. 1979

Colman, E.A.M. *The Dramatic Use of Bawdy in Shakespeare*. Longman, 1974.

Comfort, A. *The Joy of Sex*. Crown, 1972.

Dally, P. *The Fantasy Game*. Avon, 1976.

Daly, M. *Gyn/Ecology*. Beacon, 1979.

Doke, C.M., and Vilakazi, B.W. *Zulu-English Dictionary*. 1964

Douglas, M. *Purity and Danger*. Methuen, 1984.

Eisiminger, S. "Colorful Language." *Verbatim*, IV, 1, 1979.

Farmer, J.S., and Henley, W.E. *Slang and Its Analogues* (1904). Reprinted by Kraus.

Foucault, M. *The History of Sexuality*. Vol. 1. Pantheon, 1978.

Franklin, J. *A Dictionary of Rhyming Slang*. Routledge & Kegan Paul, 1960.

Freud, S. *The Complete Psychological Works*. Norton, 1976.

Fryer, P. *Mrs Grundy: Studies in English Prudery*. Corgi, 1965.

_____. *Private Case — Public Scandal*. Secker & Warburg, 1966.

Grose, F. *Dictionary of the Vulgar Tongue* (1811). Reprinted by Ayer, 1963.

Hankey, C. "Naming the Vulvar Part." *Maledicta*, IV, 2, 1980.

Harrap's French-English Dictionary of Slang and Colloquialism. 1970.

Harrison, F. *The Dark Angel*. Sheldon Press, 1977.

147

Healey, T. "A New Erotic Vocabulary." *Maledicta*, IV, 2, 1980.

Henke, J.T. *Courtesans and Cuckolds*. Garland Press, 1979.

Jay, T.B. "Sex Roles and Dirty Word Usage: A Review of the Literature and a Reply to Haas." *Psychological Bulletin*, 88, 3, 1980.

Johnson, S. *A Dictionary of the English Language* (1755). Reprinted by Ayer, 1980.

Kearney, P.S. *The Private Case*. Landesman, 1981.

Lakoff, G., and Johnson, M. *Metaphors We Live By*. University of Chicago Press, 1980.

Landau, S.I. "Sexual Intercourse in American College Dictionaries." *Verbatim* 1:1, 1974.

Landy, E.E. *The Underground Dictionary*. Simon & Schuster, 1971.

Maledicta: The International Journal of Verbal Aggression, 1977–.

Marcus, S. *The Other Victorians*. Norton, 1985.

Miller, C., and Swift, K. *Words and Women*. Doubleday, 1977.

Moers, E. *Literary Women*. Oxford University Press, 1985.

Montagu, A. *The Anatomy of Swearing*. MacMillan, 1967.

Morris, D. *The Human Zoo*. Dell, 1970.

Niemueller, A.F. *American Encyclopaedia of Sex*. Panurge Press, 1935.

Oxford Dictionary of English Etymology. Clarendon Press, 1969.

Oxford English Dictionary with new Supplements.

Paros, L. *The Erotic Tongue*. Madrona Publishers, 1984.

Partridge, E. *Dictionary of Historial Slang*. Penguin, 1972.

_____. *Dictionary of Slang and Unconventional English*. Macmillan, 1985.

_____. *Here There and Everywhere*. Hamish Hamilton, 1950.

_____. *Shakespeare's Bawdy*. Routledge & Kegan Paul, 1968.

_____. *Slang Today and Yesterday*. Methuen, 1970.

_____. *Usage and Abusage*. Penguin, 1963.

Pothermus, T. (ed.). *Social Aspects of the Human Body*. Penguin, 1978.

Pythian, B.A. *A Concise Dictionary of English Slang*. Hodder & Stoughton, 1973.

Rainbird, E. *The Illustrated Manual of Sexual Aids*. Minotaur Press, 1973.

Random House College Dictionary. 1982.

Rawson H. *A Dictionary of Euphemisms and Other Doubletalk*. MacDonald & Co., 1981.

Rodgers, B. *Gaytalk*. Paragon Books, 1972.

Rossi, W.A. *The Sex Life of the Foot and Shoe*. Ballantine Books, 1978.

Rosten, L. *The Joys of Yiddish*. McGraw, 1968.

Sagarin, E. *The Anatomy of Dirty Words*. Lyle Stuart, 1962.

Silverstein, C., and White, E. *The Joy of Gay Sex*. Simon & Schuster, 1978.

Simons, G.L. *A Place for Pleasure*. Harwood Smart, 1975.

The Slang of Venery. Privately published, 1916, British Library.

Spears, R. *Slang and Euphemism*. Jonathan David, 1981.

Spender, D. *Man Made Language*. Methuen, 1985.

Sulloway, F.T. *Freud: Biologist of the Mind*. Basic Books, 1983.

Tannahill, R. *Sex in History*. Stein & Day, 1982.

Thass-Thienemann, T. *The Subconscious Language*. Washington Square Press, 1967.

The Visual Dictionary of Sex. Pan, 1978.

Webster's Ninth Collegiate Dictionary. Merriam-Webster, 1983.

Webster's Third New International Dictionary. Merriam-Webster, 1976.

Wentworth, H., and Flexner, S.B. *Dictionary of American Slang*. Crowell, 1960.

Wilson, R. *Playboy's Book of Forbidden Words*. Playboy Press, 1972.

Wright, P. *The Language of British Industry*. Macmillan, 1974.

Young, W. *Eros Denied*. Corgi, 1968.

INDEX

Entries in this index cover the text only, and not the glossary. Furthermore, terms that appear in boldface in the text, all of which appear in the glossary, are cited here only if they are substantively discussed in the text.

aggression 24, 53–54, 65, 68, 75, 88
Akkadian 3
Allen, W. 20
Aman, R. 81
American Heritage Dictionary 8
anality 19–20
androcentrism 5, 6, 21, 24, 46, 51
Anglo-Saxon 7, 9
animality 30–31, 34, 43–44, 49,
    54–56, 68, 76
Aphrodite 82
ars erotica 10
Ash, M. 40
Australian 37, 51, 52, 57

Bailey's Universal Etymological Dictionary 8, 49
Barnhart's Dictionary of New English 4–5
Bataille, G. 16
bible/biblical 15, 60, 71, 84
birds 42–43, 79
body 17, 19, 20, 31, 44
breasts, terms for 50–52
British Museum 13, 29
Buñuel, L. 20

Chambers Twentieth Century Dictionary 8, 34
Chaucer 64

cheating 24–26, 49, 68
Cleland 44
clitoris, terms for 49–50
clothing 58, 76
Clytemnestra 50
cock 53, 54
color 61, 85, 86
culture 17, 18, 29, 33, 40–42, 46, 49,
    57, 63
cunt 16, 39, 47, 48

Daly, M. 6
dancing 18, 34, 47, 49
death 16–17, 32
dick 53, 59, 82
Douglas, M. 18
Dutch 24, 73, 86

Egyptian 15
Elizabethan 21, 31, 35, 38, 41, 48,
    50, 51, 77, 87
Ellis, H. 10
euphemism 11
excretion 19–20

Farmer and Henley 60
Fliess, W. 56
Florio, J. 8
flowers 42

food 20-21, 32-33, 45-46, 57, 62-65, 68, 76, 85-87
foreskin, terms for 61
Foucault, M. 9, 14, 19
French 3, 7, 9, 31, 46, 49, 56, 58, 64, 70-71, 74, 75, 78, 80, 81, 86, 87, 88, 89
Freud/Freudian 10, 14-16, 18, 19, 23, 25, 31-32, 48, 55, 56
Fryer, P. 14
fuck 7-10, 23-26, 29-30, 37

gender 3-6
German, Germanic 3, 5, 24, 37, 39, 46, 50, 52, 55, 56, 58, 60, 62, 79, 81, 85, 88
Greek 50, 59, 63, 74, 75, 79, 80
Grose, F. 8, 30, 35, 39, 44, 46, 48, 77, 88

Hebrew 3, 60, 61
Hermes 82
Hotten 86

incest 21
instruments 57
Irish 89

jazz 34
Johnson, S. 8, 60

Kant, E. 1
Kirby, J. 4
Krafft-Ebing, R. 10

Lacan 56
Latin 1, 3, 7, 9, 24, 32, 35, 39, 49, 50, 52, 55, 56, 61, 64, 67, 68, 69, 71, 74, 77, 84-86

Makeba, M. 35
Maledicta 26, 40, 41, 81
Marx, K. 4
menstruation 21-22
Merriam-Webster see Webster's
metaphysics 26
Miller and Swift 5
Millet, K. 4
Moers, E. 41
Montagu, A. 8
Monty Python 36
Morgan, 5
Morris, D. 13
music 34-35, 47, 58

naming 6, 47, 59-61, 80
nature 17, 18, 33, 40
New Collins Dictionary 8, 24, 36
Nguni 35
nipples, terms for 52
Norse 85

Oedipus 21
orality 19-21
Oxford Dictionary of English Etymology 23, 34, 39
Oxford English Dictionary 8, 23, 34, 39, 40, 88

Partridge, E. 8, 12, 30, 33, 36, 39, 40, 44, 51, 54, 60, 61, 63, 65, 79, 86, 88
Penguin Dictionary 8
phenomenology 1-2
pregnancy 21-22
prick 16, 53
puberty 21-22
pubic hair, terms for 49

Random House Dictionary 8, 34
religion 7, 19, 61, 70, 75, 77-78, 83
repression 13-14
Rodgers, B. 50, 65, 71, 82

Rossi, W. 17
rhyming slang (Cockney) 12, 36, 37,
    47, 51–52, 60, 63–64, 71, 73, 76,
    78

Sandburg, C. 12
Sanskrit 56
science 10
scientia sexualis 10
Scottish 59, 61
screw 25
semen, terms for 64–65
sexism 4–5
Shakespeare(an) 29, 30, 31, 33, 41,
    44, 45, 49, 50, 51, 64, 65, 66, 73,
    77, 85, 86
Skinner's Etymologicon Lingua Anglicanae
    8
slang 11–13
The Slang of Venery 25, 29, 49, 75, 87
South African 71, 82
Spender, D. 4
sport 18, 27, 46–47

success 27
Sumerian 3

taboo 10–11, 14–17
Tannahill, R. 7, 22
testicles, terms for 62–64
Thass-Thienemann, T. 14–16
Turkish 87
venereal disease, terms for 89
violence 24–25, 29, 53

*Webster's Third New International Dic-
    tionary* 8, 34, 39
Webster's Ninth Collegiate 24, 34
Wentworth and Flexner 11, 13, 81,
    88
Wilde, O. 72
Wilson, T. 4

Yiddish 37, 45, 46, 55, 56, 58, 79
Young, W. 14

DATE DUE

NOV 29 1988			